THE SOCIAL COSTS OF NEOLIBERALISM

ESSAYS ON THE ECONOMICS OF
K. WILLIAM KAPP

The Social Costs of Neoliberalism

Essays on the Economics of K. William Kapp

By Sebastian Berger

SPOKESMAN
Nottingham

First published in 2017 by
Spokesman
Russell House
Bulwell lane
Nottingham NG6 0BT
England

Phone 0115 9708318
Fax 0115 9420433
www.spokesmanbooks.com

Copyright Sebastian Berger

All rights reserved. No part of this book may be reprinted or reproduced or utilised in any form or by any electronic, mechanical or other means, now known or hereafter invented, including photocopying and recording, or in any information storage or retrieval system, without permission in writing from the publishers.

A catalogue record is available from the British Library.

ISBN 978 0 85124 864 6

Printed in Nottingham by Russell Press (www.russellpress.com)

CONTENTS

Acknowledgements   9

Preface   12

1 Social Economics vs. the Social Costs of Neoliberalism   15
    1.1 Introduction
    1.2 The Birth of 'Social Costs' out of the Spirit of the Socialist Calculation Debate
    1.3 The Fatal Flaws in the Market's Calculus
    1.4 The Graduate Institute of International Studies and the Institute for Social Research
    1.5 The Early International and Environmental Focus
    1.6 'Social Costs and Social Returns: A Critical Analysis of the Social Performance of the Unplanned Market Economy'
    1.7 'Private,' 'Free,' or 'Business' Enterprise
    1.8 'Shifting,' 'Externalizing,' or 'Socializing' Costs?
    1.9 The Substantive Rationality of Planning: Social Minima, Social Benefits, and Social Knowledge
    1.10 The Life of Kapp's Ideas in the Material World: Environment and Development, Science and Technology, Law and Economics
    1.11 Conclusion

2 Social and Institutional Economics vs. Formal Economics   40
    2.1 Biographical Background
    2.2 The history of the manuscript and Kapp's intellectual project
    2.3 A Final Note on Changes to the Manuscript

3 The Discourse on Social Costs: Heterodox vs. Neoliberal Theories   52
    3.1 Introduction
    3.2 Kapp's Heterodox Theory of Social Costs
    3.3 Looking Back to Forge the Future of Heterodox Economics
    3.4 The Socialist Calculation Debate
    3.5 The Social Costs of Markets and the Social Benefits of Planning
    3.6 The Social Costs of Markets
    3.7 Social Benefits of Planning
    3.8 Substantive Rationality and Social Knowledge
    3.9 The Open System Approach and Circular Cumulative Causation
    3.10 Social Costs and the Critique of Neoclassical Economics
    3.11 The Brave New World of Social Costs
    3.12 Conclusion

4 Social Costs: Kapp's Impossibility Theorem vs. Neoliberalism   76
   4.1 Introduction
   4.2 Kapp's 'impossibility thesis' vs. liberalism a là Mises and Hayek
   4.3 The influence of American institutionalism:
       ex ante social controls vs. ex post Pigouvian taxes
   4.4 Neoliberal feedback à la Knight, Coase, Stigler, Calabresi,
       Buchanan and Beckerman
   4.5 Responding to neoliberalism: Kapp's 'impossibility thesis' reformulated
   4.5.1 Impossibility of expressing the absolute value of human life
   4.5.2 Impossibility of expressing complex and cumulative
       causation and uncertainty
   4.6 Conclusion

5 Kapp's 'Social Costs', Clark's 'Cost Shifting' and Neoliberalism   94
   5.1 Introduction
   5.2 The Kapp-Clark Correspondence in Context
   5.3 J. M. Clark's Theory of Overhead Costs and Cost Shifting
   5.4 The Kapp-Clark Correspondence on Social Costs
   5.5 Institutionalism vs. Neoliberalism: The Discourse on Social Costs
   5.6 Conclusion

6 Kapp and Polanyi on Substantive vs. Formal Economics   115
   6.1 Introduction
   6.2 Biographical Parallels
   6.3 The context of Polanyi's influence on Kapp's two integral projects
   6.4 The Kapp-Polanyi correspondence and Kapp's two integrated projects
   6.5 Conclusion

7 Kapp's Theory of Social Costs and Ernst Wiechert's Poetry   130
   7.1 Introduction
   7.2 On Economic 'Double Truth'
   7.3 The Double Truth as a Set of Avoidable Tragedies
   7.4 Opening Economics to the Creative, Esthetic,
       and Ethical Potential of Experiential Knowledge
   7.5 How the Experiential Knowledge of Art and
       Poetry Can Inspire Economics
   7.6 The Economist Kapp and the Poet Wiechert:
       A Case Study of an Inspirational Friendship
   7.7 Wiechert's Poetic Pedagogy:
       The Spiritual Bond Between the Artist and the Young
   7.8 The Importance of Courage and a Free Heart
   7.9 Enduring Ideals and Islands of Comfort vs. the Danger of Careerism
   7.10 Kapp's Reform Proposals for Education and Teaching Economics

    7.11 Wiechert's Romanticism, or Nature, Religion,
         and the Simple Life as Lasting Sources of Inspiration
    7.12 The Political Consequences of Wiechert's Romanticism
    7.13 Kapp's Economics, or the Humanization and
         Integration of Social Knowledge
    7.14 Conclusion

8. Social Costs as a Psychological Problem   151
    8.1 Introduction
    8.2 Elsner's philosophy of economics, or:
         recovering what's 'lost in calculation'
    8.3 Earlier calls for a psychology of neoclassical economists
    8.4 Open psychological questions
    8.5 Lost in fear: rationalization, repression, compensation,
         isolation, and projection
    8.6 Algorithm as myth and knowledge culture, or:
         losing experiential authority, the 'feminine,' and community
    8.7 Archetypes and complex formation, or: the lost shadows
    8.8 'Max U.': a phallocentric hero without soul and full natural body
    8.9 Cognitive dissonance, cognitive capture, and double truth, or:
         losing history, wisdom and the care for the self
    8.10 Psychology of neoclassical economists as priests
    8.11 Persecuting blasphemers and losing openness
    8.12 Conclusion

9 Social Costs, Open Systems, and Circular Cumulative Causation   178
    9.1 Circular Cumulative Causation (CCC)
    9.2 Open System Approach (OSA)
        9.2.1 Thermodynamics and Openness at the
           More Complex Level of Human Society
        9.2.2 The 'Biocultural Concept of Man'
        9.2.3 The Non-Metaphorical Character of the OSA
    9.3 'Political-Economic' Institutionalism
        9.3.1 Social Costs as a Result of the
           Open System Character and of Circular Cumulative Causation
        9.3.2 'Political Institutionalism'
        9.3.3 'Systemic' Policy
    9.4 Conclusion

10 Social Costs and Myrdal's Circular Cumulative Causation   188
    10.1 Introduction
    10.2 The Origin of CCC
    10.3 Meaning and Methodology
    10.4 Minimizing Social Costs via Economic Planning

10.5 Differences to Veblen's and Kaldor's CC
10.6 Conclusion

11 Social Costs and Lowe's Instrumental Analysis — 197
11.1 Kapp's Theory of Social Costs
11.2 Linking Kapp's Approach with Lowe's Instrumental Analysis
11.3 Implications for Environmental Policy
11.4 Research Project: 'Political Institutionalism'
11.5 References

12 Social Costs and Hayden's Social Fabric Matrix for Policy-Making — 206
12.1 Introduction
12.2 Framing Social Costs: The Need for General Systems Analysis and the Limitations of Utility Theory
12.3 A Normative Matrix for Social Costs: Primary Criteria and Socioecological Indicators
12.4 Kapp's Humanist Approach to Policymaking and Social Costs
  12.4.1 The Complexity Theory of Social Costs and the Limitations of Utilitarian Policies
  12.4.2 Rational Humanism and Primary Criteria
  12.4.3 Social Minima and Socioecological Indicators for Measuring Social Costs
12.5 Conclusion

13 Social Costs of Salmon Fisheries: A Circular Cumulative Causation Analysis with Policy Implications — 221
13.1 Introduction
13.2 CCC as a methodology for fisheries
13.3 A CCC-analysis of salmon's life cycle, salmon depletion, and farmed salmon
13.4 The social costs of salmon depletion and of farmed salmon
13.5 CCC's 'real term' method and its implications for the theory of social costs
13.6 From increasing pecuniary returns to sustainable socio-economic and ecological returns: the quest for new forms of democratic governance
  13.6.1 Prospects for an institutional-political EE approach to fisheries
  13.6.2 Free market environmentalism and EE's critique
  13.6.3 From 'command and control' to 'community-based management' regimes
13.7 Conclusion

Notes — 248

Acknowledgements

This publication project can be traced back to the encounter between K. William Kapp and Ken Coates – the late president of the Bertrand Russell Peace Foundation. They met in the early 1970s and Coates came to appreciate the special value of Kapp's work. In 2008 Spokesman republished for the Russell Peace Foundation Kapp's essay 'Market against Environment' as part of a collection of the most influential works in its history: *The Spokesman – Democracy – Growing or Dying?* (Coates 2008). Coates characterizes Kapp's work as 'celebrating industrial democracy' and 'profound scholarship' that gave rise to an 'early and profound concern' of trade unions to encourage environmental protection. Kapp's text had served Coates as a key text for a conference on Socialism and Environment convened by the Russell Peace Foundation whose expert participants agreed to establish the Socialist Environmental and Resource Association. The introduction to the article describes Kapp as 'one of the foremost authorities on the economics of pollution and environmental control.' Thanks to the support of Tony Simpson, the current editor at the Russell Peace Foundation, this book project could be realized under Spokesman's umbrella.

This work has been supported by the K.Wm. and L. Lore Kapp Foundation for the Humanization and Integration of the Social Sciences. Many thanks are due to Annika Froese for her assistance in preparing the articles in this book for publication. Special thanks also go to Laura Johnson from Taylor and Francis for her support in obtaining permissions and digital files.

The individual chapters in this book are identical to the previously published articles and book chapters. The titles have been adapted to create a flow in this book's table of contents.

Chapter 1: 'K. William Kapp's Social Theory of Social Costs' was originally published in, *History of Political Economy*, Vol. 47 (suppl 1), pps. 227-252. Copyright 2015 Duke University Press. Republished by permission of the publisher. (Journal website: www.dukeupress.edu)

Chapter 2: 'Introduction' (2011). In S. Berger and R. Steppacher (Eds) *The Foundations of Institutional Economics – by K. William Kapp*, Routledge. – with permission from Taylor & Francis

Chapter 3: 'Introduction' (2015). In S. Berger (Ed.) *The Heterodox Theory of*

Social Costs – by K. Wm. Kapp, Routledge. – with permission from Taylor & Francis

Chapter 4: 'The Social Costs Discourse: Kapp's Impossibility Thesis vs. Neo-liberalism' (2012). In W. Elsner, et. al. (eds) *Social Costs Today – Institutional Economics and Contemporary Crisis*, Routledge. – with permission from Taylor & Francis

Chapter 5: 'The Making of the Institutional Theory of Social Costs: The Clark-Kapp Correspondence' (2013). *American Journal of Economics and Sociology*, Vol. 72, pp. 1106-1130.

Chapter 6: 'Karl Polanyi's and K. William Kapp's Substantive Economics: Important Insights from the Polanyi-Kapp Correspondence' (2008). *Review of Social Economy*, Vol. 66, pp 381-396. (Journal website: www.tandfonline.com/loi/rrse20)

Chapter 7: 'Experiential Knowledge and Poetic Economics, or: How the Poet Ernst Wiechert inspired the Economist K. William Kapp' (2015). *Journal of Economic Issues*, Vol. 49, 3: 730-748.

Chapter 8: 'Social Costs and the Psychology of Neoclassical Economists' (2016). In Gräbner, C., Heinrich, T. and Schwardt, H., (eds) *Policy Implications of Recent Advances in Evolutionary and Institutional Economics: Essays in Honor of Wolfram Elsner*. London/New York: Routledge. – with permission from Taylor & Francis

Chapter 9: 'European Contributions to Evolutionary Institutional Economics: The Cases 'Open Systems Approach' (OSA) and 'Cumulative Circular Causation' (CCC). Some Methodological and Policy Implications' (2007) (with Wolfram Elsner). *Journal of Economic Issues*, Vol. 41, pp 529-537.

Chapter 10: 'Circular Cumulative Causation à la Myrdal and Kapp – Political Institutionalism for Minimizing Social Costs' (2008). *Journal of Economic Issues*, Vol. 42, pp 357-365.

Chapter 11: 'Toward a Political Institutionalist Economics: Kapp's Social Costs, Lowe's Instrumental Analysis, and the European Institutionalist Approach to Environmental Policy' (2007) (with Mathew Forstater). *Journal of Economic Issues*, Vol. 41, pp 539-546.

Chapter 12: 'The Normative Matrix of Social Costs – Linking G. Hayden's Social Fabric Matrix Approach to Economic Policymaking with K. W. Kapp's Theory of Social Costs' (2009). In W. Elsner, S. Fullwiler and T. Natarajan (Eds) *Policy Analysis and the Social Fabric Matrix: Applications and Case Studies*, Springer. – with permission from Springer.

Chapter 13: 'Unnatural Depletion and Artificial Abundance: A Circular Cumulative Causation Analysis of Salmon Fisheries and Some Implications for Political Ecological Economics' (2009) (with Edward Glavin IV). In S. Berger (Ed.) *The Foundations of Non-Equilibrium Economics: The Principle of Circular Cumulative Causation*, Routledge. – with permission from Taylor & Francis.

Preface

The present volume is a comprehensive collection of previously published articles encompassing a decade of research on the economics of K. William Kapp. The initial inspiration to this publication was provided by other books that introduce the economics of thinkers who were close to Kapp, such as Gunnar Myrdal, Karl Polanyi, and Thorstein Veblen. And, since there is no monograph on the economics of Kapp, the current book is a provisional substitute to a future monograph that delivers an up-to-date overview. The archival research reveals hitherto unknown links in the discourse on social costs between Kapp and other economists and establishes the meaning and significance of his ideas for contemporary discussions on the social costs of neoliberalism. This, however, is not meant to be a substitute but rather an appetizer for reading his original works on the social costs of business enterprise.

One of the goals is to revitalize research interest in Kapp's economics. More recent articles by Gerber (2016) and Neves (2016) illustrate the continued debate surrounding Kapp's ideas. The same is true of the renewed publication of his book 'The Social Costs of Private Enterprise' in the French edition 'Les Coûts Sociaux de L'Entreprise Privée' (Kapp 2015) and the inclusion of Kapp's approach in the 2015 DUKE Conference on 'Market Failure in Context' (Marciano and Medema 2015).

A second aim is to correct misinterpretations of his work. This refers to recent attempts that fuse Kapp's work with ideas of neoliberal economists such as Ronald H. Coase (Niglia/Vatiori 2007). The textual and archival evidence presented in this book leaves no doubt that these attempts are ill-informed and not in the spirit of Kapp, who fought against the rise of neoliberalism, in particular the work of Hayek and Mises, who are considered to be the masterminds of the neoliberal thought collective (Mirowski and Plehwe 2015). Within contemporary evolutionary economics in Europe there are neoliberal as well as ordoliberal strands (see for example Witt 1996) whose understanding of externalities is incompatible with Kapp's approach.

This leads us up to the title of this volume that points out the relevance of Kapp's work in the contemporary context of resurgent neoliberalism.[1] At a time when the worsening of social, ecological and financial crises would require more social control of the corporate system, the world witnesses the take-over of government by corporations (Mirowski 2013;

Galbraith 2008; Monbiot 2016). These authors point to the fact that neoliberalism produces recurring crises characterized by literally exploding levels of social costs, which, according to Mirowski, are instrumentalized to propose and install, through emergency measures that bypass a lengthy parliamentary decision process, additional market solutions for problems created by markets in the first place. The result is that further realms of the social and natural are usurped into the market. (For this hypothesis see Mirowski 2013; Klein 2008.) The proposal to remedy social costs through a governmentally imposed social entrepreneur framework that makes 'profits a tool for change' falls into this neoliberal category. (For such a proposal see Colander and Kupers 2016.) While not identical in outlook or policy prescriptions, many books dealing with the financial crisis of 2008 frame the issue through the concept of market failure and external costs. All this points to the potential of reintroducing Kapp's argument on social costs, especially since he forged it to target the neoliberal doctrines of Hayek and Mises. Many of the key elements of his theory of social costs resonate with the above mentioned analyses. Firstly, the market system is a system of 'unpaid' or 'socialized' costs, which indicates the impossibility of rational allocation from a societal perspective in such a system. The omission of accounting for the social costs of markets and the lack of prevention strategies undercut sustainable development paths and, instead, produce recurring socio-economic and ecological crises. Rather than being an efficient information processor the market system destroys knowledge that cannot be adequately expressed in algorithmic and monetary terms. Kapp pointed out the anti-humanist and anti-scientific character of this system that subordinates human health and wellbeing to markets, regardless of scientific knowledge on environmental toxicology that supports the victims of damage. Furthermore, he warned that the neoliberal proposal to find market solutions to the problem of social costs is an excuse for endless delays and 'too little too late' and invites corruption through special interests. Essentially, Kapp argued that the entire tendency of the liberalism à la Hayek and Mises is to avoid any recognition that market rationality has anything to do with rising levels of social costs and the deterioration of the natural and social environments. His proposal to prevent social costs via social controls of technology and investment decisions is a major challenge to neoliberalism and stems from his participation in the socialist calculation debate. For Kapp social and democratic planning of the economic system and enforcement of socio-ecological safety standards was the alternative to neoliberalism, and the precondition for human freedom, security and well-being.

References

Colander, David and Kupers, Roland (2016) *Complexity and the Art of Public Policy: Solving Society's Problems from the Bottom Up*, Princeton University Press.

Galbraith, James K. (2009) *The Predator State: How Conservatives Abandonned the Free Market and Why Liberals Should Too*, New York: Free Press.

Gerber, Julien-Francois (2016) 'The Legacy of K. William Kapp,' *Development and Change*, 47, 4: 902-917.

Kapp, K. William (2015) *Les Coûts Sociaux de l'Entreprise Privée*, Paris: Les Petits Matins.

Klein, Naomi (2008) *The Shock Doctrine – The Rise of Disaster Capitalism*, New York: Picador.

Marciano, Alain and Medema, Steven G. (2015) *Market Failure in Context, Annual Supplement to Volume 47, History of Political Economy*, Durham and London: Duke University Press.

Mirowski, Philip (2013) *Never Let A Serious Crisis Go To Waste*, Verso.

Mirowski, Philip and Plehwe, Dieter (2015) *The Road From Mont Pelerin: The Making of the Neoliberal Thought Collective*, Cambridge: Harvard University Press.

Monbiot, George (2016) hhttp://www.theguardian.com/books/2016/apr/15/neoliberalism-ideology-problem-george-monbiot

Neves, Vitor (2016) 'What Happened to Kapp's Theory of Social Costs? A Case of Metatheoretical Dispute and Dissent in Economics,' *Review of Political Economy*, Vol. 28, 4: 488-503.

Witt, Ulrich (1996) 'Innovations, Externalities and the Problem of Economic Progress,' *Public Choice* 89, 113-130.

1
Social Economics vs. the Social Costs of Neoliberalism

1.1 Introduction

This article deals with the theory of social costs by K. William Kapp, namely, the origin, gestation, and further development of *The Social Costs of Private Enterprise* (1950). This article analyzes archival material to show that Kapp viewed Social Costs as a continuation of his contribution to the socialist calculation debate (Kapp 1936), in which he defended the socialist position on the possibility of rational planning, including the need to prevent social costs ex ante. In this defense he proposed a 'countervailing impossibility thesis,' according to which social costs are proof that the market calculus disregards social needs, which cannot be rational from the perspective of society. Kapp understood his position in the debate as defending Max Weber's notion of the substantive rationality of planning against Ludwig von Mises's 'impossibility thesis.' During his career Kapp refined his defense of the substantive rationality of planning. The result of this refinement is a foundation for social economics, which Kapp viewed as synonymous with the intellectual project of American institutional economics. This foundation consists of a framework for social-democratic planning based on theories of social costs and benefits, social needs, social value, social minima, socio-ecological indicators, and social knowledge. While the socialist calculation debate is the origin of Kapp's defense of planning, he continuously developed it to take account of instances where public administration in Soviet Russia and India fell short of being substantively rational. Kapp never adopted the polarization of capitalism versus socialism. Instead he envisioned a social-democratic framework that effectively ties market, state, and civil society actors to a substantive rationality, that is, social minima. This approach is also dubbed 'new rational humanism' because it aims to guarantee social minima that are rooted in existential human needs. The latter are analyzed in a new science of integrated social knowledge on the existential biological and cultural structure of the human being in society. Thus, Kapp's social economics provides a crucial link to ecological economics, environmental sociology, and philosophical anthropology. Hence, Kapp developed a genuinely social theory of social costs, which originated as an explicit defence of the substantive rationality of planning to prevent social costs and guarantee social minima, which became the foundation of a comprehensive theoretical framework of social economics.

1.2 The Birth of 'Social Costs' out of the Spirit of the Socialist Calculation Debate

The trajectory of the social costs discourse in the twentieth century is crucially shaped by the reaction of the Chicago School to American institutionalism, including Kapp's institutional theory of social costs (Berger 2012, 2013; Franzini 2006). What has not been sufficiently registered is that this ideological conflict is an extension of the socialist calculation debate of the 1920s and 1930s, which was the cradle of Kapp's theory of social costs. In this debate, his dissertational treatise 'Planwirtschaft und Aussenhandel' ('The Planned Economy and International Trade') (Kapp 1936) sided with the socialists. This work has never been translated into English, and thus the present analysis sheds new light on the genesis of Kapp's theory of social costs.

The thesis of the present article, namely that Kapp's dissertation contains the nucleus of the theory of social costs, is confirmed by the introduction to *The Social Costs of Private Enterprise* (Kapp 1950b, xxvii–xxviii):

> The basic idea of the present study was first advanced in a highly tentative manner in the author's attempt to deal with the problem of economic calculation in connection with his analysis of the economic relations between a foreign trade monopoly and private exporters and importers.

Kapp argued in his dissertation that Mises's (1920) thesis about the impossibility of a rational economy under socialism needs to be countered with an impossibility thesis regarding the market economy. This thesis should be that the economic calculus based on market prices does not meet the requirement of the economic principle from the perspective of society. Kapp sought to defend the possibility and necessity of rational planning by pointing out the one-sidedness and the resulting blind-spots in the Mises argument about the superior rationality of markets. In an unpublished interview (Kapp n.d.a) Kapp explained that he understood the emergence of his argument on social costs to be the result of various factors, including the 'great debate initiated by Ludwig v. Mises and Max Weber,' the economic calculation controversy, his background of dealing with problems of economic planning, and his critical attitude toward a 'free enterprise economy.' Kapp's own explicit understanding of the nucleus of his argument as a case of 'Weber vs.

Mises' on the rationality of the price system is also confirmed in 'Social Costs and Social Benefits—a Contribution to Normative Economics' (Kapp 1963b). Arguing that markets are only formally rational but not from the perspective of society, Kapp adopted Weber's analytical framework of the conflictual relationship between formal and substantive rationality. In Kapp's 'countervailing thesis,' social damages serve as proof of the impossibility of markets to rationally allocate goods and services from the perspective of society. Thus, in this light they reflect the market's purely formal rationality, which from the perspective of society appears limited, biased, and even arbitrary.

1.3 The Fatal Flaws in the Market's Calculus

The dissertation presents three distinct arguments why a calculus based on market prices only formally meets the requirements of the economic principle while failing to do so from a societal perspective. First, it attends to the issue that insolvent needs are disregarded in a 'free exchange-economy' by quoting the second edition of Carl Menger's (1923, 49) *Grundsätze der Volkswirtschaftslehre* (Principles of Economics). The latter maintains that in business, even the most compelling and urgent needs of the destitute have no weight at all, even among financially comfortable people who are the most sympathetic. The business world disregards the genuine human needs of the population while eagerly pursuing the needs of those who are able and willing to pay. Second, Kapp notes that the market calculus is a source of error and irrationality in the formation of individual valuation, quoting again Menger (1923, 3) on illusionary, undeveloped, and pathological needs. Psychological manipulation of consumers through advertisement means, according to Kapp, that the economic principle is only fulfilled formally because less important needs are satisfied at the cost of more important ones.

Third, Kapp argues – partly with reference to A. C. Pigou (1929, 186, 197) – that the disregard for numerous damages under an economic calculus of market prices means that this calculus is uneconomic from the standpoint of society while being completely consistent with the economic principle that secures the profitability of the private business. The numerous social damages mentioned are the disruption of national health; increases in crime, accidents, and employment-related illnesses and accidents; inadequate protection of motherhood; excessive smoke concentrations; noise pollution; unhealthy construction work; retardation of scientific progress because of patents; advertisement; and premature resource depletion. In a footnote to this closing section on social costs, Kapp (1936, 42) anticipates his future research agenda, which was to materialize in *Social Costs*:

> It would be an interesting task for statistics to develop correct methods for the capturing of disadvantages and damages which accrue to society in a free market economy due to the activity of independent entrepreneurs that is solely based on the principle of highest profitability.

The above limitations of an economic calculus based on market prices necessitates, in Kapp's view, economic planning for social benefits. That the valuation of goods according to market prices frequently disregards societal needs and interests reflects a basic incapacity of markets to incorporate these needs in its calculus. In this perspective, economic viability from a societal perspective cannot be achieved by markets alone. As evidence for this conclusion, Kapp refers to social policies in capitalist economies, which compensate retroactively for social damages via laws, and charitable measures. Kapp further concludes that the planned economy can calculate potential damages beforehand and take them into consideration in economic decisions. This conclusion is the origin of Kapp's later fully developed argument about the necessity to prevent social costs ex ante and thus to guarantee the fulfilment of social needs. As examples of social needs, Kapp initially considers foremost the defense against dangers that threaten the existence of society, such as epidemics, illnesses, enemy attacks, but also agencies that improve the general welfare, public health, and the cultural level of society. The important task for the planned economy is, according to Kapp, to establish principles for the valuation of goods based on the needs and goals of society. Just like in the case of social costs above, it is a footnote that indicates the future course of study on social valuation:

> Because this question would exceed the frame of this work a systematic treatment of the system of economic calculation on the basis of 'social value' should be reserved for a later treatment. (Kapp 1936, 46)

Kapp traces the problem of social valuation to Albert Schäffle's *Bau und Leben des Sozialen Körpers* (The Structure and Life of the Social Body) (1881), and Friedrich Wieser's (1924, 116) 'Theorie der Gesellschaftlichen Wirtschaft' ('The Theory of the Social Economy'). In conclusion, Kapp's argument on social costs can be traced back to the socialist calculation debate, in which it was forged as a critique of the formal rationality of the market calculus and a justification for economic planning that guarantees the fulfilment of social needs.

1.4 The Graduate Institute of International Studies and the Institute for Social Research

Kapp's early work was supported by the Institut universitaire des haute études internationals (IUHED, Graduate Institute of International Studies) in Geneva. Archival research indicates that Kapp had attempted to enroll at the University of Frankfurt to work on his doctorate in 1933. The university's enrollment form, however, asked for evidence of Aryan descent, and perhaps the rise of Nazism is the principal reason that Kapp emigrated together with his future wife, Lili Lore Masur, who was Jewish, to pursue doctoral studies at IUHED. The latter also provided a haven for 'concerned liberals' in the 1930s, some of whom became leading protagonists in building the neoliberal flagship organization, the Mont Pèlerin Society (Mirowski and Plehwe 2009). The preface to his dissertation expresses Kapp's gratitude to Mises for his continuous suggestions and stimulations, and both Mises and Eugene Stanley of the University of Chicago for the friendly interest they took in his work. The fact that Kapp's argument on social costs emerged at this particular institute buttresses my thesis about its origin. As an economist with socialist leanings,[2] Kapp used the phenomenon of social costs to defend the socialist position on planning against Mises's antisocialist thesis.

Kapp also relied for support on the so-called neo-Marxist Frankfurt School, with which he was acquainted in its Geneva exile between 1933 and 1936. Reconstituted as the Institute for Social Research at Columbia University, it supported Kapp's work on social costs financially and was most likely decisive in providing Kapp with a teaching position at Columbia. The principal reason for this affiliation is that Kapp's framing of social costs as a problem of rationality is in line with what Michel Foucault ([1979] 2008, 106) dubbed the 'post-Weberian' project of the Frankfurt school, to investigate the irrational rationality of markets. Previous archival research shows that Kapp was a close friend of Friedrich Pollock, the economist of the Frankfurt school (Berger and Forstater 2007), and his dissertation cites the latter's research on the increased capabilities of planning that result from improved statistical methods and technologies (Kapp 1936, 25). Pollock also influenced *Social Costs*:

> I also wish to acknowledge gratefully a grant-in-aid which I received from the Institute of Social Research at Columbia University from November 1943 to May 1944. In this connection I wish to record my gratitude to Dr. F. Pollock, Associate Director of the Institute of Social Research, who read the entire manuscript and made many valuable suggestions related to specific phases of the study. (Kapp 1950b, xxx)

It was also Pollock who invited Kapp to participate in a leading role in the formation of the newly founded Institute for Social Research in Frankfurt in the 1950s.[3] Furthermore, *Social Costs* references leading authors of the Frankfurt School, such as Erich Fromm and Max Horkheimer. The position of *Social Costs* within the intellectual project of the Frankfurt School's post-Weberianism turns it into an important link between sociology and economics. In conclusion, the institutional context reflects the origin and core of his argument on social costs. The doctoral candidate Kapp used the latter to launch a post-Weberian attack à la Frankfurt School on Mises's liberalism in order to defend the necessity for economic planning.

1.5 The Early International and Environmental Focus

The close affiliation of IUHED with the League of Nations and ILO also proved decisive for the early international and environmental orientation of Kapp's research on social costs. On the one hand, it provided Kapp with an early learning experience on how to insert his economics within the context of international organizations of outstanding importance. See, for example, his membership on the expert committee that prepared the United Nations conference on the human environment in Stockholm, and his membership on the Standing Committee of the Social Science Council of UNESCO. Combined with his dissertation's discussion of pollution and resource depletion, his early international orientation led to Kapp's work on the League of Nation's discussions on natural resources. As a research assistant of John B. Whitton (Princeton University) between January and September 1937, Kapp prepared the 'Memorandum on the Efforts Made by the League of Nations towards a Solution of the Problems of Raw Materials' (1937) and submitted it to the 1937 International Studies Conference held in Paris under the auspices of the International Institute for Intellectual Cooperation. Following an invitation from the International Industrial Relations Institute in The Hague, Kapp delivered a report on the work of the League of Nations Committee for the study of the problem of raw materials at the institute's conference in 1937. Later Kapp also published *The League of Nations and Raw Materials, 1919-1939* (1941). His relatively early involvement with issues of environmental disruption and natural resources as economic themes continued after his immigration to the United States, where he initially concentrated on social damages in agriculture, which lead him to also see the interrelatedness with water and air pollution (see Kapp n.d.a). This explains *Social Costs*' environmental focus, that is, its five chapters on issues such as air and water pollution, renewable and nonrenewable resources, and resource utilization. This special attentiveness to nature and the environment earned him the recognition as one of the earliest economists to comprehensively analyze environmental problems and even as augur of the environmental crisis.[4]

However, this early interest in the environment may be only partly related to the influence of Pigou's work and the research opportunities at IUHED. Rather, it is documented that Kapp's susceptibility to the theme of industrial society's relationship with nature antedates the 1930s. The profound and lasting ethical influence of his teacher, the famous German novelist Ernst Wiechert, is acknowledged in a series of articles and also documented in their extensive post–World War II correspondence (Berger, forthcoming). Kapp highlights Wiechert's lessons on the great importance of nature as refuge, inspiration, and mental and physical restoration, but also the ethics of 'love for all suffering creatures.'[5] The focus on nature is, thus, deeply rooted in Kapp's biography since his formative years in the 1920s.

1.6 'Social Costs and Social Returns: A Critical Analysis of the Social Performance of the Unplanned Market Economy'

Archival material shows that in the 1940s Kapp continued to develop his defense of the socialist position in the socialist calculation debate by elaborating the social cost argument as a critique of the market calculus and a rationale for economic planning. Two unpublished drafts of the introduction to *Social Costs* state that the intention is to provide a critique of the unplanned market economy, equilibrium economics, and capitalism:

> As an analysis of the social inefficiency of the unplanned market economy the study was bound to assume the character of a critique not only of capitalism but also of traditional equilibrium economics. (Kapp n.d.b)

The unpublished project outline 'Social Costs and Social Returns: A Critical Analysis of the Social Performance of the Unplanned Market Economy' restates this aim with reference to the liberalism of Mises and Friedrich Hayek:

> Social Costs and Social Returns: A Critical Analysis of the Social Performance of the Unplanned Market Economy – In harmony with the faith of 19th century liberalism traditional equilibrium economics states that the unregulated forces of supply and demand in an unplanned market economy

tend to lead to an optimal allocation of scarce resources among competing ends and objectives. This doctrine continues to be regarded by many as an apparently scientific foundation for all arguments against positive intervention with the economic process in the capitalist economy; its strength is attested by the current success of the books by Hayek and Mises [...] This study offers a critique of the basic premises of 19th century economic liberalism by examining the social performance of the unplanned market economy in the light of several facts which are usually omitted and neglected in economic theory [...] In the first place it attempts to indicate the limitations of all economic calculations in terms of private costs and private returns. To allocate economic resources merely in accordance with private costs and private returns defeats any endeavour to find a rational solution to the economic problem. (Kapp n.d.c)

These materials clearly show that Kapp continued his defense of the socialist position from the socialist calculation debate by developing the argument on social costs as a critique of liberalism while adding the targets 'capitalism,' the 'unplanned market economy,' and 'equilibrium economics.' This is also confirmed in a letter to John M. Clark, which laments the strength of the liberal tradition reflected in the considerable response enjoyed by the recent works – presumably Hayek's *Road to Serfdom* (1944) and Mises's *Bureaucracy* (1944) – of these 'intransigent economic liberals [Hayek, Mises, and Robbins]' (Kapp to Clark, December 12, 1945, quoted in Berger 2013).

The above unpublished outline also pitches the project against the 'prophets of gloom [Hayek and Tocqueville]' who believe that economic planning would imply an inevitable road to serfdom. However, chapter 2 of the final version of *Social Costs* states that the important questions raised by the 'current debate on the 'road to serfdom' were only indirectly related to the problems under discussion in *Social Costs* and are thus not addressed in more detail in the book (Kapp 1950, 24). This makes sense when we take into consideration that Kapp separated the initial project, publishing *Social Costs*, while leaving unpublished the sections on social benefits. Only the latter would have been directly related to Hayek's critique of planning in 'Road to Serfdom.' The unpublished second part was described in the initial project outline as

> the re-orientation of economics; [...] [exploration of] the possibilities for the setting up of valid criteria for economic planning and the formulation for economic policy, and perhaps to prepare the way for the elaboration of a positive theory of social value are the chief ultimate purposes of this inquiry. (Kapp n.d.b)

Kapp aimed at developing a theory of social benefits

> derived from the gratification of collective needs; from international economic policies designed to achieve a balanced economy [...] and from the improvement of transportation facilities [...] scientific research, multiple purpose projects (such as TVA), and the maintenance of a social minimum with respect to essential foodstuffs, medical care, housing, and education. (Kapp n.d.b)

The decision not to publish the part on planning for social benefits raises questions as to the reasons for excluding this important material. After all, economic planning for social benefits was the larger goal, for which the argument on social costs had merely been intended as a rationale with respect to Mises's thesis. Likewise, in the Kapp-Clark correspondence *Social Costs* was deemed only a first step for the development of a social economics based on theories of social benefits and social valuation (Berger 2013).

What happened to the important social benefits part of the initial project? Previous archival research (Berger 2013) evidences the critical nature of John M. Clark's comments on Kapp's draft manuscript. In a nutshell, Clark considered Kapp to have failed in providing any detailed formulation and evaluation of the potentials and limitations of a 'collectivist alternative.' Clark urged him to consider that every system, including alternative collectivist ones, would have imperfections and that the desired comprehensive social accountancy might not come about in such a system and that the dispute would be shifted from the 'machinery of the markets' to the 'political machinery.' The unpublished project outline provides further reasons for delaying the work on social benefits. It states that providing solutions via social benefits for each instance of social costs would have unduly enlarged the manuscript, destroyed the continuity of the text, and raised the important issue of liberty, which needs a separate treatment (Kapp n.d.c).

The absence of a discussion of freedom in *Social Costs* was also a point of critique made by Frank Knight, who noted, however, that this issue had been dealt with in a separate article published in the same year, that is, 'Economic Planning and Freedom' (Kapp 1950a; Knight 1951). Presumably, the decision to publish *Social Costs* without a discussion of social benefits of planning made a treatment of the issue of freedom in the planned economy unnecessary. This also explains Kapp's above comment that the issues raised by Hayek's *Road to Serfdom* are not directly related to *Social Costs*, which is solely a critique of the unplanned market economy and capitalism. In a later interview Kapp (n.d.a) mentioned as further reasons for the separation of the initially intertwined projects that completing the entire argument on social benefits would have taken too long at the time and that he had completed only three chapters. He also explained that he viewed his work on development planning in India in the late 1950s and early 1960s as a continuation of this work. This view is confirmed by the chapter 'Social Costs and Social Benefits: Their Relevance for Public Policy and Economic Planning' published in his book on economic planning in India (Kapp 1963c).

1.7 'Private,' 'Free,' or 'Business' Enterprise

The Social Costs of Private Enterprise is Kapp's most significant publication in terms of scholarly impact. The work was reviewed widely, most notably by Frank Knight (1951) and John M. Clark (1950), and it attracted responses from economists such as James Buchanan (1962), Guido Calabresi (1961), and Wilfred Beckerman (1972) (for a discourse analysis, see Berger 2012). Google Scholar lists around 630 citations, while the second enlarged and revised edition, which was titled *The Social Costs of Business Enterprise* (Kapp 1963a), shows upward of 220 citations.

Social Costs exerted a significant influence on the community of scholars forming under the banner of ecological economics (Ropke 2004), especially those working on the environmentalism of the poor (see, e.g., Martinez-Alier 2002), and the integration of social-ecological economics (Spash 2011), but also environmental sociologists (Foster 2010). Even leading environmental economists like Allen Kneese relied on *Social Costs* in his critique of Pigou's and Coase's theories of externalities: 'A perspective more like that of the present paper is found in Kapp' (Ayres and Kneese 1969, 282n1, 295). The group of scholars who awarded most recognition to Kapp's work on social costs is found in the American institutionalist movement, reflected most notably in the works of James Swaney (2006) and Marc Tool (1978, 1):

> Dr. K. William Kapp and his forty-year career as a front rank institutional economist [...] [established] the relevance of the holistic, institutional mode of thinking to the complex and urgent problems of environmental deterioration and economic development. Indeed, Kapp was among the first to explore the interdependent significance of these two problems.

This appreciation was also reflected in Kapp's contribution to the formation of the Association for Evolutionary Economics and his collaboration with Gunnar Myrdal on the (unsuccessful) formation of an international association of institutional economists (see Berger and Steppacher 2011 for details). Upon arrival in the United States in 1937, Kapp endeavored to connect his arguments on social costs and benefits with the conceptual frameworks of the American institutionalists. In fact, he even developed the book project *The Foundations of Institutional Economics* with the initial working title 'The Foundations of Social Economics.' This clearly demonstrates Kapp's recognition of the identity of the American institutional movement and his project of social economics (see Berger and Steppacher 2011). Kapp explicitly placed *Social Costs* in the tradition of social and institutional economics, notably Thorstein Veblen's theory of business enterprise, in the preface to the second enlarged and revised edition, which was titled *The Social Costs of Business Enterprise* (1963a, xxvii):

> The change of the title to *Social Costs of Business Enterprise* is intended to express more explicitly the affinity of our analysis to the intellectual tradition of [...] institutional economic theory [...] [It was] Veblen who, as early as 1921, called for an investigation by economists in consultation with the technical expert, 'of the various kinds and lines of waste that are necessarily involved in the present businesslike control of industry.'

Kapp viewed Veblen's theory of social waste as consistent with his own views since the socialist calculation debate. Namely, social waste and damages are viewed as evidence of a systemic problem that needs to be remedied via systemic social controls. This is consistent with the finding that the theory of social waste is a 'source theme' of American institutionalism (Rutherford 2011, 36; this volume), which expresses the view of the Progressive Era's experts that there are inherent market flaws and not just market failures (Leonard, this volume). But also the significant influence of John M. Clark's social economics is acknowledged by Kapp (1950b, xxvii):

> His [Kapp's] interest in the problem of social costs was further stimulated by J. M. Clark's contributions to 'Social Economics' as well as by the results of the unique and still largely neglected research carried out under the auspices of the National Resources Planning Board. Professors J. M. Clark and Robert Lynd read an earlier draft of the introductory and concluding chapters and have offered critical comments, which are gratefully acknowledged.

Unfortunately, Kapp decided to publish this second enlarged and revised edition of *Social Costs* in India with Asia Publishing House, which explains the relatively low level of attention it received in the United

States, especially when compared with the first edition, which was published by Harvard University Press. This decision must be seen in the light of the Fulbright appointments at the Gokhale Institute of Politics and Economics and the University of Rajasthan during which he conducted research on economic planning for social benefits in India (1963c). It may be surmised that he viewed the revised *Social Costs* not only as complementary to the latter but also as important support for the case for economic planning in India.

Further archival evidence suggests that the terms *private enterprise* and *free enterprise* (used in Kapp n.d.d) were eventually discarded because they were perceived to be 'too ambiguous' in an economy characterized by large-scale government involvement (Kapp n.d.a). One might wonder why Kapp did not use a more radical title, such as 'The Social Costs of Capitalism,' since his initial project outline aimed at a critique of capitalism. The early preference for the Weberian framework since his dissertation and his insistence on the need for detailed institutional analysis are significant here, as they suggest a preference for the approach of the younger German historical school (Weber) and the American institutionalists (Veblen, Clark) over the conceptual framework and terminology of Marxism. However, this distinction may not be that decisive, since even the so-called neo-Marxist Frankfurt school was associated with a post-Weberian intellectual project (see above). Additionally, references to Marx abound in *Social Costs*, and Kapp published three of his major books on economic planning in countries with socialist or communist governments, that is, Soviet Russia (1936), India (1963c), and China (1974). The latter is favorable to Maoist economic planning, especially the recycling and zero-waste schemes, and relies on Marx's theory of social use value as a theoretical framework. Most likely, the decision to avoid the more radical title 'The Social Costs of Capitalism' in the United States of the 1940s was partly related to the 'red scare era' characterized by severe repression of economists of socialist or communist orientation (Lee 2009).

1.8 'Shifting,' 'Externalizing,' or 'Socializing' Costs?

The search for the appropriate terminology in the 1940s also continued with regard to social damages, as Kapp tried to position his work within the US institutionalist movement. While Kapp and Clark agreed on the concept of cost shifting as a rationale for social economics and social controls, they disagreed on what to call the shifted portion of the total costs of production:

[Your definition of] 'social' values and costs differs from mine in applying to non- market quantities only, where mine [Clark's] included also the quantities the market 'measures.' (Clark to Kapp, December 4, 1945; quoted in Berger 2013)

In the literature, this important difference between Kapp's and Clark's definition of the concept of social costs has unfortunately been conflated by describing Clark's 'shifted costs' as 'social costs' (see, e.g., Prasch 2005). Distinguishing, as Kapp did, private costs from social costs (social losses, damages, inefficiencies) emphasizes that the logic of maximizing private returns is a built-in incentive for businesses to *socialize* as many costs as possible. According to Kapp, adding social to private costs results in total costs. This is an important terminology turn from the original notion of 'shifted costs':

> The term [social costs] covers all direct and indirect losses suffered by third persons or the general public as a result of private economic activities. (Kapp 1950b, 13)

This difference in defining social costs is significant, since Clark's definition of social costs as nonmarket plus market costs is in the neoclassical tradition of Pigou. This neoclassical conceptualization of social costs is deemed incompatible with the project of social economics by Kapp and the principal reason for its rejection. Commentators noted early on that Kapp's definition is inconsistent with Pigou's (Pearce and Sturmey 1966, 152n1). While Kapp noted that Pigou had radicalized his political-economic conclusions ('bankruptcy of capitalism' and 'extending public ownership') (Pigou, quoted in Kapp 1963a, 38), he viewed Pigou's conceptual framework as imbued with the limitations of the neoclassical theories of price and value, and closed system and equilibrium preconceptions. The latter preclude an adequate understanding of the circular cumulative causation of social costs, that is, complex causal relationships that determine the magnitudes and qualities of the damages. The term *external costs* is seen as a consequence of neoclassical preconceptions that suggest that the issue at hand is a relatively minor and temporary aberration from a functioning mechanism, remediable with ad hoc measures within the existing system. Kapp criticized the reform proposals for environmental control that emerge from the 'polluter pays principle' that underlies all market-based (taxes, bargaining) and even tort law-based approaches to social costs. The main point of critique was that these solutions address the problem of social costs *ex post* without emphasis on prevention. While he acknowledged that taxation of polluters is better than nothing, he viewed this approach as ineffective, piecemeal, and too conservative. (Kapp 1971, n.d.e) Conversely, Kapp's understanding of social costs was more akin to the American institutionalists' conception of social costs as large-scale and systemic problems caused by the institution of business enterprise, which require far-reaching changes at the system level. In reassessing twenty years of discussions on *Social Costs*, Kapp maintained the fundamental point of dispute in the preface to the 1971 edition:

> The Social Costs of Private Enterprise undertakes to diagnose the causes that tend to give rise to the disruption of our physical and social environment. […] a system of decision-making operating in accordance with the principle of investment for profit cannot be expected to proceed in any way other than by trying to reduce its costs whenever possible and by ignoring those losses that can be shifted to third persons or to society at large. Predictably, this critical view, which runs counter to the presuppositions and biases of conventional economic analysis, has not met with general approval. Thus, various alternative explanations for the occurrence of social costs have been advanced. These have one thing in common: to exonerate the principle of investment for profits from any causal connection with environmental disruption. (xiii-xiv)

Stating the fundamental point of dispute as the principle of investment for profits mirrors Veblen's terminology and reiterates the view from the socialist calculation debate that social costs are evidence of a systemic flaw in the rationality of markets. This is also interpreted as a fundamental conflict between individual and social interests (Kapp 1963b), which has not only the power to shape history:

> The political history of the last 150 years can be fully understood only as a revolt of large masses of people (including business) against the shifting of part of the social costs of production to third persons or to society. (Kapp 1950b, 16)

It also means that the relative power positions of companies and industries reflect their ability to socialize costs. The extent to which the victims can leverage countervailing power determines the extent of social costs (Kapp 1963b). Thus, Kapp's theory is a social conflict theory of social costs.

1.9 The Substantive Rationality of Planning: Social Minima, Social Benefits, and Social Knowledge

His theory of social costs led Kapp to far-reaching conclusions presented in *Social Costs'* final chapter, 'Toward a New Science of Political Economy.' Principal among them is the demand to 'return to philosophy,' referring to the words of Max Horkheimer: 'Economic science must overcome 'the horizon of contemporary society'" (Kapp 1950b, 246-47). This demand is specified in 'The Broadening of the Scope of Economic Investigations,' 'The Reformulation and Enlargement of Basic Concepts,' and 'Social Choices, Social Evaluation, Social Value.' The task of this new science included the objectification and quantification of social costs. The principal way to achieve this goal was to investigate social costs as deficiencies in the satisfaction of scientifically derived and socially determined minima of adequate living conditions (Kapp 1963b, [1975] 2011). Social minima reflecting social needs can be scientifically derived:

> In the field of air and water pollution it is possible to work out minimum standards of public health in the form of maximum permissible levels of concentration of pollutants. Social costs and social objectives can be identified in terms of existing deficiencies by comparing the actual state of pollution with the maximum permissible concentration of pollutants. Similarly, it is possible to work out safe social minima or maximum rates of depletion of renewable resources (e.g. wildlife and fisheries) as well as water and soil by the definition of a critical zone beyond which any increase of depletion would give rise to an irreversible process of destruction of the resource. Minimum standards of requirements can be defined also in such fields as public health, medical care, education, housing, civilian defense, transportation and recreation. (Kapp 1963b, 195)

Thus, social minima and indicators are the main policy tools for the planning of social benefits. The initial unfinished manuscript of social benefits from the mid-1940s had already included a chapter on social minima such as the extent of unsatisfied social needs, the obsolescence of residential urban dwellings, inadequate medical care, and deficiencies in the field of public health (Kapp n.d.f). Kapp defined four main characteristics of the social benefits of planning for social minima that result from the existence of social needs and make them a necessary object of government action because private enterprise will not provide them: they are highly defused, cannot be withheld, accrue to all members of society, and are indivisible (Kapp 1963b). This approach to social benefits is explicitly rooted in Weber's concept of substantive rationality:

> Substantive rationality [...] measures the extent to which a given group of persons is or could be adequately provided with goods by means of an economically oriented course of social action. (Kapp 1963b, 190)[6]

Thus, substantive rationality meant for Kapp an approach to economic planning that guarantees social minima. In contrast to Weber, Kapp argued that substantive rationality can be objectified via a scientific inquiry into need satisfaction, such that Weber's caveat about the infinite possible value standards under a regime of substantive rationality is unwarranted. Kapp's effort to objectify and quantify social costs and benefits in a substantive and scientific manner was also directed against Mises's argument about the alleged lack of rationality in economic planning. Kapp (1963b) maintained that the price system's quantitative character is only seemingly objective and rational because in actual fact it is highly arbitrary (manipulation of consumers and disregard for the poor, social damages, and needs). In other words, Kapp continued the defense of the socialist position since his dissertation against Mises's impossibility thesis. Yet the quest to scientifically objectify and quantify social costs and benefits also aimed at providing an alternative to the purely monetary appraisal of social costs in neoclassical economics. Social minima, according to Kapp, objectify and quantify social costs and benefits by removing them from the realm of pure ideology into the realm of science and the pragmatic test.

Kapp acknowledged that the problem of social costs and benefits would always remain partly political in nature because of the necessity of social evaluation of essential and less essential human needs. Here, Kapp (1963b) referred to the need for a democratic theory of consumption based on majority votes and referendums.[7] Based on Weber and Otto Neurath, Kapp adopted the position that substantive rationality can be based on an economic calculation in real terms that compares real physical units of available resources. Yet the potential inefficiencies of substantive rationality are also acknowledged in terms of delays, coercion, and vested interests in the political system. This realistic view of the issues faced by economic planning is characteristic of Kapp's work since the 1960s when he conducted empirical research on economic planning and public administration in India (Kapp 1963c).

Thus, in conclusion, the argument on social costs maintained the central target of the dissertation. Relying on Weber's critique of formal rationality and Veblen's critique of pecuniary principles, Kapp (1963b) continued to attack Mises's purely formal defense of the rationality of the price system. Adopting Otto von Neurath's proposal for planning in real terms, Kapp solidly tied himself to the very socialist position that had been the reason for Mises's initiation of the socialist calculation debate. Kapp epitomized in important respects the Progressive Era expert who has a 'faith in the scientific state,' sees himself as a 'forward-looking modernist,' believed himself to be an 'ethical economist,' a 'guide to the social good' with the 'public interest at heart' (Leonard, this volume).

Kapp's ([1975] 2011) plea for a 'new science of political economy' and 'return to philosophy' materialized in the above-mentioned unfinished book project 'Foundations of a Social Economics' but also *Towards a Science of Man in Society–a Positive Approach to the Integration of Social Knowledge* (1961). In fact, this concern was so important to Kapp that it later became the main mission statement of the Kapp Foundation for the Integration and Humanization of the Social Sciences. Joining the issues of economic planning and a positivist approach to a unified social science had previously been a project associated with Neurath, but Kapp did not acknowledge this source of inspiration in *Science of Man* (for a discussion of this link, see Spash 2012). Instead, the final chapter closes with references to 'realtypical' and Gestalt analysis (Weber, Spiethoff) and substantive economics (Polanyi 1957). Thus, Kapp's approach to social knowledge is best understood as part of a means-ends instrumentalism (Kapp 1963b, [1975] 2011; Berger and Forstater 2007). His own recognition of the kinship with instrumental analysis, that is, the theory of economic knowledge for controlled economic systems, is decisive here (Kapp 1976; Lowe 1965). In this, social knowledge about the dynamic structure of human needs in society is part of the process of scientifically deriving means, while social minima are part of the process of socially determining normative ends. Kapp's democratic approach to social control is strongly influenced by John Dewey and thus differs from the notion of politically unaccountable expert control enacted by many Progressive Era economists (Leonard, this volume). Throughout his works Kapp (2011, 88n9) explicitly targeted Mises's instrumentalism, that is, his 'purely positivist [read: value-free], formal and subjectivist procedure [i.e., praxeology],' revealing once more the continuity of his main intellectual thrust since the socialist calculation debate but also *Social Costs*. The latter doubts that Mises would be prepared to apply his definition of economics as a science of human action (means-ends) to social choices and evaluations, that is, 'decisions of government in matters of economic policy' (see Kapp 1950b, 252). Kapp's integrated and social conceptualization of knowledge is a contribution to the 'economics of scientific knowledge' (Mirowski and Sent 2002) that provides an alternative to purely individualist conceptualizations of knowledge, such as personal knowledge (Polanyi 1958) and commodified knowledge (Hayek 1945).

1.10 The Life of Kapp's Ideas in the Material World: Environment and Development, Science and Technology, Law and Economics

The major impact of Kapp's ideas emerged during the 1970s and 1980s, which is mainly attributable to their ability to attract organizational and financial support.[8] Most notable are Kapp's influential membership on the expert panel for environment and development, which helped prepare the 1972 UN conference on the human environment, and his chairmanship of the German ministerial commission on green technologies. His vision is credited as inspiring the conception of at least four major organizations still operating today, that is, the Socialist Environment and Resource Association (SERA), the Centre for Environment and Development in Paris, the European Association for Evolutionary and Political Economy (EAEPE), and the German Association for Ecological Economics (VÖÖ). Significant also was the fact that Kapp's work on social costs attracted financial support from the Institute for Social Research and the Fulbright Foundation. Additionally, since the early 1980s the K. William and Lore L. Kapp Foundation for the Humanization and Integration of the Social Sciences continued to support research and to be involved in the awarding of the Kapp Prizes of EAEPE and VÖÖ. Additionally, collected volumes on Kapp's economics flourish in the heterodox economics community (Gerber and Steppacher 2011; Ramazzotti, Frigato, and Elsner 2012).

Richard Gaskins (2010) has recently pointed out that a major source of support for Kapp's 'whole-society' perspective of social costs and precautionary *ex ante* approach of social controls of technologies exists within public health studies of injury and disease. This seems correct, as Kapp explicitly referred to the kinds of technological controls effective in the industries of food, pharmaceutics, and nuclear power as ways to reduce social costs and guarantee social minima:

> In this context the burden of proof that a new technology, a new product, a new process, and a particular input (and output) pattern are safe would have to rest in principle upon the producer and not upon the damaged person or society. Institutionalized agencies would have the function and responsibility to anticipate, appraise, and judge beforehand the hazards and benefits of alternative technologies, techniques, and locations. On the basis of such an assessment it would be possible to direct investments with respect to both permissible choice of factor inputs and the location of specific industries, in accordance with criteria that take account of the full range of the costs and consequences of new techniques for the individual and society as well as the world community. (Kapp 1971, xxi)

Kapp concluded that this approach would imply radically new forms of decision making and planning by institutions responsible to society and more responsive to human needs. The individual allocation and investment decision, the private choice of technology, and the selection of the site of production would be replaced. A detailed framework for technological controls was elaborated during Kapp's chairmanship of the German ministerial commission Governmental Furtherance of Environmentally Friendly Technologies (Kapp [1975] 2011): (1) goal formulation, which involved (a) dealing with goal conflicts, (b) societal assessment of alternative technologies as a prerequisite of selecting an objective, and (c) choice of goal and participation in research policy decisions; (2) problems in coordinating research, which involved (a) coordination of research on the national level and (b) international cooperation; (3) financing the research and promoting the diffusion of environmentally sound technologies, entailing (a) possibilities of financing research, (b) state profit sharing, (c) state support of research projects with great risk and relatively small prospects of commercial utilization, (d) state research institutes, (e) measures of promoting the dissemination of environmentally sound technologies, methods, and products, (e1) legal and institutional bases, (e2) dissemination of information about environmentally sound technologies, (e3) new patent and license regulation, and (e4) financial aids to promote the dissemination of environmentally sound technologies; and (4) from the causation principle to the objective principle: technology as a dependent variable.

Another application of Kapp's theory pointed out by Gaskins (2007) occurred within the field of law and economics (for references to Kapp in legal scholarship, see Kimball 1959, 934; Koplin 1955, 840). Kapp (1950b, 63) had clearly exposed the problems with legal solutions to social costs in the case of work injuries, such as the inability of victims to receive their rewards because of insolvent employers or private insurance companies. Citing the 1939 report of the National Resource Committee, Kapp also noted that court action failed to resolve problems such as water and air pollution because of the problems of large numbers of affected parties, prohibitively expensive legal fees, and the burdensome if not impossible proof of specific damages, their amounts, and the possibility of abatement (80-81). The 'liability law solution,' Mises's preferred solution (Dawson 2013; Cordato 2004), is criticized just like the 'bilateral market approach,' which is the preferred solution of Coase and Stigler (Coase 1960; Medema 2011), as an instance of the ideology of individual decision making underlying the 'polluter pays principle' (see above for Kapp's rejection of this principle) (Kapp n.d.e).

Partly because of the influence of J. M. Clark, legal realists adopted a perspective on social costs akin to that of Kapp (Gaskins 2007). They recognized the complexity of social cost cases and supported the idea of a 'community responsibility' for social costs in the form of a social insurance scheme. The latter was viewed a public law alternative to tort law, which would introduce the responsibility to prevent social costs ex ante, resorting to, for example, 'criminal penalties, industrial health and safety laws, and a comprehensive prevention strategy aimed at reducing injuries and environmentally caused diseases' (Gaskins 2007, 4). This kind of community responsibility proposed by legal realists for the account of social costs of a community is today recognized by New Zealand's Accident Compensation Corporation (ACC), based on three remediation strategies, that is, 'prevention, rehabilitation and compensation, stressing that order of priority' (Gaskins 2010, 39). Trying to prove the defendants' fault or negligence, or even establishing causality according to tort law in complex economy-environment interactions with time lags and cumulative circular interactions, is viewed as erratic, inconsistent, time consuming, and administratively expensive. The chances of becoming a victim is viewed as a statistical inevitability because of the injury-generating practices of complex industrial societies and a risk of social progress, and is not due to individual fault. The simplistic, individualistic, and linear view of causation and compensation of the nineteenth-century fault principle is deemed inappropriate to deal with the complexity underlying social costs because the attempt to disentangle the multiplicity of causations behind individual social cost cases is either very inefficient or even ineffective because of being impossible or too time consuming. Additionally, the unnecessarily expensive administration of legal solutions to cases of social cost makes it cost inefficient. An inconsistency of legal rulings across similar cases is likewise problematic. That is, tort law is perceived as unsuitable for dealing with social costs because it leaves a large part of the social costs unpaid for, that is, a social costs deficit. ACC aims to make it impossible that social costs stay with the victim and are not compensated for unless the victim's claim can pass the court's fault test. Insidious avoidance strategies of defendants with deep pockets are likewise unnecessary. While the ACC's prevention strategy remains underdeveloped because of conflicts over the distribution of costs of preventing social costs, it maintains Kapp's idea that the most efficient and just solution to social costs is prevention via effective health and safety regulation (Gaskins 2010, 39-45).

1.11 Conclusion

The article has demonstrated that K. William Kapp provided a genuinely *social* theory of social costs. This genuinely social character is the result of a consistent effort to defend the socialist position from the socialist calculation debate, that is, the possibility of substantively rational planning to prevent social costs. The core argument is that social costs reflect the violation of social needs by the market's calculus. Substantive rationality in planning is needed to guarantee the fulfillment of social needs. Social needs are scientifically objectified and quantified via the elaboration of social minima, that is, minimum adequate living conditions. The latter are rooted in the structure of existential human needs, which are investigated in a science of integrated social knowledge. Social costs, according to Kapp's view, are a genuinely social, that is, complex macro-phenomenon, resulting from circular cumulative causation between the open economic system and its social and natural environment. Consequently, Kapp's theory of social costs is not based on the 'polluter pays principle' underlying individualist and ex post solutions to social costs, such as neoclassical taxation or bargaining, or Mises's tort law solution. Instead, Kapp proposed and developed a framework for systemic social legislation that prevents social costs *ex ante* via safety limits, social minima, and technological controls. Today, the continued presence of his approach in economic discourse and its application to policymaking are a testament to the power of Kapp's ideas.

References

Ayres, Robert, and Allen Kneese (1969) 'Production, Consumption, and Externalities.' *American Economic Review* 59 (3): 282-97.

Beckerman, W (1972) 'Environmental Policy and the Challenge to Economic Theory.' In *Political Economy of the Environment: Problems of Method.* Paris: Ecole pratique des hautes etudes and Mouton.

Berger, Sebastian (2008) 'Karl Polanyi's and Karl William Kapp's Substantive Economics: Important Insights from the Kapp-Polanyi Correspondence.' *Review of Social Economy* 66 (3): 380-96.

(2012) 'The Discourse on Social Costs: Kapp's Impossibility Thesis vs. Neoliberalism.' In *Social Costs Today: Institutional Analyses of the Present Crisis,* edited by Wolfram Elsner, Pietro Frigato, and Paolo Ramazzotti. London: Routledge.

(2013) 'The Making of the Institutional Theory of Social Costs: Discovering the K. W. Kapp and J. M. Clark Correspondence.' *American Journal of Economics and Sociology* 72 (5): 1106-30.

Forthcoming. 'Culture and Economics: How the Poet Ernst Wiechert inspired Kapp's Humanist Economics.' *Journal of Economic Issues.*

Berger, Sebastian, and Mathew Forstater (2007) 'Towards a Political Institutionalist Economics: Kapp's Social Costs, Lowe's Instrumental Analysis, and the European Institutionalist Approach to Environmental Policy.' *Journal of Economic Issues* 41 (2): 539-46.

Berger, Sebastian, and Rolf Steppacher (2011) Introduction to *The Foundations of Institutional Economics,* by K. William Kapp, 0-13. Edited by Sebastian Berger and Rolf Steppacher. Abingdon: Routledge.

Buchanan, James M (1962) 'Politics, Policy, and the Pigovian Margins.' *Economica* 29 (113): 17-28.

Burczak, Theodor (2011) 'A Socialist Spontaneous Order.' In *Hayek, Mill, and the Liberal Tradition,* edited by Andrew Farrant, 130-47. London: Routledge.

Calabresi, Guido (1961) 'Some Thoughts on Risk Distribution and the Law of Torts.' *Yale Law Journal* 70 (4): 499-553.

Clark, John M (1950) 'The New Economic Community.' *Yale Review* 40 (1): 171-74.

Coase, Ronald (1960) 'The Problem of Social Costs.' *Journal of Law and Economics* 3 (October): 1-44.

Cordato, Roy (2004) 'Towards an Austrian Theory of Environmental Economics.' *Quarterly Journal of Austrian Economics* 7 (1): 3-16.

Dawson, Graham (2013) 'Austrian Economics and Climate Change.' *Review of Austrian Economics* 26 (2): 183-206.

Foster, John Bellamy (2010) *The Ecological Rift: Capitalism's War on Earth.* New York: Monthly Review Press.

Foucault, Michel (1979) (2008) *The Birth of Biopolitics.* Basingstoke: Palgrave Macmillan.

Franzini, Maurizio (2006) 'Social Costs, Social Rights, and the Limits of Free Market Capitalism: A Re-reading of Kapp.' In *Social Costs and Public Action in Modern Capitalism: Essays Inspired by Karl William Kapp's Theory of Social Costs,* edited by Wolfram Elsner, Pietro Frigato, and Paolo Ramazzotti, 56-71. London: Routledge.

Gaskins, Richard (2007) 'Social Insurance and Unpaid Costs of Personal Injury: A Second Look at K. William Kapp.' Paper presented at the 2007 conference of the European Society for Ecological Economics, Leipzig.

2010. 'Accounting for Accidents: Social Costs of Personal Injury.' *Victoria University of Wellington Law Review* 41:37-50.

Gerber, Julien-François, and Rolf Steppacher, eds. (2012) *Towards an Integrated Paradigm in Heterodox Economics: Alternative Approaches to the Current Eco-Social Crises.* Basingstoke: Palgrave.

Goodwin, Craufurd (2008) 'Ecologist Meets Economist: Aldo Leopold, 1887-1948.' *Journal of the History of Economic Thought* 30 (4): 429-52.

Hayek, Friedrich (1944) *The Road to Serfdom.* Chicago: University of Chicago Press.
— (1945) 'The Use of Knowledge in Society.' *American Economic Review* 35 (4): 519-30.

Kapp, K. William. n.d.a. 'Interview by The Economist.'
— n.d.b. 'Draft Introduction.' Unpublished manuscript.
— n.d.c. 'Project Outline.' Unpublished manuscript.
— n.d.d. 'The Social Costs of Free Enterprise.' Unpublished manuscript.
— n.d.e. 'Environmental Control and the Market Mechanism.' Unpublished manuscript.
— n.d.f. 'Social Returns.' Unpublished manuscript.
— (1936) *Planwirtschaft und Aussenhandel.* Geneva: Georg & Cie.
— (1937) *Memorandum on the Efforts Made by the League of Nations towards a Solution of the Problems of Raw Materials.* Submitted to the Tenth Session of the International Studies Conference of the International Institute of Intellectual Cooperation. Geneva: Geneva Research Center.
— (1941) *The League of Nations and Raw Materials, 1919-1939.* Geneva Studies vol.12, no. 3. Geneva: Geneva Research Center.
— (1950a.) 'Economic Planning and Freedom.' *Weltwirtschaftliches Archiv* 64: 29-54.
— (1950b.) *The Social Costs of Private Enterprise.* Cambridge, Mass.: Harvard University Press.
— (1961) *Toward a Science of Man in Society: A Positive Approach to the Integration of Social Knowledge.* The Hague: Martinus Nijhoff.
— (1963a.) *The Social Costs of Business Enterprise.* London: Asia Publishing House.
— (1963b.) 'Social Costs and Social Benefits: A Contribution to Normative Economics.' In *Probleme der normativen Ökonomik und der wirtschaftspolitischen Beratung,* edited by E. v. Beckerath and H. Giersch, 183-210. Berlin: Duncker & Humblot.
— (1963c.) *Hindu Culture, Economic Development, and Economic Planning in India.* Bombay: Asia Publishing House.
— (1971) Introduction to the 1971 edition of *The Social Costs of Private Enterprise.* New York: Schocken Books.
— (1974) *Environmental Policies and Development Planning in Contemporary China and Other Essays.* Paris: Mouton.
— (1976) 'The Open System Character of the Economy and Its Implications.' In *Economics in the Future,* edited by Kurt Dopfer, 90-105. London: Macmillan.
— (2011) 'Science and Technology in the Light of Institutional Analysis.' In *The Foundations of Institutional Economics,* edited by Sebastian Berger and Rolf Steppacher, 203-44, Abingdon: Routledge.

Kimball, Spencer L. (1959) 'Traffic Victims: Tort Law and Insurance by Leon Green.' *Michigan Law Review* 57 (6): 933-37.

Knight, Frank (1951) 'Review of *The Social Costs of Private Enterprise,* by K. William Kapp.' *Annals of the American Academy of Political and Social Science* 273:233-34.

Koplin, H. T. (1955) 'Conservation and Regulation: The Natural Gas Allocation

Policy of the Federal Power Commission.' *Yale Law Journal* 64 (6): 840-62.
Lee, Frederic S. 2009. *A History of Heterodox Economics: Challenging the Mainstream in the 20th Century*. London: Routledge.
Lowe, Adolph (1965) *On Economic Knowledge: Towards a Science of Political Economics*. New York: Harper and Row.
Martinez-Alier, Joan (2002) *Environmentalism of the Poor: A Study of Ecological Conflicts and Valuation*. Cheltenham: Edward Elgar.
Medema, Steven G. (2011) 'A Case of Mistaken Identity: George Stigler, 'The Problem of Social Costs,' and the Coase Theorem.' *European Journal of Law and Economics* 31 (1): 11-38.
Menger, Carl (1923) *Grundsätze der Volkswirtschaftslehre*. 2nd ed. Vienna: Holder-Pichler-Tempsky.
Mirowski, Philip (2013) *Never Let a Serious Crisis Go to Waste*. London: Verso.
Mirowski, Philip, and Edward Nik-Khah (2008) 'Command Performance: Exploring What STS Thinks It Takes to Build a Market.' In *Living in the Material World*, edited by Trevor Pinch and Richard Swedberg, 89-130. Cambridge, Mass.: MIT Press.
Mirowski, Philip, and Dieter Plehwe, eds. (2009) *The Road from Mont Pèlerin: The Making of the Neoliberal Thought Collective*. Cambridge, Mass.: Harvard University Press.
Mirowski, Philip, and Esther-Mirjam Sent, eds. (2002) *Science Bought and Sold: Essays in the Economics of Science*. Chicago: University of Chicago Press.
Mises, Ludwig von (1920) 'Die Wirtschaftsrechnung im Sozialistischen Gemeinwesen.' *Archiv für Sozialwissenschaften* 47 (1): 86-121.
   1944. *Bureaucracy*. New Haven, Conn.: Yale University Press.
Pearce, D. W., and S. G. Sturmey (1966) 'Private and Social Costs and Benefits: A Note on Terminology.' *Economic Journal* 76 (301): 152-58.
Pigou, Arthur Cecil (1929) *The Economics of Welfare*. 3rd ed. London: Macmillan.
Polanyi, Karl (1957) *Trade and Markets in the Early Empires*. Glencoe, Ill.: Free Press.
Polanyi, Michael (1958) *Personal Knowledge: Towards a Post-critical Philosophy*. Chicago: University of Chicago Press.
Prasch, Robert (2005) 'The Social Costs of Labor.' *Journal of Economic Issues* 39 (2): 439-45.
Ramazzotti, Paolo, Pietro Frigato, Wolfram Elsner, eds. (2012) *Social Costs Today: Institutional Analyses of the Present Crisis*. London: Routledge.
Ropke, Inge (2004) 'The Early History of Modern Ecological Economics.' *Journal of Ecological Economics* 50 (3): 293-314.
Rutherford, Malcolm (2011) *The Institutionalist Movement in American Economics, 1918-1947*. Cambridge: Cambridge University Press.
Schäffle, Albert (1881) *Bau und Leben des Sozialen Körpers*. Vol. 3. Tübingen.
Spash, Clive (2011) 'Social Ecological Economics: Understanding the Past to See the Future.' *American Journal of Economics and Sociology* 70 (2): 340-75.
   (2012) 'Towards the Integration of Social, Economic, and Ecological Knowledge.' In *Towards an Integrated Paradigm in Heterodox Economics:*

Alternative Approaches to the Current Eco-Social Crises, edited by Julie-Francois Gerber and Rolf Steppacher, 26-46. Basingstoke: Palgrave Macmillan.

Swaney, James A. (2006) 'Policy for Social Costs: Kapp vs. Neo-classical Economics.' In *Social Costs and Public Action in Modern Capitalism: Essays Inspired by Karl William Kapp's Theory of Social Costs*, edited by Wolfram Elsner, Pietro Frigato, and Paolo Ramazzotti, 106-25. London: Routledge.

Tool, Marc (1978) 'Review of *Economics in Institutional Perspective: Memorial Essays in Honor of K. William Kapp.' Journal of Economic Issues* 12 (4): 891-901.

Wieser, Friedrich (1924) 'Theorie der Gesellschaftlichen Wirtschaft.' In vol. 1, pt. 2, of *Grundriss der Sozialökonomik*. Tübingen.

2
Social and Institutional Economics vs. Formal Economics

The year 2010 marks the 100th anniversary of Karl William Kapp's birth and provides this publication of his *Foundations of Institutional Economics* with a special occasion. Yet, as will be explained below, this book does not merely serve a commemorative purpose. This introduction leaves to future research the task of a more comprehensive evaluation of Kapp's contribution to economics, and of his potential significance to modern pluralist and heterodox economics. It focuses instead on understanding Kapp's book within the context of his intellectual project and his personal biography. In this, the introduction answers to questions that have arisen from the manuscript's history: for instance, why was the author unable to complete this work for sixteen years? and why should this material be published at this point in time after being stored largely unnoticed in the Kapp Archive for well over thirty years?[9] Thus, the introduction is a continuation of the 'rational reconstruction' of (European) institutionalism[10] and supports the thesis that Kapp's book was part of a largely unexplored project within 20th century institutionalism. The goals of this project were to 'institutionalize' institutional economics internationally via organizations of importance; to move the development discourse in the direction of democratic planning of social welfare minima, technology and the environment; and to prevent the global rise of 'formal' economics. While more research is needed, the following investigation indicates that the standard narrative about the demise of institutional economics after WWII should be amended,[11] and stimulates interesting questions as to what can be learned for the future of institutional economics.

2.1 Biographical Background

K. William Kapp was a leading 20th century economist who is best known for his book *The Social Costs of Private Enterprise* (1950), which significantly influenced the discourse on institutional reforms to prevent environmental disruption. Today, such international organizations of economists as the European Association for Evolutionary Political Economy and the European Society for Ecological Economics associate themselves with Kapp, and his ideas are again part of the discourse on social costs and economic crises.[12] Born on October 27, 1910 in Königsberg, Karl William Kapp grew up during the epoch of Imperial Germany and the Weimar Republic. His father, August Wilhelm Kapp, worked as a philosophy teacher, held a doctoral degree in physics, and was portrayed as a distinguished humanist socialist by Ernst Wiechert, who was a prominent humanist poet and also Karl William's teacher at the 'Hufgymnasium.' Karl William, or 'Ted' as close friends called him, studied 'Staatswissenschaft' (consisting of law and economics) at the universities of Berlin and Königsberg. As early as 1933, he and Lili Lore Masur (who would become his wife and co-author) left Nazi-Germany for Geneva, where William completed his doctoral degree in economics at the Geneva Postgraduate Institute of International Studies and became acquainted with the exiled 'Frankfurt School.' The Frankfurt School eventually formed the Institute for Social Research at Columbia University and provided the Kapps with a scholarship in 1937, allowing their emigration to the United States of America, where Kapp held appointments at Columbia University, New York University, the City University of New York, and Wesleyan University in Connecticut. Between 1958 and 1963, the Kapps undertook three Fulbright research visits to India and the Philippines before receiving an appointment at the University of Basel (Switzerland) in 1965. Kapp retired in 1975 and died on April 26, 1976.

Kapp started the current project at the age of 50 after his first research visit to India, where he had directly experienced the significance of its Hindu culture and institutions to its economic development.[13] He had just finished a long-standing research project that tied together the insights of the emerging fields of cultural anthropology and social psychology in his framework to integrate social knowledge (*Theory of Man in Society* (1961)), emphasizing the crucial role played by culture and institutions in adequately satisfying bio-cultural human needs. This cultural-institutional orientation can be traced back to Kapp's position as co-editor of the *Introduction to Western Civilization* project at Columbia (1946), and was being solidified at the beginning of the sixties with increasing reliance on Veblen's institutional economics: e.g. the enlarged and revised second edition of *The Social Cost of Business Enterprise* (1963), in honor of Veblen's *Theory of Business Enterprise* (1904).

2.2 The history of the manuscript and Kapp's intellectual project

Kapp began working on the manuscript in 1960 while teaching graduate courses in institutional economics at Brooklyn College.[14] The first document referring to the project outline is a letter to Karl Polanyi in 1960.[15] Addressing Polanyi's efforts to develop a 'teaching program in institutionalism and its theoretical implications,' Kapp noted:

> Dear Karl: [...] as you will have seen from my outline I am trying to do precisely that for the so-called American 'School' that goes back to Veblen. This does not mean that I am not fully aware of the fact that your group has done work along similar lines. I have always felt that our work converges in all important respects [...] [Your work] is much more in the tradition of Veblen's institutionalism than is usually realized. [...] In short, my study is not going to stop with the older institutionalists and I hope I have made this clear in my outline. I have always felt that one of the reasons why institutionalists did not make greater headway in the past was due to the absence of any systematic-theoretical treatment of our thought and the absence of suitable first-rate reading materials. In short, you are right, a 'Reader' is necessary.[16]

The project outline mentioned in this letter had originally been submitted to the administration of Brooklyn College[17] with the title 'American Institutionalism: The System of Economic Analysis of Veblen and His Followers.' In answering his critics who accused institutional economics of being 'at best an impressionistic description of an ever changing economic environment' Kapp admitted the problem that institutional economics 'is not fully recognized as a distinct approach to the formulation of questions and the ordering of ideas,' and that it had failed to systematize its approach. Consequently, Kapp derived the goal of systematizing institutional analysis to demonstrate the 'common view of the economic process' and to bring together 'those ideas and theories which can be shown to be logically interconnected.' Other goals were

> to [...] [improve] institutionalist thought [...] [by making] explicit the systematic character and logical connections between the various parts of American institutionalist thought would perfect this branch of our knowledge by giving it greater clarity, greater accuracy and greater comprehensiveness. [...] in those fields of analysis which are still open theoretical issues in our discipline such as the question of external (social) costs and external (social) economics, private wants and public purposes, public investment criteria.

Clearly, his hope was that 'insofar as we succeed in systematizing American institutionalist thought, our study may carry conviction to other members of the profession and represent a challenge to rejuvenate and broaden the scope of modern economic analysis.' Kapp applied for a 'release for one year from teaching and administrative duties' to 'advance the actual writing of the manuscript' that he optimistically anticipated to finish within a 'period of three years.' These two documents show that Kapp deemed his book the 'systematic-theoretical reading material' necessary for a mid-20th century project to advance institutional economics while 'not stopping with older institutionalism.'

In a letter to Edgar Salin dated January 12, 1963, Kapp referred to his project as 'Foundations of Social Economics' with which he hoped to develop a system of modern social economics based on an empirical-institutional methodology. Obviously, Kapp found it useful to make 'social' synonymous with 'institutional' economics. This terminological move can be understood in the light of John Maurice Clark's *Preface to Social Economics*, which inspired Kapp to distinguish his approach from formal neoclassical economics and to define his agenda, leading to the publication of his article 'Social Economics and Social Welfare Minima' (1965; see appendix). In *Social Costs of Business Enterprise* (1963), Kapp also increasingly referred to Clark's arguments to stress the social value dimension of the problem of social costs. According to Kapp, both social and institutional economists perceive the economy as an

> open system [...] Social economics has a greater impact on practical affairs than is usually realized. It can be shown that the economic policies of the New Deal, contemporary labor legislation, social security schemes, public utility, anti-trust and security-exchange regulations, and policies designed to mitigate economic fluctuations have all been strongly influenced by social economics. Therefore, social economics may prove equally fruitful in the analysis and ultimate solution of persistent contemporary economic problems, such as social inefficiencies and social costs reflected in unused capacity and unemployment, the neglect of public benefits and the starving of the public sector, the increasing disparities between rich and poor countries, and the changing nature of international economic relations.[18]

Just as in the initial project outline, this quote shows that Kapp explicitly places his project in the tradition of the American institutional economists who designed the seminal programs of New Deal and security-exchange regulation. Kapp's goal was to renew this legacy in relation to such newly emerging issues as social costs, poverty, and economic development. One of the ways in which Kapp sought to further his project was to participate in the early attempts of U.S. institutional economists to form an association:

> Dear Professor Gambs: Returning from a one year's stay at the University of the Philippines I find several communications of the Wardman Group [...] I am delighted about the establishment of this group of dissenting economists

and I am glad to see that you included my name in the list of original members. I think that we have long needed such an organization in the U.S. May I suggest that we devote ourselves [...] to two things which seem to me of great importance at the present time. First, the preparation and publication of a selection bibliography of works, annotated and classified by subject matter which were written in the tradition of social or institutional economics during the last two years. Second, I think that we could render no greater service to the propagation of social economics than to encourage the preparation of teaching materials such as readings and textbooks [...] As far as the ultimate name of the society is concerned I am inclined to agree with Myrdal that 'Veblen Society' may be too narrow despite the overwhelming influence which Veblen has indeed exercised and continues to exercise at least in America. I feel that the name 'Association to Study the Reconstruction of Economics', although pointing to what is needed and is actually on the agenda, may have a methodological ring which may not appeal to a sufficiently large group of members of the profession. If 'Institutional Economics' is not satisfactory why not use 'Social Economics' in contradistinction or juxtaposition to 'Pure' or 'Positive' Economics which deliberately abstracts precisely those socio-cultural factors and influences which make economic processes what they are: dynamic, evolutionary, structured and embedded in a broader framework of society and culture. I have begun to use the term 'Social Economics' in the new edition of 'History of Economic Thought – A Book of Readings' Barnes and Nobles 1963. [...] Incidentally, Social Economics also comes close to 'Sozialökonomik' – a term which Max Weber used on the Continent. [...] I hope to stay in close touch with the Wardman Group.[19]

The correspondence with leading American economists reveals not only that he suggested 'social economics' as an appropriate name for the organization,[20] but that Kapp increasingly perceived this project as being directed against the rise of 'formal economics.' In this context, he considered Max Weber's notions of substantive rationality and social economics[21] useful because they can be used to emphasize the importance of higher norms, e.g. social minima or the social (value) dimension of developmental and environmental problems (see appendix).[22] Kapp also furthered his project by promoting it to one of the leading European economists, Gunnar Myrdal:

Dear Professor Myrdal: [...] My own research plans center around an admittedly ambitious undertaking which carries the tentative title 'Foundations of Social Economics'. It is concerned partly with the demonstration of the strength and validity of the principle of circular causation as a main hypothesis for the study of socio-economic processes and partly with a further elaboration of my previous studies dealing with social costs, social benefits and economic planning. I intend to show that there is an alternative to model-building and reasoning in terms of hypothetical constructs and that the principle of cumulative causation together perhaps with an empirical typology constitute a realistic approach to scientific discovery and explanation of institutional regularities and sequences of occurrences. I am enclosing a tentative outline of my project in order to indicate the trend of my current thought.[23]

The emphasis on circular cumulative causation (CCC) underlines the fact that Kapp considered Myrdal's analytical framework[24] to be of strategic importance for his intellectual project as *the* antithesis to formal economics' equilibrium concept. CCC accentuates growing socio-economic disparities and environmental disruption, providing a rationale for improved social controls and institutional reforms.[25] Kapp's letter also points out the similarities between their research agendas on 'institutional problems' arising from international trade between unequal systems:

> What impresses me in particular is the realistic framework in which you place the contemporary problem of international trade and financial relations. On a more limited scale, indeed within the different context of the Thirties, I once tried to answer some of the institutional problems which arise in international trade relations between countries with foreign trade monopolies and business enterprise economies. In fact, my dissertation (1936) at the Geneva Postgraduate Institute of International Studies was concerned with problems of this kind.

The context of this and the following correspondence is that by the early 1960s Myrdal and Kapp were considered leading developmental economists who had undertaken research projects in developing countries and participated in the ensuing development debates. On the one hand, both economists understood that the 'development era' posed the threat of formal economics spreading to developing countries and they warned students there not to become 'conformists to the inherited doctrines of the West.'[26] On the other hand, they recognized the unique opportunity to 'institutionalize' institutional economics internationally by forming a broad international organization:

> Dear Professor Kapp: I have long felt that we are kindred souls and I am quoting you in a big book on South Asia [*Asian Drama*] [...] This is just to thank you for your most interesting and inspiring article 'Social Economics and Social Welfare Minima', which you kindly sent me. [...] the time would be right for an international association of institutional economists parallel to the

Econometric Society. One difficulty is that most American institutionalists are so provincial and believe that everything started with Veblen – and almost finished with him.[27]

This letter marked the beginning of the active collaboration between Kapp and Myrdal's research group at the Institute for International Economic Studies with the purpose of organizing institutional economics on an international level with special emphasis on development planning. Most likely, Kapp's programmatic article on social economics inspired Myrdal to further cooperate with his 'kindred soul.' Kapp's proposal of 'social welfare minima' to guarantee the satisfaction of existential human needs overlapped with Myrdal's life-long work on development planning for poverty relief. Consequently, Kapp placed at the center of the present manuscript his argument for deriving and using the concept of minimum adequate living conditions as the central development criteria (instead of monetary indicators) (see chapters four and five).[28] Yet, Myrdal's attitude towards the American institutionalists foreshadowed some of the problems of forming an international organization.[29] A similar attitude surfaced in a letter by Erich Jacoby (Myrdal's colleague at the institute in Stockholm). Their skepticism towards the early American association is indicative of some of the problems of organizing institutional economics on a broad international basis. Jacoby was especially concerned about the term 'evolutionary' and the 'way of thinking' of the early AFEE economists:

> Dear Professor Kapp: [...] We feel also that we should take the initiative for the creation of an Association of Institutional Economists which could make a contribution to the reinterpretation of the ideas of Thorstein Veblen, Cummings and Wiksell in the light of the problems which we have to face today, particularly in the underdeveloped countries. Your suggestions, therefore, are very welcome and Gunnar Myrdal and I are prepared to work closely together with you. During our conversations in Rome and Basel we have also mentioned the newly established Association for Evolutionary Economics which is moved by the same dissatisfaction with the present trend of contemporary economics though I do not believe, after short study of the first volume of the Journal of Economic Issues, that their way of thinking in all relevant aspects is identical with ours. Personally I feel that the emphasis placed on 'evolutionary' instead of 'institutional' is to some extent misleading and might weaken the possibilities which an association of institutional economists might also have in Eastern European countries. There is, however, no doubt that we have to take into consideration the new American association when we wish to build up an association of institutional

economists. […] we should take the first steps to establish an organization of institutional economists on a broad international basis […] At a somewhat later stage we will also have to talk with our American friends. I wish to assure you that it will be a great pleasure for Gunnar Myrdal and myself to work closely together with you in this venture.[30]

Likewise, Kapp rejected biological metaphors and did not apply the 'evolutionary' adjective. Together with Myrdal, he preferred the accentuation of 'institutional' forces in circular and cumulative dynamics and deemed the term 'institutional' as universal enough for an organization that could integrate economists from different regions of the world and from a diversity of ideological backgrounds, particularly during the Cold War and the development era.[31] Interestingly, Kapp did not incorporate theories that were quite popular in mid-20th century American institutional economics, such as Clarence Ayres' 'Veblenian dichotomy' or the Texas institutionalist argument on resources and technology.[32] Instead, Kapp's *Foundations* became a unique synthesis of Veblen and mid-20th century European economic theories, most of which were linked to or grew out of the development discourse. The important conclusion seems to be that Kapp and his European collaborators aimed at establishing a broad international organization, with a focus on economic development issues that seemed to be at odds with parts of the early American association.

The importance that Jacoby's letters assigned to winning the support of the Deputy Chairman of the Planning Commission of the Government of India is another indication for the project's focus on economic development issues:

> My dear Kapp: […] In the meantime I have written to Professor D.R. Gadgil, the Deputy Chairman of the Planning Commission of the Government of India, who is today probably Asia's most outstanding economist. As you know, Gunnar and I have talked with him about the possibility of establishing such an association and we would like to have his close cooperation before we take a public initiative. Gunnar Myrdal is greatly interested in this whole matter and feels very strongly that it is the right moment to act and that the initiative should emanate from Stockholm, of course in very close cooperation with you.[33]

In seeking Gadgil's cooperation, this group of economists showed an understanding of the importance of political-institutional support. Upon returning from conference travel to the Netherlands and Cambridge, Jacoby reported back to Kapp not only that many economists were very enthusiastic about an organization of institutional economists that will 'comprise the east and the west,' but also that 'Professor Gadgil [...] seems to be very happy to be associated with the project' which gives 'the green signal to start the work.' In order to include the US institutional economists, Jacoby asked Kapp for a copy of 'Gamb's speech and other material about the evolutionary economists in the USA. I need particularly the character of this organization. The periodical has not impressed me very much.'[34] In response, Kapp once again mentioned his book: 'My dear Jacoby: [...] I applied for and was granted a leave of absence for the coming academic (winter) semester. [...] I shall use this time to give some thought to the problems of institutional economics – particularly to my old idea of a systematization of institutional theories.'[35] And: 'Dear Professor Myrdal: [...] I have taken a leave of absence for the coming winter semester 68/69 in order to do some writing on institutionalism.'[36] It is evident that Kapp continued to view his book as part of their common project, which was well underway by 1968 when Kapp wrote to the American institutionalist Louis Junker that 'nothing is more important than to work out the theoretical Foundations of institutionalism.'[37] Following Myrdal's invitation, Kapp delivered a preliminary overview of these foundations in his 'In Defense of Institutional Economics' lecture in Stockholm (see appendix), for which Myrdal organized the speedy publication in the 'Swedish Journal of Economics.' Shortly after Kapp's lecture, however, Jacoby reported that their project was suddenly facing a problem that would prove to be insurmountable:

> I have today to tell you that Statens Rad för Samhällsforskning has informed us that they have no possibility to support Gunnar Myrdal's and my proposition for the preparatory work required for the formation of an international association of institutional economists. Gunnar Myrdal and I are very sad about this decision, which makes it impossible for us at this time to take the initiative for the formation of such an association. This, of course, does not affect our sincere belief that the setting up of such an association is urgently needed and that we will support to all possible extent any movement in this direction.[38]

Kapp replied by expressing the hope 'that this is only a postponement and not a decision against the project altogether. [...] I understand that a project of this kind should not be treated as a part-time matter, and I also realize that it requires some financing.'[39] Despite this failure, Kapp still expressed confidence about his book project in a letter to Myrdal:

'Meanwhile I hope to be able to complete the first draft of my analysis of the Foundations of Institutional Economics within the present year.'[40] Only six months later, Kapp asked the leading US institutional economist Joseph Dorfman for advice in finding a suitable publisher: '[the book is primarily addressed] to economists and social scientists of the English speaking world, and particularly in America [...] I expect the manuscript to be ready towards the end of 1970.'[41]

Kapp also wrote Myrdal: 'By 1972 I hope to have completed my study on the foundations of institutional economics of which I enclose an outline in the form of chapter headings.'[42] He planned to include a chapter on the interrelation of social costs and environmental disruption with the underlying problems of science and technology:

> [the book's last][43] chapter on institutionalism and the price system [...] is partly a treatment of the problem of social costs and partly a discussion of planning in real terms and a chapter on the role of science and technology in the light of institutional analysis [...] [because] social costs falsify market criteria of choice and in general support wrong criteria of planning and policy making thereby helping to misdirect and delay the development process [...] my studies on the role of science and technology in the development process. My interest is [...] to explore the role and effects as well as the prerequisites for their acceptance, diffusion and application in a particular country.

And again, in another letter to Myrdal: 'My work on institutionalism will stress among other things the role and significance of science and technology and I see in this not only a fruitful, but less explored field of investigation, particularly with reference to underdeveloped countries.'[44] Kapp's interest in environmental disruption was 'still very much alive' and he assured Myrdal that he would pursue this 'problem individually, and as a member of the standing committee of the Social Science Council of UNESCO.'[45] It may be inferred that Kapp considered organizations of outstanding importance, such as UNESCO, as platforms to promote institutional economics' arguments within the development discourse. A case in point is his participation in the United Nations' panel of experts on 'Environment and Development' in preparation for the historic 1972 U.N. Conference on the Human Environment in Stockholm, which resulted in the institutionalization of the United Nations Environmental Program (UNEP). In this, Kapp worked closely with and became an inspiration for Ignacy Sachs (special advisor to the secretary general) who was in the process of formulating his theory of 'Ecodevelopment' while founding the International Research Centre on Environment and Development.[46] Another example is Kapp's leading role in a German governmental commission for 'Social and Economic Change,' proposing a democratic furtherance of green technologies (see appendix). In addition, Kapp's participation and speech during the international workshop of the worker's union 'IG Metal' in Germany inspired the formation of the Socialist Environmental and Resource Association (SERA) in England.[47]

This involvement in the discourse on environmental disruption and technology, however, caused further delays in Kapp's book manuscript. As a result, Kapp even deemed it necessary to devote parts of his retirement to its completion:

> Dear Gunnar: [...] As you know I am going to retire at the end of October [...] I intend to devote myself to an old project of mine: The Foundations of Institutional Economics. I hope to be free from this task by the beginning of 1976. May I finally ask you whether it would be possible to send to my assistant Dr. Rolf Steppacher your reprints. He is very much concerned with institutional economics and would be very grateful to you [...][48]

Kapp's book manuscript, then, was part of a larger project, the goal of which was to 'institutionalize' institutional economics internationally, and to move the development discourse towards democratic planning and social minima. This project also intended to prevent the global rise of formal economics that considered economic ends as outside the scope of democratic decision making. As we have seen, this project failed in many ways. In the meantime, however, several international organizations have emerged that are to some extent concerned with the issues identified by Kapp, such as the European Society for Ecological Economics. Yet, recent research indicates that the project's neoliberal antithesis, promoted chiefly by the Mont Pelerin Society, has been more successful in producing and promoting the arguments that have dominated international economic discourse and transformed the global socio-economic system.[49] Remarkably, the two projects existed simultaneously for some time; Myrdal, in fact, eventually shared the Bank of Sweden Prize with Friedrich A. von Hayek, the leading figure of the Mont Pelerin Society.

The success of the neoliberal project has been linked to the financial, social, and environmental crises of ever increasing magnitudes and the resulting large-scale destruction and redistribution of wealth, as well as the withering away of democracy. These phenomena have lead to unprecedented levels of dissatisfaction with the status quo of the economy, suggesting an opportunity for a new 'double movement.'[50]

Kapp and Myrdal proposed such change via democratic economic planning and saw a central role for the United Nations, without naively overlooking the dangers of ineffective administration.[51] The present reconstruction of Kapp's project thus aims to stimulate the debate about suitable strategies for revitalizing the legacy of institutional (social) economics that once provided the ideas for, and gave birth to, progressive institutional change, such as the New Deal and effective security-exchange regulation.

2.3 A Final Note on Changes to the Manuscript

The editors reached the decision to publish this manuscript in 2008. It soon became clear that major editorial work was necessary. The references were largely incomplete and choices had to be made among different chapter titles that were found in different versions of the manuscript. In addition, the subchapter 'Towards a Theory of Institutional Change' was originally planned as an individual chapter, but since its text neither contained subchapters nor introduction, it was added as a subchapter to the one on institutions. The English language of the manuscript also needed revision for stylistic coherence and readability. After all, Kapp was not an English native speaker, and the style may have suffered due to the manuscript being developed over a period of sixteen years in various countries. These linguistic edits were minor, however, and concerned excessively repetitive or unclear parts of the text. The subchapter 'The American Influence: Pragmatism, Darwinism, Brooks Adams' of 'Intellectual Antecedents of Institutional Economics' was missing from the manuscript and could not be replaced with other materials. The three missing chapters of the manuscript, 'Substantive vs. Formal Rationality', 'The Central Hypothesis of Institutional Economics: Circular Causation', and 'Institutionalism and the Price System,' could be substituted with Kapp's published articles on these issues (see appendix).

3

The Discourse on Social Costs: Heterodox vs. Neoliberal Theories

'Social Costs [is] the story of my life'[52]

3.1 Introduction

This book is about K. William Kapp's theory of social costs. Based on unpublished and previously untranslated articles from the Kapp Archive this volume reconstructs this major contribution to heterodox economics. This contribution is important because much is at stake in the struggle to gain hegemony over the interpretation of the social damages arising from the economic system. The accepted boundaries of the discourse on social costs are today the neoclassical works of Pigou and Coase. (Aslanbegui/Medema 1998) It is therefore not surprising that the tremendous social costs of recent crises are interpreted mainly through these 'market-compatible' lenses. What are the alternatives?

This book publication contributes to the intellectual project of heterodox economics that seeks to overcome the neoclassical bias of today's conversation on social costs. Kapp's theory of social costs is valuable in this regard precisely because it is the most comprehensive alternative to the above theories, serving as a crucial building block of heterodox economics. More than any other economist Kapp dedicated a lifetime worth of intellectual effort to forge a heterodox theory of social costs. In fact, the genealogy of the discourse on 'social costs' largely mirrors the genealogy of his intellectual biography. The significant scholarly and policy impact of Kapp's work between the early 1950s and the late 1970s demonstrates its potential for the heterodox economics movement, which seeks to develop and implement effective solutions to social costs. Recovering Kapp's theory of social costs is important for heterodox economics because it proposes solutions to and asks questions about social damages that go far beyond the narrow neoclassical confines of the contemporary conversation. For heterodox economics to change the conversation on social costs it is necessary to make clear why the currently dominating neoclassical theories are a dead end, that there are heterodox alternatives, and their practical value for preventing social costs and for advancing heterodox economics. These tasks were taken up by Kapp and are the subject of this introduction.

3.2 Kapp's Heterodox Theory of Social Costs

One of the ways to understand the dominating neoclassical narrative on social costs is to ask what lies at its fringe, and beyond its boundaries. Indeed, heterodox economics can be interpreted as the excommunicated 'other' of neoclassical economics, (Dow 2011) which serves in the first place to give neoclassical economics a clear identity. Of course, this definition is not accepted by every self-identified heterodox economist. (Mearman 2011) Yet, recent research suggests that heterodox economists are not just united in their rejection of neoclassical orthodoxy but are in fact more in agreement on policy and theory than neoclassical economists. (Di Maio 2013) This would support Fred Lee's view that a coherent heterodox economic theory is slowly but steadily emerging.

In the first instance this volume showcases that Kapp would have wholeheartedly agreed with Lee's definition of heterodox economics as blasphemy, that is, as a radical critique of neoclassical economics. (Lee 2009) This means that Kapp would reject those positions in the contemporary debate that identify heterodoxy with pluralism or an 'anything goes' that is inclusive of neoclassical economics. (For the pluralism debate in heterodox economics see Mearman 2012; Lee 2010.) Quite to the contrary, one of the explicit goals of his theory of social costs was to refute neoclassical economics and its theories of social costs and externalities in their entirety for their faulty logic, ineffective policy proposals, and its hidden normative-apologetic character. Kapp was perhaps the first economist to discuss social costs as an outcome of neoclassical economics itself. (See this volume's chapters 6; Kapp 1950) Such a project is likewise suggested by Lee (2013). Kapp continuously refuted neoclassical economics throughout his work, since his dissertation's critique of Ludwig von Mises' neoliberal[53] impossibility thesis (see this volume's chapters 2 and 3; for an analysis of Kapp's interactions with neoliberal economists see Berger 2013; 2012). Consequently, proposals to reconcile Kapp's with Coase's neoliberal theory of social costs must be considered groundless. (For such an attempt see Niglia/Vatiori 2007)

Secondly, this volume demonstrates that Kapp's work is a contribution to Lee's project to systematically develop the blasphemous position by crafting heterodox theories that are based on insights from several traditions and can serve as powerful alternatives to neoclassical economic theories. While Kapp was mainly affiliated with the movement of social and institutional economics his was an approach that integrated insights from those heterodox traditions that he considered part of the 'substantive' or 'holistic' school, such as Marx, Veblen, Weber, and List. He neither believed in creating another dogma as a closed system of knowledge that would only repeat the neoclassical plight, nor a postmodern-pluralist cacophony. Rather, he developed an integrated system of social knowledge that remains open because it takes its lead from a given problem situation, as for instance, the socialization of production costs. (Kapp 1985) His theory of social costs is thus an ideal building block for an open-system-approach to heterodox economics.

Kapp's open-system-approach (OSA) to social costs and social knowledge (see chapters 9 and 11 in this volume; Berger/Elsner 2007) is the main reason for the wide acceptance of Kapp's theory of social costs by contemporary heterodox economists from a variety of intellectual backgrounds, such as Marxist environmental sociologists and ecological economists, (Foster 2010; Martinez-Alier 2002) as well as institutional economists. (Elsner/Frigato/Ramazzotti 2012) OSA is acknowledged as one of the key concepts of Ecological Economics (Carpintero 2013) and endorsed by economists who propose an integrated heterodox economics as an alternative to neoclassical economics. (Spash 2012; Gerber/Steppacher 2012) Even the environmental economist Alan Kneese acknowledged the superiority of Kapp's theory of social costs over that of Pigou and Coase. (Kneese 1969) Kneese adopted the radical critique of Cost-Benefit-Analysis which had initially been developed by Kapp (see chapter 12 this volume) and which is today one of the defining characteristics of heterodox Ecological Economics. (Carpintero 2013) Thus, Kapp's theory of social costs serves as a sturdy bridge between various heterodox paradigms. Its flexibility and attractiveness allowed Kapp to move in a variety of intellectual circles, countries, and institutional contexts. While this makes it impossible to fit him into one paradigmatic box the following sections reconstruct the defining aspects of Kapp's heterodox theory of social costs.

3.3 Looking Back to Forge the Future of Heterodox Economics

Despite the above signs of esteem among heterodox economists, Kapp's theory of social costs is largely forgotten, and has so far even failed to attract the attention of historians of economic thought. This contrasts with Kapp's leading role in the discourse on social costs between roughly 1950 and 1980. This contrast can be understood as a result of the demise of the institutional economics movement, (Rutherford 2011) the suppression of heterodox economics, (Lee 2009) and the great neoliberal transformation of the economics profession. (Mirowski 2013) Furthermore, the prohibitively high epistemic costs of trying to reconstruct past theories (Yalcintas 2013) contributes to Kapp's continued eclipse.

The reconstruction of past theories and concepts can be justified on the basis of the notion that ideas or their unrealized potentials are either lost or not fully realized due to incommensurabilities in the evolution of science. (Bernstein 1991; Elsner 1986) The goal of a 'rational reconstruction' (Rorty 1984) is to recover these losses with a view to influence the contemporary conversation, in this case the conversation on social costs. This follows in the footsteps of Lee's Post Keynesian price theory (Lee 1998), which can be described as 'looking back to see the future.' The latter has been explicitly proposed with regards to the work of Kapp by the leading socio-ecological economist Clive Spash (2011). The reconstruction is based on unpublished articles from the Kapp Archive and untranslated materials, which were selected so that the reader can follow the genealogy of Kapp's argument on social costs and its application in a variety of contexts.

3.4 The Socialist Calculation Debate

Chapters 2 and 3 constitute the first English translation of the core chapters on theory from Kapp's dissertation. (Kapp 1936) Kapp considered these chapters to include the nucleus of his theory of social costs. (1950, p. xxvii-xxviii) The latter began as a critique of economic calculation based on market prices in the context of the Socialist Calculation Debate (SCD). This context sheds light on the root of the dispute between Kapp's heterodox and neoclassical/neoliberal theories of social costs. In fact, it shows that the heterodox theory of social costs was born out of an attempt to counter Mises' polarizing and dogmatic impossibility thesis regarding socialist planning and the resurgence of (neo)-liberalism in general. This attempt was at the same time a defense of the socialist position on the possibility necessity of using economic planning to prevent social costs and create social benefits. Later, in the 1960s, leading members of the 'Neoliberal Thought Collective' (NTC) (Mirowski/Plehwe 2009) criticized Kapp's theory for blaming social costs on markets. (see Berger 2013; 2012 for an analysis of these interactions) This neoliberal counter-revolution on social costs may be viewed as a continuation of SCD as its protagonists, such as Mises and Hayek, became leading architects of NTC and the Chicago School. (See Mirowski 2009; Van Horn/Mirowski/Stapleford 2011)

In chapter 2 Kapp argues that instead of trying to refute Mises's thesis regarding the impossibility of rational allocation under socialism a 'countervailing thesis' regarding the market economy should be developed and empirically validated. This thesis holds in essence that economic calculation based on market prices cannot be rational from the perspective of society because it systematically socializes costs and ignores the substantive (material) nature of the economic process. Chapter 8 evidences that Kapp understood the genealogy of his theory of social costs as part of the debate between Weber and Mises on the rationality of the price system. Chapter 7 corroborates this interpretation as it juxtaposes Weber's substantive rationality and Mises's formal rationality.

However, instead of Weber's concept of substantive rationality the dissertation relies only on the substantive and socio-economic arguments developed by Menger, Wieser, Schäffle, List, and Polanyi[54], evidencing the large influence of Austrian economics discourse on the formation of Kapp's initial argument. In addition, Kapp references Pigou on the numerous social damages of markets which systemically undermine the gratification of social needs: the disruption of national health, employment related illnesses and accidents, inadequate protection of motherhood, excessive smoke concentrations, noise pollution, unhealthy construction work, retardation of scientific progress due to patents, advertisement, and premature resource depletion. Based on these socio-economic and substantive arguments Mises's 'rationality' of the price system is exposed as a merely *formal* rationality. The latter is not rational from a societal perspective because markets socialize costs and disregard the needs of the poor, both of which work against the gratification of social needs. Substantive rationality inverts the perspective and thereby exposes the hidden irrational sources of Mises's formal rationality. The rationality of markets now appears as a system that ignores and even represses social knowledge because it is not of interest from the point of view of private ownership. Market rationality thus leads to a violation and disregard of social needs and values. This reveals a veritable will to ignorance inherent in Mises's formal rationality. (See Mirowski 2013 for a different interpretation of the neoliberal will to ignorance as an epistemological challenge)

The myopic rationality of markets necessitates, according to Kapp, economic planning based on the precautionary principle to prevent social costs and guarantee the satisfaction of social needs. In defending the necessity and possibility of substantively rational planning, Kapp predominantly drew on the works of socialist economists, such as Friedrich Pollock, Emil Lederer, and Otto von Neurath. While social policies in liberal-capitalist economies compensate retroactively for social damages, precautionary planning can prevent social costs and thus guarantee the gratification of social needs. Planning thus yields important social benefits, which Kapp described in a subsequent book project.

3.5 The Social Costs of Markets and the Social Benefits of Planning

Chapter 3 shows that by the early 1940s Kapp had developed his SCD argument into a full scale book project with the working title 'Social Costs and Social Returns – A Critical Analysis of the Social Performance of the Unplanned Market Economy.' Because the term social returns was later dropped for 'social benefits' (see chapter 7) this project is here referred to as 'Social Costs/Social Benefits' (SC/SB).

The first goal of this project was to provide an empirically grounded critique of '19th century liberalism' (with explicit reference to the works of Hayek and Mises), the 'unplanned market economy,' 'capitalism,' as well as 'equilibrium economics' and 'conventional economic theory.' The second goal was to develop a theory of the social benefits of planning that would be 'derived from the gratification of collective needs [...] and the maintenance of a social minimum with respect to essential foodstuffs, medical care, housing, and education.' This theory would require the development of valid criteria 'for [...] economic policy, and perhaps to prepare the way for the elaboration of a positive theory of social value.' (Chapter 3) This part is directed at and strongly disagrees with the tenets of the 'prophets of gloom' – especially Hayek – that economic planning implies an inevitable road to serfdom. (Chapter 3)

The SB portion of SC/SB remained unfinished and unpublished for a number of reasons. One of them may be that John M. Clark had criticized Kapp for failing to provide any detailed formulation and evaluation of the potentials and limitations of a collectivist alternative. (Berger 2013) Further reasons are given by Kapp himself in chapter 4 which states that providing solutions to each instance of social costs via the social benefits of planning would have unduly enlarged the manuscript, destroyed the continuity of the text, and raised the important issue of liberty, which required a separate treatment. Chapter 8[55] reveals that only three chapters were finished by the mid-1940s and that completing the entire manuscript on social benefits would have taken too long. It also evidences that Kapp viewed 'Hindu Culture, Economic

Development and Economic Planning in India' (Kapp 1963) as the completion of this work on SB. Therefore, this book's key chapter on 'Social Costs and Social Benefits: Their Relevance for Public Policy and Economic Planning' is reprinted in the present volume (chapter 7).

Since the 1940s Kapp perceived the theory of social costs merely as a stepping stone towards a social economics that includes theories of social valuation (social accounting), social needs, social knowledge, social minima, social benefits, and social controls. Kapp explicitly pursued the project of social economics outlined by John M. Clark (Berger 2013) under the working title 'The Foundations of Social Economics,' which was posthumously published. (Kapp 2011) This work elucidates how Kapp sought to integrate the basic insights of European and American socio-economic traditions, namely, the works of Karl Marx, Max Weber, Thorstein Veblen, and their mid-20th century followers. (Kapp 2011) Kapp's publications *Readings in Economics* (1949) and *History of Economic Thought* (1956) narrate a development of the history of economic ideas that culminates in social economics as the pinnacle of economic thought.

3.6 The Social Costs of Markets

The above SC/SB project resulted in the publication of Kapp's main work on social costs, published as *The Social Costs of Private Enterprise* (SCPE) in 1950. The second enlarged and revised edition was entitled *The Social Costs of Business Enterprise* (1963) (SCBE). Chapter 4 evidences that the title *The Social Costs of Free Enterprise* was also given consideration. As chapter 8 evidences the term 'business enterprise' was eventually chosen because large scale government involvement in the economy had already rendered the terms 'private' and 'free' enterprise inappropriate for analytical purposes. Additionally, the preface of SCBE declares that the theory of social costs was in the tradition of Veblen's *Theory of Business Enterprise* (1904) as: 'Veblen [...] called for an investigation [...] 'of the various kinds and lines of waste that are necessarily involved in the present businesslike control of industry.' (Kapp 1963, p. xxvii) In this view the system's organizing principle of investment for profits acts as a systemic incentive to socialize costs of production by shifting them to society, third parties and future generations. Chapter 4 defines social costs:

> 'the term "social costs" refers to all those harmful consequences and damages which third persons or the community sustains as a result of productive processes, and for which private entrepreneurs are not held accountable. These social losses may be reflected in damages to human health; they may

find their expression in the destruction or deterioration of property values and the premature depletion of natural wealth; or they may be evidenced in an impairment of less tangible values.'

This definition of social costs is consistent with John M. Clark's notion of 'cost shifting' (Berger 2013) and adopts the view held by American institutionalists that social costs are systemic and large-scale problems inherent in the business-like control of industry, that is, Veblen's 'principle of investment for profits.' (Rutherford 2011) Consequently, only systemic solutions in the form of institutional reforms and social controls can effectively remedy social costs.

In conclusion, SCPE integrates Kapp's earlier Weberian argument from the SCD (see above) with Veblen's argument. Chapter 7 demonstrates that Kapp understood these two arguments as essentially the same for his analytical purposes. However, SCPE and SCBE also abound with references to Karl Marx's *Capital* volumes I-III, and one of Kapp's last articles on social costs highlights Marx's prescient insight:

> 'No matter how economical capitalist production may be in other respects, it is utterly prodigal to human life […] Capitalism loses on one side for society what it gains on another for the individual capitalist' (Marx, *Capital*, vol. III, 1909, p. 104 in Kapp 1970: 844)

In fact, the editorial preface of the Polish translation of SCPE extols Kapp's work and deems it to be consistent with Marxism. (Unpublished Manuscript 1: Kapp Archive) Additionally, SCPE includes a chapter on the conceptual history of social costs, which traces its development from classical economists, the socialists, Marx, the German Historical School, and Veblen to the social economists. Consequently, Kapp provides an integrative basis for a heterodox theory of social costs.

Kapp's understanding of social costs leads him to various insights. For instance, in the same vein as Karl Polanyi's 'double movement' Kapp states that the 'political history of the last 150 years […] [is] a revolt of large masses of people (including business) against the shifting of part of the social costs of production to third persons or to society.' (Kapp 1950, p. 16) This makes clear that Kapp's theory of social costs is a social conflict theory, that is, the extent of the victims' ability to leverage countervailing power determines the extent of social costs. In this view, the relative success and positions of companies and industries reflect their power to socialize costs. (For this view see also chapter 7)

3.7 Social Benefits of Planning

We recall that Kapp's dissertation (chapter 2) had already hinted at his intention to develop a theory of social benefits that accrue from planning, the prevention of social costs, and the gratification of social needs. As already mentioned this idea became part of the above SC/SB project (chapter 3) but was abandoned by the mid-1940s and largely forgotten since. In order to reconstruct this aspect of Kapp's theory the three completed yet unpublished chapters on social benefits from the initial SC/SB manuscript are presented in chapter 5. This reconstruction of the 'lost' SB portion is important because it evidences that Kapp did not just develop a theory of the social costs as a critique of markets and an argument for precautionary planning. Importantly, he also developed a theory of the social benefits of planning, which is a vital complement to the theory of social costs. The main reason for this is the fact that social benefits arise from the gratification of social needs by means of economic planning. The prevention of social costs contributes to the gratification of social needs and thus provides social benefits. Social costs and social benefit are thus interrelated. These chapters take inspiration from Friedrich List (see also Kapp 1962) whose argument on the social benefits of balanced economic development planning still resonate in the contemporary Neo-Listian and circular-cumulative-causation literature. (Berger 2009; Selwyn 2009)

Chapter 8 evidences that Kapp considered only three chapters on social benefits to be completed. From their stage of development it follows with considerable certainty that these are the chapters on international policies (chapter 5.3), transportation (chapter 5.4), and multi-purpose projects (chapter 5.5). The chapters on collective needs, social minima and science that are part of the table of contents (chapter 5 1) remained as torsos and do not constitute publishable material. The torso on social minima is fully developed and published in Kapp 2011 and Kapp 1965. The torso on science became part of SCPE, later work on science and technology (Kapp 1977; 2011), and chapter 12 on the organization of science along environmental goals. The torso on collective needs is published here as an exception because it illustrates Kapp's understanding of collective needs, as an early version of his concept of social needs.

Chapter 5.2 develops the dynamic understanding of collective needs in the light of their historical emergence. Public health measures to prevent epidemics, education, social security, and national self-sufficiency are examples of the generally accepted set of common interests, that is, 'the object of a genuine collective need.' Kapp recognizes that it is the trans-boundary character of problems, such as epidemics, and the complexity of modern production processes that give rise to *Wagner's Law* of increasing public activity and the collectivization of ends observable in all advanced countries. Thus, collective needs result from life in complex communities, they are dynamic and grow due to growing complexities. Another factor is the increase of influence of the working class thanks to democracy, which has lead to the recognition of a common responsibility for the weak members of society. Kapp argues that the gratification of collective needs and the protection of the weak against socially harmful effects of competition yield social benefits. In the end, collective needs are a matter of political practice. In addition, there are common interests of a less tangible kind, such as the ethical and humanitarian aspirations of a community, which are collective needs and which have economic implications.

Chapter 5.3 highlights the social benefits of protectionism, and the inseparability of the political-economic sphere that includes concerns over security, sovereignty, and the dangers of dependency. Kapp argues that the social benefits of protectionism include the development of genuine productive capabilities and powers that are the true source of wealth because they produce general prosperity. Further social benefits of protectionism are independence, a balanced economy, and the prevention of economic vicious cycles that result from foreign competition, price wars, dependency and migration.

Chapter 5.4 emphasizes the social benefits of social provisioning of transportation in the form of lower transportation costs, new settlements, national unity, national wealth, enhanced land values, and increased rewards to general industry. The definition of social benefits is advanced as '[effects that] are largely inappropriable to private producers and consumers' or 'cannot be easily appropriated by private producers, but rather accrue to society as a whole.' These social benefits of transportation ultimately have positive effects on private balance sheets as they are 'intrinsically connected.' The main arguments advanced for the social benefits of a well-planned and integrated transportation system are the large fix costs of projects, large overhead costs, higher efficiency and economies of scale.

Chapter 5.5 discusses the social benefits of multi-purpose projects, such as soil conservation, stream and water projects, and flood controls. Their social benefits include: the reduction of run-off of rainfall, maintenance of groundwater stores, equalization of stream flows, protection of wildlife, prevention of sedimentation of rivers and reservoirs, reduction of floods, positive health effects, conservation of land values, irrigation, and pollution abatement. These multiple purposes are of a 'social character' and their 'beneficial effects accrue to other people, or to the community as a whole.' Kapp adopts the complexity perspective regarding the interrelatedness of regional or national ecosystems, which was developed by the National Resource Committee and Richard T. Ely.

3.8 Substantive Rationality and Social Knowledge

Chapter 7 bases the theory of the social benefits of planning on Weber's notion of substantive rationality (see also Berger 2008 for this aspect of Kapp's theory):

> 'Substantive rationality [...] measures the extent to which a given group of persons is or could be adequately provided with goods by means of an economically oriented course of social action.' (Kapp, chapter 7)

In dealing with the phenomena of social costs and social benefits scientifically, Kapp heeded Weber's caveat of the ethics of conviction and his banning of social values from science. Weber's notion of substantive rationality and favorable remarks on Otto Neurath's planning in real physical terms of resources became the basis for Kapp's quest to render the phenomena of social costs and social benefits accessible to scientific, meaning, quantitative and objective treatment. This evidences once more Kapp's continued association with the very theoretical position that had triggered Mises's response and had thereby initiated the SCD (see above). Kapp's idea was to investigate social costs and social benefits in terms of the satisfaction of scientifically derived minima of adequate living conditions. In this view social costs are a violation of social minima and social-environmental safety standards that reflect social needs rooted in human needs. The project of a scientific theory of social costs and social benefits was thus tied up with the substantive investigation of human needs and behavior. The latter was explicitly launched against Mises's purely formal theory of behavior, that is, praxeology, (Kapp 1985; 2011) and against the neoclassical theory of behavior, namely, hedonism. (Kapp 1985; 2011) Hence, Kapp translates Weber's substantive rationality into a 'rational humanism' that considers the gratification of substantive human needs as the goal of an explicitly normative economics (Kapp 1985), and a step towards a democratic theory of consumption (chapter 7). Both consist of a process of deliberation that relates ends to means, that is, Kapp's adaptation of John Dewey's version of American pragmatism. The latter's insistence on pragmatic revisions in the light of empirical tests, realist theory, empirical relevance, and the rejection of universal validity and absolute certainty became programmatic for Kapp's approach. (Kapp 1985; 2011)

Investigating the relationship between human needs and the quality of the natural and social environment necessitated, according to Kapp, the integration and humanization of social knowledge and social science. (Kapp 1961) This meant bringing to bear all relevant insights from philosophical anthropology, social psychology, and existential philosophy on the unique bio-cultural openness of the human being and the existential needs that result therefrom. This integrated view of biological and cultural/social aspects of existential human needs was part of the quest to scientifically establish social minima and safety standards that guarantee the gratification of basic human needs. If fully enforced, these standards and minima would yield social benefits and preempt social costs. Kapp traced this differentiation between basic and higher needs back to the works of Veblen, Menger, and Maslow.

The proposal to integrate social knowledge on basic bio-cultural needs, however, must be seen in the light of Otto von Neurath's positivist project of the unification of knowledge. (Spash 2011) The influence of positivism on Kapp's theory of social costs and social benefits is also evident in chapter 7, which develops a detailed defense of the use of theoretical terms in scientific inquiry and its relation to observable phenomena. The concept of social costs captures a variety of tangible and less tangible phenomena that have in common that they are causally related to the principle of investment for profits and formal rationality. Following the 'conceptual turn' in positivism in the 1950s based on Carnap's insight concepts cannot be reduced to the sense data of observable properties of physical systems. Therefore, the ontological status of theoretical terms is a real entity because it refers to implicit structures as underlying unitary causes that are linked to explicit and empirical phenomena, also referred to as a depth-realist position. (Steinmetz 2005)

This nuanced understanding of the problem of social costs and social benefits as a systemic problem that demands institutional reform, substantive rationality, and social knowledge avoids the simplistic dualisms of capitalism vs. socialism, or state vs. market. Kapp's work on the social benefits of economic development planning in socialist countries such as Soviet Russia (1936), India (1963), and China (1974) also dealt with the social costs that emerge due to ineffective public administration (1960).

3.9 The Open System Approach and Circular Cumulative Causation

Chapters 9 and 10 develop and apply the concept of open systems for purposes of the sustainable development debate. Chapter 9 argues that the normative goal of the development process is the protection and improvement of environment, as well as the prevention of its deterioration in the form of social costs. The means are an inventory of ecological conditions and comprehensive public planning, that is, 'eco-development.' This chapter develops the connection between normative economics of long term ecological development planning and the fundamental vision of the open systems character of the economy. Kapp argues that the open-system-approach (OSA) perspective correctly conceptualizes the substantive and interrelated character of economic problems. OSA constitutes Kapp's fundamental vision for economics that requires a transdisciplinary and integrated approach, the long term determination of normative goals, deliberation and action oriented research.

Chapter 10 was presented at the Bellagio Center in 1967, which was sponsored by the Rockefeller Foundation and hosted a number of high profile meetings,[56] underscoring the significance that was attributed to Kapp's work. It showcases that Kapp perceived economic development to be a system of circular cumulative causation between various elements of the socio-economic system. In this system perspective, rapid economic growth can actually be abortive to the development process if it is accompanied with high social costs and not supported by viable institutional arrangements that guarantee the satisfaction of existential needs. An 'open system' perspective is necessary to identify tensions in the development process and to adapt strategies to guarantee 'survival needs.' Kapp applies Bertalanffy's definition of a system to the economic development process, adding valuable insights beyond the seminal 'The Open System Character of the Economy' that earned Kapp his status as an open system thinker. (Berger/Elsner 2007) Namely, it demonstrates how Kapp blended his systems thinking, which he developed since the early 1950s in the wake of the general systems theory movement (Kapp 1985) with the 'circular cumulative causation' (CCC) theory of the economic development process. The blend of OSA and CCC is unique to Kapp and based on his own work on complex and interrelated problems and systems since the 1940s. Gunnar Myrdal received the 1972 Bank of Sweden Prize in Memory of Alfred Nobel partly for his work on CCC, notably his 'Asian Drama' (1968), which he had sent Kapp for review prior to its publication. (For the collaboration between Kapp and Myrdal see Berger/Steppacher 2011; see Berger 2009 for the similarities between Kapp's and Myrdal's development theory and CCC)

3.10 Social Costs and the Critique of Neoclassical Economics

Chapter 6 constitutes Kapp's pioneering attempt to formulate an argument on the social costs of neoclassical economics. This chapter was partly published in SCPE, which as we recall was intended as a critique of neoclassical economics (see chapter 3). Its current form presents novel material on Kapp's critique of neoclassical economics. Chapter 13 is one of Kapp's latest formulations of the critique of neoclassical economics as a form of ideology, which takes its central inspiration from Veblen. Both critiques have gained momentum in the wake of the Great Financial Crisis of 2008 in movements such as 'rethinking economics,' 'new economic thinking,' and 'reteaching economics.' They are also reflected by various recent heterodox book publications, such as 'The Social Costs of Markets and Economics' (Lee 2013) and 'The Crimes of the Economy – A Criminological Analysis of Economic Thought.' (Vincenzo Ruggiero 2013)

Chapter 11 develops the critique of neoclassical theories of social costs, that is, its market-based and closed-system approach, its polluter-pays-principle and cost-benefit analysis. This article was partly used for a keynote address at the meeting of the UNESCO's International Social Science Council in Kyoto in 1975. As a standing member of this organization Kapp participated in these meetings at least since 1970 where he met with other economists, such as Ignacy Sachs and Allen Kneese who pioneered the analysis of environmental disruption as a consequence of interactions between the socio-economic and ecological system. (Tsuru 1970) In this article Kapp develops a critique of the solutions to social costs that rely on taxation, tort law and bargaining, all of which are based on the neoclassical 'Polluter-Pays- Principle' (PPP). We recall that Kapp relied on Pigou's treatment of social damages in his dissertation's argument on social costs (see above) and SCBE (Kapp 1963) acknowledges Pigou's call for the socialization of the means of production in the face of increasing social costs. This reflects Kapp's ambiguous attitude towards Pigou's work. While acknowledging the latter's increasingly radical political-economic conclusions and initially relying on his assessment of social damages,

SCPE (Kapp 1950) and several later articles roundly reject Pigou's taxation solution and his concept of externalities. The tort law solution was likewise consistently rejected by Kapp. (Kapp 1950; Berger 2013) Chapter 11 shows that Kapp also objected to the 'bilateral market' solution since the early 1970s. This is remarkable since the latter only slowly made its way into the mainstream (for a history of the 'Coase Theorem' see Medema 2011) and evidences Kapp's astute awareness of new developments in neoclassical theories of social costs. In the context of this critique Kapp, however, does not refer to Coase or Stigler, but to Buchanan's dogmatic insistence that 'individual decision making' delimits the scope of economics. Buchanan had previously rejected Kapp's theory of social costs and gone on to develop his own approach to externalities. (Buchanan 1962) In turn, Kapp criticizes Buchanan's methodologically individualist approach to social costs as ineffective because treating each case of social costs in isolation inhibits the recognition of the problem's systemic scope and its complex causation. In this context Kapp reiterates his argument from SCD on the flaws in the rationality of the price system and the distortions to which it gives rise. Thus, market solutions to social costs are arbitrary because they rely on the ability to pay, which relies on the arbitrary distribution of income. Kapp attacks the anti-scientific, dehumanizing, and anti-democratic animus of the PPP. He also considers the PPP to be ineffective due to the slow legislative process, high implementation costs, and the lack of a prevention strategy. Moreover, the PPP is highly vulnerable to the influence of (neo-) 'liberal' lobby groups:

> 'An additional problem endemic to regulatory agencies is that their decisions may be influenced by liberally financed interest and pressure groups, which may engage in selective research and release of information, counter-information, denials, and counter-denials which render the search for correct and impartial decisions difficult or impossible.' (chapter 11)

The PPP is also deemed unjust because it does not guarantee improvements. Yet, Kapp admits that the PPP would be 'important' if the alternative is to not do anything at all about social costs, which would be even worse. Addressing the issue of the determination of the level of the charges under the PPP Kapp identifies the vast requirements of data gathering as a major problem, that is, the knowledge requirements for the estimation of the damages and the costs of the measures of public action. The PPP faces the problem of determining a fixed level of charges in relation to uncertain variables. Kapp concludes that this is the principle reason why direct measures are advantageous because they can actually guarantee the prevention and reduction of social costs and do not merely shift the costs to consumers. They also avoid the issue of avoidance strategies, such as shifting pollution from water to air. With regard to the option to compensate social costs via liability law Kapp notes several inadequacies. The latter are due to the complexities involved that make the burden of proof and the costs involved in it prohibitive and inefficient. Inconsistent rulings across similar cases of social costs are also a major problem with the legal solution. (For the similarities between Kapp and the legal realist position on social costs see Gaskins 2007; 2010) Instead of legal solutions Kapp refers to the possibility of radical changes to the socio-legal structure that would require ex ante technological assessment and impact studies that guarantee safety standards and social minima. Yet, Kapp is aware that the latter faces stiff opposition from producers (chapter 11).

As Kapp points out in chapter 9 the PPP reflects a faulty understanding of the substantive and interrelated character of the problem of social costs. This faulty understanding is the closed system approach. What is required instead is the recognition of the open system character of the economy with its circular and cumulative causation, which require a multi-disciplinary and integrated scientific approach that has as its goal the protection, prevention and improvement of the human environment. In assessing 20 years of discussions on SCPE with neoclassical economists, Kapp was able to identify the root of the disagreement in his view

> 'that the institutionalized system of decision-making in a system of business enterprise has a built-in tendency to disregard those negative effects on the environment [...] Predictably, this critical view, which runs counter to the presuppositions and biases of conventional economic analysis, has not *met* with general approval. Thus, various alternative explanations for *the* occurrence of social costs have been advanced. These have one thing in common: to exonerate the principle of investment for profits from any causal connection with environmental disruption.' (Kapp 1971, p. xiii-xiv)

3.11 The Brave New World of Social Costs

Kapp's critique of the PPP notwithstanding it is today the predominant approach to social costs, which are increasingly deferred to the legal and the market system, especially in the United States. The foundation for the legal approach to social costs is Mises's praxeology, which is viewed as a pure logic that can be applied without regard to ethical predispositions (rule utilitarianism). (Gunning 2000, pp 6, 8) It is helpful to recall that

Kapp made his objection to Mises's praxeology a point of departure for his version of substantive rationality and the integration and humanization of social knowledge in continuation of his dissertation's anti-Misean argument during the SCD (see above). Mises's adopts Pigou's terminology of 'external costs' but places it under the rubric of 'limits of property rights' and defines them as 'consequences of action that the agent is not held accountable [for].' Further, he admits that the agent 'will not bother in his planning about all the effects of his action. He will disregard [...] those costs which do not burden him.' (Mises in Gunning 2000, p. 10) Yet in his research Mises does not devote any considerable attention to the theme that 'the property system is a system of rights to control actions that have external effects.' (Gunning p. 11)

Based on these foundations, social costs are deferred to judges and tort law to determine 'which rights to control actions that have external effects should be defined and enforced.' (Gunning, p. 14) In this, PPP is interpreted as the applicability of tort law that makes the victims of externalities whole in a way that fully addresses the grievance, eliminates the emissions, and confines them to the polluters own property. (Cordato 2004, p. 12) When in doubt about property rights the advice is that courts ought to enact the 'first come first served principle' to reduce the uncertainty of plans of first users by enhancing the amount and quality of information. The usefulness of Coase's market-rule for establishing initial rights 'to the person or persons they believe would end up with the rights after a hypothetical zero-transactions costs exchange' is acknowledged. (Gunning, p. 15-16) To be sure, even these authors state that 'nothing [...] warrants the view [of an] active and interventionist government. [...] the assignment of initial legal rights is a function of government in the light of the goal of maintaining a property system in the entrepreneur economy.' (Ibid, p. 17) Some authors in this tradition, however, reject Coase's outcome utilitarian, which is perceived to be at odds with Mises rule utilitarianism (praxeology). Their goal is to avoid any possibility that 'politicians determine what is and isn't pollution and what the appropriate emissions targets are.' (Cordato 2004; p. 15)

The discussion on the merits of Coasian bargaining notwithstanding, the core tenet of the legal solution is that all damages are conceived as human interpersonal conflicts. Environmental disruption, for example, is thus viewed as 'human problems of mutual plan formulation and the achievement of goals.' (Cordato 2004, p. 7) The tenet that human conflict should be minimized via the assignment of property rights is deduced from Menger's Principles (1st edn), and inserts the notion of 'legal failure' for 'market failure'. (ibid, p. 8) The logical yet quixotic conclusion is that social costs do 'not exist either as measurable or even theoretical concept[s]' because they are purely subjective. (Cordato 2004, p. 5) This perspective guides the legal approach to environmental policy, in which 'externalities are a pseudo problem.' (Dawson 2013, p. 184) This approach is adamant that science is too uncertain to provide definitive solutions for governmental rules that reduce or prevent social costs. (Dawson 2013)

What these proposals fail to mention is that courts and tort law cannot escape the necessity of establishing causality, which requires scientific proof about causality between the polluter and polluted. Consequently, the strategy of proponents of the legal solution to social costs has been to frame the legal use of science in such a way that it can never become dangerous to corporations. (See Mirowski 2011 for an analysis of this strategy) In this scheme, the so-called 'sound science' movement engineers the use of science in court to banish what neoliberals declare as 'junk science,' meaning social cost science speaking in favor of the victims of corporate cost shifting. For instance, Federal Rules of Evidence in the US apply criteria for the admissibility of scientific experts and evidence, and impose prior conditions of testability and whether the science has been generally accepted. Judges are turned into arbiters who block 'junk science' and ensure 'sound science.' The litigants with the biggest financial resources can now

> 'issue seemingly endless pre-trial challenges to the quality of the science of the opponent [...] [placing] the burden on the plaintiff to validate each and every study referenced in the case [...] 'sound science' [...] restores the asymmetric bias toward corporate science [in the courtroom].' (ibid, p. 302)

Additionally, the Shelby Amendment to the freedom of information act is used by business organizations to harass and challenge publicly funded scientists whom they dislike, using legal challenges to turn science with policy implications into an ordeal of legal maneuvers and threats. Since there is no freedom of information act for corporate funded research it is immune to subpoena and reinforces the asymmetry to corporate research. The net result of the 'sound science' argument is in fact a degradation of the quality of the entire scientific research base in cases on social costs. 'Sound litigation science' is viewed as responding to the market demand and as superior to slow academic science, which brings science home to the market. (Mirowski 2011)

The above account demonstrates that the PPP is an ex post strategy of dealing with social costs via tort law and the ex post assignment of property rights based on 'first come first served' or the 'Coase-rule.' In practice this approach turns the problem of social costs into an issue of the market for science. (See Mirowski 2013 for this analysis) This essentially means that the market is the only entity holding sufficient knowledge to deal with social costs, that is, an epistemological challenge of the publicly funded system of science and the democratic governmental process. The challenge consists in willfully accepting human ignorance because humans as either scientific experts or democratically elected representatives cannot be trusted to understand social costs because they are too complex. Essentially, this view holds that social costs are solved by markets in the fullness of time and spreads doubt and confusion about science and intellectuals. Markets know better and market solutions have to be developed and implemented. This step buys important time as these schemes take many years to be designed and implemented before it becomes evident that they do not work to resolve the social cost problem (see e.g. Cap & Trade and Geoengineering). The net result is that private property rights that had to be assigned in the process have commodified further realms of the social and natural environment.

A parallel development is that the increasing pressures caused by the social cost of ecological or financial crises create moments of emergency, in which standard rules are suspended and PPP-based solutions can be imposed without democratic accountability: social costs thus impose a road to delimiting democratic controls and imposing a kind of 'liberal dictatorship.' (See Farrant/MacPhail/Berger 2012) The term used by German Chancellor Angela Merkel is the 'market-compatible' democracy, which refers to imposing solutions for social costs that would never stand the test of a democratic referendum. Democratic and scientific solutions to social costs are kept impotent. (For a theory of the neoliberal state see Mirowski 2013; p. 335-350)

3.12 Conclusion

The reconstruction of Kapp's theory of social costs provides an important contribution to the project of building an integrated heterodox economics as an alternative to neoclassical economics and the neoliberal economic system. Kapp's theory serves this purpose particularly well since it integrates key insights on social costs from several important heterodox economic traditions – Marx, Weber, Veblen – to counter not only neoclassical and neoliberal theories of social costs, but also to critique the rationality of the market system. Kapp's contribution is important today as social costs are dramatically increasing and neoclassical theories have proven their ineffectiveness in reducing, preventing or mitigating social costs. In fact, they have become instrumental in usurping further realms of society into the market by enforcing the PPP. If Kapp is right about the PPP's fatal flaws, this regime will lead to higher levels of social costs. The great value of Kapp's theory is that it provides a sophisticated articulation of an alternative approach of effective precautionary social controls of the economic system to prevent social costs. The key points of the foregoing reconstruction of Kapp's theory of social costs may be summarized in brief:

1. Markets socialize costs to third parties, future generations, and society as a whole.
2. Social costs are large-scale and systemic problems requiring systemic and comprehensive remedies at the macro and societal level. Social costs are not minor temporary failures of an otherwise functioning and harmonious system, and can thus not be effectively remedied via ad hoc and ex post measures.
3. Social costs happen behind the back of the victims and are one-sidedly forced upon them in situations characterized by power asymmetries. Social costs are not voluntary exchange relationships between equals.
4. Social costs are subject to circular and cumulative causation between the open economic system and its social and natural environment, which makes them non-linear, unevenly spread out along the time axis, hidden for considerable periods of time, and often irreversible. Social costs are not linear and direct causal relationships, which makes it often impossible to determine their exact causality or value ex post.
5. Social costs do not have exchange value, because human life and health are not exchangeable commodities. Human life and health have an absolute value and are of a substantive kind.
6. Social cost prevention and reduction are matters of institutional reform and their extent depends upon the level of countervailing power that can be leveraged via social controls.
7. Instituting precautionary safety standards and social minima can protect human life and health ex ante, guarantee the gratification of basic human needs, and thereby effectively prevent social costs, and create social benefits. Protective measures reflective of existential human needs are a matter of the integration and humanization of social knowledge.

Kapp's theory may be differentiated from PPP-based theories by way of the following typology:

Typology of Social Costs				
	Neoclassical (Pigou)	*Neoliberal (Coase)*	*Libertarian (Mises)*	*Heterodox (Kapp)*
Social Costs	Accidental, minor disturbance of an otherwise harmonious and rational system		Accidental 'legal failure' of specific property rights	Systemic socialization of costs due to profit principle; major ecological-social irrationality of markets
Ontology of the economic system	Closed system, Market exchanges, Mechanistic, Reversibility, Perfect knowledge, Risk, Individualist, Micro, Formal Rationality		Formal Rationality, Market exchanges	Open system, Entropy law, Substantive, Irreversibility, Complexity, Uncertainty, Ignorance, Social-ecological, Systemic, Macro-level
Solution	Taxes, ad hoc, ex post	Bargaining, Individualist, Private insurance markets, ad hoc, ex post	Legal system, tort law, ad hoc, ex post	Precautionary Principle, Social Controls of technology and investment decisions, Safety limits, Social Minima, Ex ante
Political Economy	Slightly interventionist: does not call into question the market as a mechanism of allocation	Strongly interventionist: constructs markets to shift power to the wealthy ('the poor sell cheap' doctrine)	Strongly anti-interventionist: power is with the large property owners	Strong social-ecological control of the mechanism of allocation: planning, prevention, controls of eco-social safety limits, counter-vailing power to protect the disadvantaged
Ethics	Outcome Utilitarianism (although Coase may also be viewed as a rule utilitarian)		Rule Utilitarianism	Humanist Ethics

References

Aslanbeigui, Nahid and Medema, Steven G. (1998), 'Beyond the Dark Clouds: Pigou and Coase on Social Costs,' *History of Political Economy*, 30, 4: 601-625.

Ayres, Robert and Kneese, Allen (1969), 'Production, Consumption and Externalities.' *The American Economic Review* 59, 3: 282-297.

Berger, Sebastian (2013) 'The Making of the Institutional Theory of Social Costs: Discovering the K.W. Kapp and J.M. Clark Correspondence.' *The American Journal of Economics and Sociology*, 72, 5: 1106-1130.

Berger, Sebastian (2012), 'The Discourse on Social Costs – Kapp's Impossibility Thesis vs. Neoliberalism,' in Elsner, Wolfram; Frigato, Pietro; Ramazzotti, Paolo (eds) *Social Costs Today – Institutional Analyses of the Present Crisis*, Routledge.

Berger, Sebastian (ed.) (2009) *The Foundations of Non-Equilibrium Economics: The Principle of Circular and Cumulative Causation*. Routledge.

Berger, Sebastian (2008), 'Karl Polanyi's and Karl William Kapp's Substantive Economics: Important Insights from the Kapp-Polanyi Correspondence,' *Review of Social Economy*, 66, 3: 381-396.

Berger, Sebastian and Elsner, Wolfram (2007), 'European Contributions to Evolutionary Institutional Economics: The Cases 'Open Systems Approach' (OSA) and 'Cumulative Circular Causation' (CCC). Some Methodological and Policy Implications,' *Journal of Economic Issues*, 41: 529-537.

Bernstein, Richard J. (1991), *Beyond Objectivism and Relativism*. University of Pennsylvania Press.

Buchanan, James M. (1962), 'Politics, Policy and the Pigovian Margins,' *Economica*, 29, 113: 17-28.

Caldwell, Bruce (2004), *Hayek's Challenge*, The University of Chicago Press.

Cordato, Roy (2004), 'Towards an Austrian Theory of Environmental Economics', *The Quarterly Journal of Austrian Economics*, 7, 1: 3-16.

Carpintero, Óscar (2013), 'When Heterodoxy becomes Orthodoxy: Ecological Economics in the New Palgrave Dictionary of Economics.' In Lee, Frederic S. (ed) *Social Costs of Markets and Economic Theory*, Chichester: Wiley.

Dawson, Graham (2013), 'Austrian Economics and Climate Change,' *The Review of Austrian Economics*, 26, 2: 183-206.

Di Maio, Michele (2013). 'Are Mainstream and Heterodox Economists Different? An Empirical Analysis.' In Lee, Frederic S. (ed) *Social Costs of Markets and Economic Theory*, Chichester: Wiley.

Dow, Sheila C. (2011), 'Heterodox Economics: History and Prospects,' *Cambridge Journal of Economics*, 35: 1151-1165.

Elsner, Wolfram (1986), *Economic Institutions Analysis – The Paradigmatic Development of Economics and the Relevance of a Recourse to the Economic Classics.(German: Ökonomische Institutionenanalyse)*. Berlin: Duncker & Humblot.

Elsner, Wolfram; Frigato, Pietro; Ramazzotti, Paolo (eds) (2012), *Social Costs Today – Institutional Analyses of the Present Crisis*, Routledge.

Connell, Carol M. (2012), *Reforming the World Monetary System: Fritz Machlup and the Bellagio Group*. London: Pickering & Chatto Publishers Ltd.

Foster, John B. (2010), *The Ecological Rift: Capitalism's War on Earth*. New York: Monthly Review Press.
Gaskins, Richard (2010), 'Accounting for Accidents: Social Costs of Personal Injury,' *Victoria University of Wellington Law Review*, 41: 37-50.
Gaskins, Richard (2007), 'Social Insurance and Unpaid Costs of Personal Injury: A Second Look at K. William Kapp' (Conference Paper European Society for Ecological Economics).
Gerber, Julien-Francois and Steppacher, Rolf (2012), *Towards an Integrated Paradigm in Heterodox Economics – Alternative Approaches to the Current Eco-Social Crises*. Palgrave-Macmillan.
Gunning, J. Patrick (2000), 'The Property System in Austrian Economics,' *Review of Austrian Economics*, 13, 2: 209-220.
Kapp, K. William (2011), *The Foundations of Institutional Economics*, edited by S. Berger and R. Steppacher, Routledge: London and New York.
Kapp, K.William (1985) *The Humanization of the Social Sciences*, edited by J.E. Ullmann and R. Preiswerk. University Press of America: Lanham (NY), London.
Kapp, K. William (1970), 'Environmental Disruption and Social Costs: A Challenge to Economics', *Kyklos*, 23 4: 833-848.
Kapp, K. William (1963a), *The Social Costs of Business Enterprise*. Bombay: Asia Publishing House.
Kapp, K. William (1963b), *Hindu Culture, Economic Development and Economic Planning in India*. Bombay/London: Asia Publishing House.
Kapp, K. William (1962), 'Friedrich List's Contribution to the Theory of Economic Development,' *The Political Science Review* (University of Rajasthan, Jaipur, India), 1, 1: 17-22.
Kapp, K. William (1961), *Toward a Science of Man in Society – A Positive Approach to the Integration of Social Knowledge*. The Hague: Martinus Nijhoff.
Kapp. K. William (1956), *History of Economic Thought – A Book of Readings*. New York: Barnes & Noble.
Kapp, K. William (1950), *The Social Costs of Private Enterprise*. Harvard University Press.
Kapp, K. William (1949), *Readings in Economics*. New York: Barnes and Noble.
Kapp, K. William (1936), *Planwirtschaft und Aussenhandel*. Genf: Georg & Cie.
Kapp, K. William, 'Unpublished Manuscript 1 – French translation of Polish Preface of *The Social Costs of Private Enterprise*.'
Lee, Frederic S. (ed) (2013), *Social Costs of Markets and Economic Theory*. Chichester: Wiley.
Lee, Frederic S. (2010), 'Pluralism in Heterodox Economics.' In *Economic Pluralism*, edited by R.F. Garnett, E.K. Olson, M. Starr, 19-35. London: Routledge.
Lee, Frederic S. (2009), *A History of Heterodox Economics – Challenging the Mainstream in the Twentieth Century*. London: Routledge
Lee, Frederic S. (1998), *Post Keynesian Price Theory*. Cambridge University Press.

Essays on the Economics of K. William Kapp

Martinez-Alier, J. (2002), *Environmentalism of the Poor – A Study of Ecological Conflicts and Valuation*. Cheltenham: Edward Elgar.
Mearman, Andrew (2012), 'Heterodox Economics and the Problem of Classification,' *Journal of Economic Methodology*, 19, 4: 407-424.
Mearman, Andrew (2011), 'Who Do Heterodox Economists Think They Are?' *The American Journal of Economics and Sociology*, 70, 2: 480-510.
Medema, Steven G. (2011), 'A Case of Mistaken Identity: George Stigler, 'The Problem of Social Costs,' and the Coase Theorem,' *European Journal of Law and Economics*, 31, 1, 11-38.
Mirowski, Philip (2013), *Never Let a Serious Crisis Go to Waste*, Verso.
Mirowski, Philip (2011), *Science-Mart – The Commercialization of American Science*. Harvard University Press.
Mirowski, Philip and Plehwe, Dieter (eds) (2009), *The Road from Mont Pelerin – The Making of the Neoliberal Thought Collective*, Harvard University Press: Cambridge (MA) / London (England).
Niglia, Guiseppe and Vatiori, Massimiliano (2007), 'K. William Kapp e Ronald H. Coase – un tentative di riconciliazione', in *Studi e Note di Economia*, Anno XII, n3, pp. 369-383.
Rorty, Richard (1984), 'The Historiography of Philosophy: Four Genres.' In *Philosophy in History*, edited by Richard Rorty, J.B. Schneewind, and Quentin Skinner. Cambridge: Cambridge University Press.
Rutherford M. (2011), *The Institutionalist Movement in American Economics, 1918-1947*. Cambridge: Cambridge University Press.
Selwyn, Ben (2009), 'An Historical Materialist Appraisal of Friedrich List and his Modern-Day Followers,' *New Political Economy*, 14, 2: 157-180.
Spash, Clive (2012), 'Toward the integration of social, ecological and economic knowledge.' In *Towards an Integrated Paradigm in Heterodox Economics*, edited by Julien-Francois Gerber and Rolf Steppacher, 26-46. Palgrave Macmillan, Basingstoke.
Spash, Clive (2011), 'Social Ecological Economics: Understanding the Past to See the Future,' *American Journal of Economics and Sociology*, 70, 2: 340-375.
Steinmetz, George (ed.) (2005), 'Introduction: Positivism and Its Others in the Social Sciences,' in *The Politics of Method in the Human Sciences*, 1-58, Duke University Press.
Tsuru, Shigeto (Ed.) (1970), *Environmental Disruption – Proceedings of International Symposium* (The International Social Science Council). Tokyo: Asahi Evening News.
Van Horn, R., P. Mirowski, and T. Stapleford (eds) (2011), *Building Chicago Economics – New Perspectives on the History of America's Most Powerful Economics Program*. Cambridge: Cambridge University Press.
Yalcintas, Altug (2013), 'The Problem of Epistemic Cost: Why Do Economists Not Change Their Mind (About the 'Coase Theorem')?,' in *Social Costs of Markets and Economic Theory*, edited by Frederic S. Lee. Chichester: Wiley.
Vincenzo Ruggiero (2013), *The Crimes of the Economy – A Criminological Analysis of Economic Thought*. Routledge.

4

Social Costs: Kapp's Impossibility Theorem vs. Neoliberalism

4.1 Introduction

Economists have tried for a long time to shape the mode of thinking about damages that arise from economic activity. As 'social costs' or 'externalities' these damages were assigned a specific place in modern society. According to historians of economic thought: 'It is now well established that the boundaries of the modern analysis of externalities were defined by A.C. Pigou's Economics of Welfare ([1920] 1932) and Ronald H. Coase's 'Problem of Social Cost' (1960)' (Aslanbeigui and Medema 1998: 1).

This intellectual history is quite symptomatic for contemporary economic discourse, in that only neoclassical and neoliberal theories are considered while K. William Kapp's fundamental critique of both of these theories is omitted. His work once received recognition even by his staunch neoliberal critic, Wilfred Beckerman:

> The economics profession in general, and those who are interested in environmental problems in particular, owe a great debt to Professor Kapp. It was he who first drew our attention to the widespread nature of external costs imposed by many productive activities and the way in which these impaired the environment, in his book on the social costs of business enterprise. This work was not duly appreciated at the time it was published because this was before concern with the environment became fashionable. (Beckerman 1972: 1)

In the words of Kapp's colleague, the institutional economist Marc Tool:

> Dr. K. William Kapp and his forty-year career as a front rank institutional economist. [...] [established] the relevance of the holistic, institutional mode of thinking to the complex and urgent problems of environmental deterioration and economic development. Indeed, Kapp was among the first to explore the interdependent significance of these two problems. (Tool 1978: 1)

Much has changed in economic discourse since the 1970s, and Kapp's arguments are – with few exceptions (Franzini 2006) – no longer part of the discourse on social costs. This chapter provides a rational reconstruction (Rorty 1984) of Kapp's argument to complement the concept's intellectual history and to broaden economic discourse beyond the limits of neoclassical and neoliberal arguments.

4.2 Kapp's 'impossibility thesis' vs. liberalism à la Mises and Hayek

Kapp's argument about social costs emerged in his dissertation, 'The planned economy and international trade' (1936), as a critique of the doctrine of liberalism and an economic accounting system based on market exchange value. Given the book's argument, it is surprising that it was written at the Postgraduate Institute of International Studies in Geneva and at the London School of Economics. According to Plehwe, the Geneva institute was an interwar institution that provided an organizational haven for 'concerned and committed liberals', such as Ludwig von Mises, who later became a founding member of neoliberal organizations, such as the Mont Pelerin Society in 1947 (Plehwe 2009). In fact, Kapp's preface even thanks Mises for the 'friendly interest' he took in the dissertation.

Kapp began his argument by addressing Mises' thesis that 'a rational economy under conditions of a centrally organized community is impossible because the removal of the means of production from the market makes their exact valuation impossible in the decisions of the central economic authorities' (Kapp 1936: 27). According to Mises, without the market and a common denominator for valuation there cannot be any economy because there is no way to determine what is rational and because production cannot be 'economical' (ibid.: 30 – 31). Kapp argued that this thesis is the focal point in the discourse on economic accounting, which in turn reflects differences in the theories of value. While he was not surprised that economists adopting a subjectivist theory of value argue that valuation becomes impossible in a planned economy, Kapp considered the socialists' reactions problematic because they mainly tried to prove Mises' thesis wrong. Instead, Kapp argued, a countervailing thesis about the market economy was needed, as well as an inquiry into the actual effects of a pure economic accounting system based on the valuation of single individuals – i.e., market exchange value (ibid.: 34).

Chapter 3 of the dissertation took up this task. Kapp built his argument upon previous contributions made by Arthur C. Pigou, Carl Menger and Karl Polanyi. The third subchapter of chapter 3, entitled 'The impossibility of reaching societal efficiency[57] based on an economic accounting of market values', argued that economic accounting based on market values does not and cannot account for the *societal* disadvantages and damages of an economic decision. Kapp used Pigou's account (Pigou 1929) of how societal disadvantages arise from economic decisions of private enterprises, referring to societal disadvantages such as health effects on workers, crime, etc., but also environmental damages caused by smoke. Kapp added to this the question about the losses due to the premature depletion of non-renewable energy and raw materials. Importantly, Kapp already outlined his future research project (*The Social Costs of Private Enterprise*, henceforth *Social Costs*) that would elaborate the different kinds of social costs more rigorously: 'It would be an interesting task for statistics to develop appropriate methods of accounting for disadvantages and damages that society has to suffer in a free market economy due to the principle of maximizing returns applied by private enterprise' (Kapp 1936: 42, fn.).

After arguing that decisions by private enterprises based on market values cause, and at the same time do not account for, social costs, Kapp proceeded to show why societal needs and interests *cannot* be expressed in the valuation of goods according to market prices. Here, Kapp built on Carl Menger's distinction between the substantive and the formal economy (Berger 2008),[58] arguing that societal needs and interests cannot find 'value-expression' in the exchange between isolated individuals (formal economy). Societal efficiency, thus, cannot be reached based on market price accounting. This constitutes the essence of what may be termed Kapp's countervailing 'impossibility thesis', directed against Mises' thesis. Kapp supported this argument by referring to the many 'corrections' that liberal-capitalist economies have to implement *ex post* via social policies to remedy losses. In a centrally planned economy, Kapp asserted, it would be possible to calculate possible damages *ex ante* and to consider these in economic decision-making. Kapp also acknowledged Karl Polanyi's influence on his dissertation in a later letter:

> Dear Karl ... Did I ever mention that your early article in reply to Mises' thesis has been very helpful to me then [!] I did my dissertation on planning and foreign trade with Mises at the Postgraduate Institute of International Studies in Geneva in the early thirties. I thought you ought to know this and that it may please you. (Kapp to Polanyi, 18 October 1962)

Polanyi participated in the early stages of the debate on possible forms of socialism in Vienna in the 1920s. In his 1922 essay, 'Sozialistische Rechnungslegung' ('Socialist accounting'), he took on Mises' argument and outlined the traits of 'rationally' planned economic production and exchange that is guided by social and democratic decision-making (Cangiani 2006: 25; Berger 2008).

While the dissertation's argument was directed against Mises' thesis,

Kapp directed his *Social Costs* (1950) also against Friedrich August von Hayek, who at the time was the leading figure in neoliberal projects, such as the Chicago School and the Mont Pelerin Society (Van Horn and Mirowski 2009). Kapp paid attention to Hayek's work since the 1930s and his dissertation – partially written at Hayek's workplace, the London School of Economics – already cited the latter's *Collectivist Economic Planning* (1935). The unpublished version of the introduction to 'Social costs' addressed itself to Mises' and Hayek's 'successful books' and their doctrine of liberalism (Kapp, unpubl. manus.), probably referring to Hayek's *Road to Serfdom* (1944) and Mises' *Bureaucracy* (1944):

> Social Costs and Social Returns: A Critical Analysis of the Social Performance of the Unplanned Market Economy – In harmony with the faith of 19th century liberalism traditional equilibrium economics states that the unregulated forces of supply and demand in an unplanned market economy tend to lead to an optimal allocation of and in many minds the presumption seems to be against purposive action in economic affairs despite all experience of depressions and other inefficiencies in the operation of the capitalist economy. This study offers a critique of the basic premises of 19th century economic liberalism by examining the social performance of the unplanned market economy in the light of several facts which are usually omitted and neglected in economic theory. […] In the first place it attempts to indicate the limitations of all economic calculations in terms of private costs and private returns. To allocate economic resources merely in accordance with private costs and private returns defeats any endeavour to find a rational solution to the economic problem. (Kapp, unpubl. manus.)

This supports the thesis that Kapp was keenly aware of the revival of the doctrines of liberalism in the works of Mises and Hayek and considered them important enough to devote an entire book to their critique. The latter took on the basic premises of economic liberalism via a full-blown empirical investigation showing how entrepreneurial outlays fail to reflect important social costs of production and are no adequate measure of total costs. Kapp's argument on social costs thus emerged as an attack on Austrian liberalism à la Hayek and Mises, while being inspired by Austrian economists, such as Polanyi and the posthumous Menger (second edition of *Principles*), as well as Pigou.

4.3 The influence of American institutionalism: ex ante social controls vs. ex post Pigouvian taxes

Kapp explicitly traced the basic idea of *Social Costs* back to his dissertation, but also to the research of the National Resources Planning Board and John Maurice Clark's *Social Economics*.⁵⁹ The Kapp–Clark correspondence evidences how Clark influenced Kapp's thinking. Kapp's copy of Allan G. Gruchy's *Modern Economic Thought: The American Contribution* (1947) shows intense underlining of the chapter on 'The social economics of John M. Clark', in particular, the concept of social value, new criteria for collective efficiency independent of price, Clark's social-liberal planning program and the democratization of the economy as a foundation of social economics. By changing the title of the second, enlarged and revised edition to *Social Costs of Business Enterprise* (1963) Kapp explicitly recognized that Thorstein B. Veblen's *Engineers and the Price System* (1921) and *The Theory of Business Enterprise* (1904) provided an analytical framework and demanded an economics that investigates the waste involved in the business-like control of industry.⁶⁰

In the tradition of American Institutionalism, Kapp argued that social costs are to be subjected to democratic decision-making (social legislation) that would enable the majority interest to put an end to this problem. He directly attacked the argument that the elimination or more equal distribution of social costs – as well as the insistence on planning – are anti-growth and anti-change. In this way, Kapp raised the question of whether the lament about the eminent end of growth – said to result from the quest for security and protection against social costs – does not reflect a movement away from social and political democracy. According to Kapp, social costs are in opposition to one of the most fundamental tenets of our professed humanistic ideals, i.e., respect for the human personality and that the human being must not become a mere instrument for some 'cause', such as growth or efficiency (Kapp 1950: 18-22). In this view, the extent to which social costs are accounted for depends on the political structure of society, requiring environmental policy and institutional reforms to minimize them:

> [Social costs] are damages [...] which under different institutional conditions could be avoided. For, obviously, if these costs were inevitable under any kind of institutional arrangement they would not really present a special theoretical problem [...] to reveal their origin the study of social costs must always be an institutional analysis. Such an analysis raises inevitably the question of institutional reform and economic policy, which may eliminate or minimize the social diseconomies under discussion. (Kapp 1963: 186)

> No democratic society can and will tolerate this subordination of the social system to the dictates of formal rationality. The universal reaction of society to the neglect of social costs [...] has taken a variety of forms [...] compelling private producers to internalize [...] social costs. (ibid.: 202)

Kapp interpreted the growing recognition given to social costs as a shift in the balance of power from those groups responsible for damages to those groups who bear the

> brunt of social losses in the past and who now are using their growing political and economic power in an effort to protect themselves against undesirable consequences. [...] The political history of the last 150 years can be fully understood only as a revolt of large masses of people (including business) against the shifting of part of the social costs of production to third persons or society. (ibid.: 16)

Kapp concluded that in modern societies there are serious obstacles to rational behavior of consumers and entrepreneurs, not least because market prices fail to measure the relative importance and magnitude of various social costs and returns. He called for a revision of neoclassical price theory, questioning its philosophical foundations and formal value theory that is confined to alternatives measurable in terms of market values. Kapp called for a new science of economics that would include social costs and returns that differ in terms of their measurability from exchangeable commodities and constitute the category of social value. Elaborating on the question of social value, Kapp later demanded a kind of 'rational humanism', i.e., substantive criteria that are sought and found in the degree of satisfaction of human needs (Kapp 1967). In this theory, particular aspects of the quality of the environment such as clean air and water would be an end in itself via scientifically derived environmental norms that reflect basic human needs. Hence, human needs become operable as social minima, and fundamental requirements of human life and survival are integral parts of the constellation of goals of economic policy. Minimum standards in the fields of public health, medical care, education, housing, transportation and recreation based on empirical data can be determined with greater agreement than usually assumed. Kapp argued that the human being and basic human needs should be the primary values and criteria, from which secondary criteria, such as social minima, ecological maximum tolerance levels, socio-ecological indicators and social controls can be derived (Kapp 1974). Kapp used this argument also in a proposal for democratic planning of science and technology (Kapp 1975).

While his work derived a major impulse from Pigou's argument, Kapp later criticized that Pigou forced the problem of social costs into the conceptual framework of neoclassical economics, despite the fact that the latter was never designed to address non-market phenomena, such as pollution. Kapp also rejected Pigou's concepts of external costs and social costs, with social costs meaning 'total costs', i.e., the sum of private costs and external costs. Instead, Kapp reserved the term 'social costs' for all those negative consequences arising from unrestrained economic activity (public and private) that are shifted to third parties, future generations or society at large, and which do not appear in cost accounts of the responsible economic unit, thus avoiding responsibility. Kapp argued that Pigou's 'external costs' is a value-laden concept within the neoclassical pre-analytical vision of a rational (market)-system in which 'external costs' are external to the system – accidental side-effects of secondary importance. This plays down the pervasive nature of the problem and suggests that it is remediable with ad hoc, *ex post* measures of taxation. Kapp criticized that the latter are essentially conservative measures that do not change the mechanism of allocation and that constitute only a minor modification of the allegedly rational system. Yet, Kapp did not fail to notice that Pigou broadened his approach in the 1940s, starting to mention 'general disharmonies' arising in production and distribution and in connection with industrial fluctuations: '[We may be] confronted with evidence of the bankruptcy of capitalism and a prima facie case for extending the range of public ownership and public operation to industries in which they have not yet been invoked' (Pigou 1947: 43-45, in Kapp 1963: 38) While Pigou's solution to the problem was to some extent interventionist and his work highlighted some of the links between economics and ethics (Aslanbeigui and Medema 1998), Kapp pointed out the limitations of this neoclassical approach.

4.4 Neoliberal feedback à la Knight, Coase, Stigler, Calabresi, Buchanan and Beckerman

Recent research has characterized neoliberalism as a transdisciplinary and international thought collective with a long-term strategy to oppose what it described as collectivism or socialism. The term 'neoliberalism' emerged in the 1930s and the movement is considered to be a child of the Great Depression, with concerned liberals feeling the need to fight the evils of planning. The Chicago School and the Mont Pelerin Society were among its key organizations since 1947, with Hayek, Mises and Buchanan, but also Stigler, as leading members. Neoliberalism rose to hegemony by the 1980s, gaining acceptance even in nominally hostile environments, such as Social Democratic Parties and the Chinese ruling elite. Crucially, neoliberalism must not be confounded with neoclassical economics because Austrian and ordoliberal segments of neoliberalism were at odds with neoclassical economics. Yet, those versions of neoclassical economics with the neoliberal policy preferences were accepted (Plehwe 2009; Mirowski 2009). While neoliberalism is not a clearly defined doctrine, some of its central tenets relevant to the discourse on social costs can be identified: (1) The market can always produce solutions for problems seemingly produced by the market in the first place; (2) the market always surpasses the state's ability as an information processor; (3) corporations can do no wrong, or at least they are not to be blamed if they do (Mirowski 2009).

In line with these tenets, the Chicago School spent the post-World War II years arguing 'for less government intervention, fewer wealth redistribution policies [...] and an across the board promotion of more private enterprise' because this would promote a more efficient allocation of resources (Medema 1998: 210). The discourse on social costs was of interest to Chicago economists from the beginning and seems to have moved upward on the neoliberal agenda in the 1960s. Although Frank Knight was not part of what became the neoliberal project at the Chicago School, starting with Hayek (Van Horn and Mirowski 2009), he was the leading economist at the interwar Economics Department at Chicago, who convinced his students of the central importance of liberal values and competitive markets, which he favored over any other political process (Rutherford 2010). In '[S]ome fallacies in the interpretation of social costs' (Knight 1924), Knight attacked Pigou's interventionist taxation solution, favoring instead a market-based solution because under conditions of 'private ownership of the factors significant for production [...] the ideal situation which would be established by the imaginary tax will be brought about through the operation of ordinary economic motives' (ibid.: 164). Knight also published a book review of Kapp's *Social Costs* (Knight 1951: 233-234), calling it socialist propaganda and lamenting that it 'does not mention freedom'. Also, Knight found a discussion of 'costs of eliminating costs' missing and that Kapp's use of the term 'waste' was problematic because waste can only be defined in reference to costs of conservation. Knight saw no practical use in criticizing the status quo if possible alternatives were not compared, and the worst defect was that the 'author is oblivious of the question as to the politico-economic organization requisite for carrying out such 'reforms'. [...] He does not say what are the alternatives and their costs' (Knight 1951: 234).

Knight was also the dissertation advisor of George Stigler, who later became a leading member of the mid-twentieth-century neoliberal Chicago School and Mont Pèlerin Society, promoting Knight's arguments on social costs in *Readings in Price Theory* in 1952 (Knight 1924). Ronald Coase admitted that Knight's ideas and terminology had greatly influenced his famous argument in *The Problem of Social Costs* (1960) (Coase 1983: 215; Medema 2010). It has been pointed out that Coase's political orientation was different from Pigou's – i.e., decidedly anti-interventionist – and that this clearly influenced his approach (Aslanbeigui and Medema 1998). Coase received a scholarship through the 'Free Market Study' funds of the neoliberal Chicago School, and can be considered as the second generation of neoliberals (Van Horn and Mirowski 2010). Coase critiqued Pigou's interventionist solution because it aimed at eliminating harmful effects via public intervention 'at all costs'. Coase's article contained a call for a closer examination of alternative policy options, viewing both market and government solutions as imperfect, and the option of doing nothing at all about social costs (Medema 2010). It was Stigler who later shaped the 'Coase Theorem', i.e., a radicalized version of Coase's argument, to serve his neoliberal purposes in the discourse on social costs. In this, Stigler also referenced Knight's anti-Pigouvian 1924 article (Stigler 1966: 119).

Conversely, Stigler's silence on Kapp's and Clark's work on social and overhead costs in *Readings in Price Theory* (Stigler and Boulding 1952) can be interpreted as an 'ignore' strategy. Instead, Stigler chose to republish Knight's almost 30-year-old, anti-interventionist 'Fallacies' (1924) article. Kapp's work must have been known to Stigler because they had been colleagues at Columbia University in the 1940s. Kapp's *Social Costs* referred to Stigler's *New Welfare Economics*, arguing that the 'compensation principle' cannot effectively encompass the phenomenon of social costs due to the immeasurability of interpersonal utility comparisons and the impossibility of guaranteeing equal satisfaction after compensation (Stigler 1943, in Kapp 1950: 40). Kapp also noticed that Stigler had rejected the Marshallian notion of external economies as early as 1941 because it involved an 'abandonment of static analysis and serves only the purposes of historical analysis' (Stigler 1941: 68-76, in Kapp 1950: 40). Likewise, Stigler must have known Clark's famous work, which was awarded the Francis A. Walker medal by the American Economic Association in 1952 'given to that living American economist who [...] has made over the course of his life the most distinguished contribution to economics' (Shute 1997; Rutherford 2011). While recent research has elevated the role played by Stigler within the neoliberal political-economic agenda of the Chicago School (Nik-Khah 2009; 2010), more research is needed concerning Stigler's strategy to attain neoliberal hegemony in the discourse on social costs. Yet, this brief intellectual history clearly shows the emergence of an increasingly coherent intellectual effort to turn the discourse on social costs to the preferred anti-interventionist direction. This effort yielded its perhaps most prominent results in the field of law and economics, influencing the way judges think about social costs.

The 'Coase Theorem', together with Guido Calabresi's 'Some thoughts on risk distribution and the law of torts' (1961), became very influential in the New Law and Economics movement, which transformed the US field of law and economics (Medema 1998). Paraphrasing Knight's concerns about the costs of eliminating social costs, Calabresi acknowledged that Kapp was probably correct in projecting a vast web of unpaid social costs, but took the position that it would be 'too costly' for our society to determine those social costs (and even more 'costly' to attempt a redistributive remedy). (Gaskins 2007: 6-7)

According to Gaskins, the US legal movement had favored Kapp over Coase until the early 1960s because of the commonalities between American-led Legal Realists and American Institutionalists. The former were based on German pioneers of 'sociological jurisprudence'. Kapp's line of reasoning fit with this tradition mainly because he had absorbed the influence of American Institutionalism at Columbia. Franzini correctly pointed out that social and human rights, as opposed to property rights, lie at the heart of Kapp's approach (Franzini 2006).

James M. Buchanan, another leading member of the neoliberal thought collective, countered Kapp's thesis even more radically, arguing that intervention cannot possibly reduce externalities:

> Such improvements in the organisation of economic activity have, almost without exception, involved the placing of restrictions on the private behaviour of individuals through the implementation of some political action. [...] If this were not the case, it is difficult to see why [...] K. W. Kapp should have entitled his work 'The Social Costs of Private Enterprise'. [...] The primary criticism of theoretical welfare economics (and economists) that is advanced in this note is that its failure to include analyses of similar imperfections in realistic and attainable alternative solutions causes the analysis itself to take on implications for institutional change that are, at best,

highly mis-leading. [...] In what follows I shall try to show that, with consistent assumptions about human behaviour in both market and political institutions, any attempt to replace or to modify an existing market situation, admitted to be characterised by serious externalities, will produce solutions that embody externalities which are different but precisely analogous, to those previously existing. (Buchanan 1962: 19)

Wilfred Beckerman, a leading neoliberal environmental economist, devoted an entire article to attacking Kapp's work, which was widely read and recognized in the emerging debate about increasing environmental degradation (Beckerman 1972; Franzini 2006).[61] The fact that Beckerman used arguments similar to Stigler's 'New welfare economics', warrants more research to determine how far this attack was not a coincidence but part of the neoliberal project. Hayek praised Beckerman as a 'competent expert' who provided a 'devastating critique' of *The Limits to Growth* report (Hayek 1974). Beckerman's direct attack illustrates most prominently the growing self-confidence with which neoliberals promulgated their ideas in the context of the ensuing environmental discourse.

In conclusion, several major protagonists of the neoliberal thought collective developed their arguments in response to Kapp's challenge of (neo-)liberalism à la Hayek and Mises. Changing the social costs discourse was on the neoliberal agenda since the 1940s, with intellectual roots developing earlier, in the interwar period. The neoliberal argument redefined the discourse in crucial ways. First, it defined the goal no longer as the elimination of harmful effects but, instead, as maximum efficiency, i.e., maximum value in terms of utility and exchange value. Thus, social costs were no longer considered a fundamental threat to society that had to be eliminated at all costs, and it was even argued that social costs cannot be eliminated at all. In comparison, Kapp's *Social Costs* had explicitly rejected the idea that the pursuit of the higher end (maximum efficiency) justified harmful effects (compensated for until equivalency is reached at the margin between costs and benefits). Kapp had also argued that history provided ample evidence for the successful struggle against social costs.

Second, by shifting the discourse away from discussing the institutional causes of social costs, and toward market-based solutions for social costs, the neoliberal thought collective boldly turned the problem upside down and prescribed as the cure what Kapp had identified as the disease. The debate was shifted away from the limitations of market-based accounting and allocation decisions, toward an idealist vision of a private bargaining system that would not develop naturally but would have to be constructed.

Third, although this was not explicitly stated by neoliberals, the state would play an important role in enforcing and determining property rights so that bargaining could work its magic. This then became the double-truth in the neoliberal intellectual effort (Mirowski 2009), insinuating an efficient and 'free-market'-based solution, while obscuring the fact that the state played an even larger and more coercive role as an omnipresent guarantor and enforcer of the necessary preconditions. The neoliberal thought collective got away with eagerly pointing out inefficiencies and costs involved in Kapp's proposal for social-democratic controls of the economy, while obscuring altogether the necessary costs of the neoliberal state.

Fourth, neoliberals did not provide an analysis of asymmetric economic power relations and corresponding economic inequality, with which the problem of social costs is imbued. This is squarely in line with the neoliberal tenet that inequality is a precondition for a well-functioning economic system, while Kapp pointed out the dangers of unequal distribution leading to a 'the poor sell cheap' doctrine that would boil down to giving corporations full sovereignty to achieve their aims, simply paying as little as they could get away with to anyone who can make a legitimate social cost claim.

In sum, this is how the neoliberal thought collective completely reformulated the problem of social costs, bearing surprising similarities with their revision of the definition of monopoly (Van Horn 2009).

4.5 Responding to neoliberalism: Kapp's 'impossibility thesis' reformulated

As shown above, Kapp had used the concept of social cost originally to refute Mises with the 'impossibility thesis' that markets do not and cannot express social costs. His empirical study, *Social Costs*, supported this thesis, directly attacking liberalism à la Hayek and Mises. As a consequence of the above-outlined neoliberal responses in the 1960s, Kapp found himself in a new position, having to reformulate his 'impossibility thesis' into an argument why markets cannot solve the problem of social costs. In 'Reply to Beckerman' (1971) Kapp first tried to remind everyone that the debate was originally focused on the fact that markets are the cause of social costs. He repeated his original argument that the maximization of net income by micro-economic units was likely to reduce the income of other economic units and of society at large, questioning the efficiency of the market as a mechanism of steering and coordinating the decisions of the various micro-economic units. The main reason for this, he argued, was that the conventional measurements (accounting systems, standards, indicators) of the performance of the economy are unsatisfactory and misleading. Kapp then addressed Beckerman, who proposed that the standard tools of economics and the logic and criteria of choice (including the aggregation of numerous (environmental) disparate items in terms of money and willingness to pay) could be used as criteria for evaluating things according to their equivalence at the margin, i.e., how much money one would accept in order to be indifferent between having the previous number of units of some 'good' and one unit less. Kapp argued that there are two 'impossibilities' that make this framework logically defective and operationally ineffective, as noted in the subsections below.

4.5.1 Impossibility of expressing the absolute value of human life
Human health, life and death do not have exchange value per se. Original physical needs, the inviolability of the individual and fundamental human requirements must not be evaluated in terms of a desire for money because it falsifies the original need and the core of the problem of decision-making (Kapp 1971). Referring to Immanuel Kant, Kapp also argued that that which cannot be exchanged has no exchange value but intrinsic absolute value. Thus, human life and survival are not exchangeable commodities and their evaluation in terms of market prices is in conflict with reason and human conscience (Kapp 1974: 132). According to Kapp, it makes no sense to ask a person how much money he would accept if he died (e.g., due to pollution) in order to be as well off as if he was alive. 'Willingness-to-pay' (WTP) as a criterion of evaluating the quality of the environment has the insidious effect of reinterpreting original human needs and requirements into a desire for money and of evaluating the relative importance of such needs in terms of criteria which reflect the existing inequalities in the wage and income structure.

Kapp favored an empirical and pragmatic approach to value. The evaluative judgment must, according to Kapp, correspond to the subject matter as it affects human health and life. Monetary criteria (WTP, compensation principle, etc.) are inappropriate because they do not evaluate characteristics which define the quality of the environment and its negative impact on human health, well-being and survival. The issue is not whether WTP can be established but whether this is cognitively responsible. Kapp argued that monetary criteria are not cognitively responsible because these evaluative criteria are detached from the evaluative criteria outside of the 'economic' discourse, and thus are irresponsible because they are untrue to the empirical fact of the matter. Quantitative standards must be correlated in an appropriate way with the defining characteristics of the qualitative definitions.

4.5.2 Impossibility of expressing complex and cumulative causation and uncertainty

WTP is further undermined by the individual's inability to ascertain the full range of short- and long-term benefits of environmental improvements, or the full impact of environmental disruption upon his health and well-being. Environmental disruption is the result of a complex interaction between the economic system with physical and biological systems. Pollutants from different sources also act upon one another, and what counts is the total toxicological situation. Complex causation relationships in environmental disruption can become disproportionate effects per unit of additional pollutant. The effects are cumulative over time with possible time lags, and there can be considerable uncertainty about future effects. These effects are not transparent to the individual, meaning that the individual does not have the information or knowledge required to make a sound judgment. Asking the individual what he is willing to pay for the improvement of the quality of the environment or what amount of compensation he is willing to accept to tolerate current and higher levels of pollution is an inadequate, ineffective and highly problematic basis for evaluating the value of environmental goals (Kapp 1971).

Kapp predicted that forcing new facts of environmental disruption into the conceptual box designed for market exchanges served to downplay the significance of the phenomena of social costs, making them appear more harmless than they are, and as a pretext for endless delays, or for doing too little too late.

4.6 Conclusion

This rational reconstruction shows that the history of the concept of social costs is from the beginning intertwined with the planning debate and the neoliberal project, and that Kapp's arguments were part of the discourse early on. Since the 1930s Kapp targeted (neo-)liberal doctrines with his empirically grounded theory of social costs, arguing, on the one hand, the impossibility of market-based solutions to social costs and, on the other, the need for social controls of the economy. Evidence shows that key figures of the neoliberal thought collective attacked Kapp's work, shrewdly turning the social cost discourse toward a pro-market direction. As is typical of the social sciences, this debate was never settled in the sense that Kapp's theory was proven wrong and was thus rightfully forgotten. Rather, the disappearance of his arguments from economic discourse may be attributed to larger developments, such as overall decline of post-World War II institutional economics (Berger and Steppacher, forthcoming), and the parallel success of the neoliberal project (Plehwe 2009). In the face of ever-greater social and environmental damages emanating from economic decision-making, reintroducing Kapp's theory could help to prevent the gradual encroachment of ideas.

References

Aslanbeigui, N. and Medema, S.G. (1998) 'Beyond the dark clouds: Pigou and Coase on social costs', *History of Political Economy*, 30(4): 601-625.

Beckerman, W. (1972) 'Environmental policy and the challenge to economic theory', *Social Science Information*, 11(1): 7-15.

Berger, S. (2008) 'Karl Polanyi's and Karl William Kapp's substantive economics: important insights from the Kapp–Polanyi correspondence', *Review of Social Economy*, 66(3): 381-396.

Berger, S. (2009a) 'The normative matrix of social costs: linking Hayden's social fabric matrix and Kapp's theory of social costs', in Natarajan, T., Elsner, W. and Fullwiler, S.T. (eds.), *Institutional Analysis and Praxis*, New York: Springer.

Berger, S. (2009b) *The Foundations of Non-equilibrium Economics*, London: Routledge.

Berger, S. and Steppacher, R. (eds.) (forthcoming), *The Foundations of Institutional Economics: by Karl William Kapp*, London: Routledge.

Buchanan, J.M. (1962) 'Politics, policy and the Pigovian margins', *Economica*, 29 (113): 17-28.

Calabresi, Guido (1961) 'Some thoughts on risk distribution and the law of torts', *Yale Law Journal*, 70(4): 499-553.

Cangiani, M. (2006) 'Freedom to plan', in Elsner, W., Frigato, P. and Ramazzotti, P. (eds.), *Social Costs and Public Action in Modern Capitalism: Essays Inspired by K. William Kapp's Theory of Social Costs*, London and New York: Routledge.

Coase, R. (1960) 'The problem of social costs', *Journal of Law and Economics*, 3: 1-44.

Coase, R. (1983) 'The fire of truth', *Journal of Law and Economics*, 26: 163.

Franzini, M. (2006) 'Social costs, social rights and the limits of free market capitalism: a re-reading of Kapp', in Elsner, W., Frigato, P. and Ramazzotti, P. (eds.), *Social Costs and Public Action in Modern Capitalism: Essays inspired by Karl William Kapp's Theory of Social Costs*, London and New York: Routledge.

Gaskins, R. (2007) 'Social insurance and the unpaid social costs of personal injury: a second look at K. William Kapp', Conference paper, 7th International Congress of ESEE, Leipzig.

Gruchy, A.G. (1947) *Modern Economic Thought: The American Contribution*, New York: A.M. Kelly.

Hayek, F.A. von (1935) *Collectivist Economic Planning*, London: G. Routledge and Sons Ltd.

Hayek, F.A. von (1944 [1994]) *Road to Serfdom*, Chicago: University of Chicago Press.

Hayek, F.A. von (1974) 'Award ceremony speech for the Bank of Sweden Prize'.

Kapp, K.W. (1936) *Planwirtschaft und Aussenhandel*, Genf: Georg & Cie.

Kapp, K.W. (1950) *The Social Costs of Private Enterprise*, Cambridge, MA: Harvard University Press. (Second, enlarged and revised edition published as (1963) *The Social Costs of Business Enterprise*, republished in 1977 and 2000 by Spokesman.)

Kapp, K.W. (1963) 'Social costs and social benefits: a contribution to normative economics', in E. von Beckerath and H. Giersch (eds.), *Probleme der normativen Ökonomik und der wirtschaftspolitischen Beratung*, Berlin: Duncker & Humblot, pp. 183-210.

Kapp, K.W. (1967 [1985]) 'Economics and rational humanism', in Ullmann, J.E. and Preiswerk, R. (eds.), *The Humanization of the Social Sciences*, Lanham and London: University Press of America.

Kapp, K.W. (1970) 'Environmental disruption and social costs: a challenge to economics', *Kyklos* 23(4): 833-848.

Kapp, K.W. (1971 [2011]) 'Social costs, neo-classical economics, and environmental planning: a reply', in Berger, S. and Steppacher, R. (eds.), *The Foundations of Institutional Economics: by K. William Kapp*, London and New York: Routledge.

Kapp, K.W. (1974 [2011]) 'Environmental indicators as indicators of social use value', published as 'Substantive vs. formal rationality', in Berger, S. and Steppacher, R. (eds.), *The Foundations of Institutional Economics: by K. William Kapp*, London and New York: Routledge.

Kapp, K.W. (1975) 'Staatliche Förderung umweltfreundlicher Technologien', *Kommission für wirtschaftlichen und sozialen Wandel 74*, Göttingen: Otto Schwarz. (Also published translated and abbreviated as 'Science and technology in the light of institutional analysis', in Berger, S. and Steppacher, R. (eds.) (2011) *The Foundations of Institutional Economics: by K. William Kapp*, London and New York: Routledge.)

Kapp, K.W. (unpublished manuscript), 'Preface' to *The Social Costs of Private Enterprise*. (Probably written in the late 1940s at New York University).

Knight, F.H. (1924 [1952]), 'Some fallacies in the interpretation of social costs', in Stigler, G.J. and Boulding, K.E. (eds.), *Readings in Price Theory*, Chicago: Homewood.

Knight, F.H. (1951) 'Review: the social costs of private enterprise', *Annals of the*

American Academy of Political and Social Science, 273: 233-234.

Medema, S.G. (1998) 'Wandering the road from pluralism to Posner: the transformation of law and economics in the twentieth century', *History of Political Economy*, 30: 202-224.

Medema, S.G. (2010) 'Ronald Harry Coase', in Emmett, R.B. (ed.), *The Elgar Companion to the Chicago School of Economics*, Cheltenham: Edward Elgar.

Mirowski, P. (2009) 'Postface: defining neoliberalism', in Mirowski, P. and Plehwe, D. (eds.), *The Road from Mont Pèlerin: The Making of the Neoliberal Thought Collective*, Cambridge, MA and London: Harvard University Press.

Mises, L. von (1944) *Bureaucracy*, New Haven: Yale University Press.

Nik-Khah, E. (2009) 'Getting hooked on drugs: the Chicago School, the pharmaceutical project, and the construction of medical neoliberalism', Conference Paper, EAEPE.

Nik-Khah, E. (2010) 'George J. Stigler', in Emmett, R.B. (ed.), *The Elgar Companion to the Chicago School of Economics*, Cheltenham: Edward Elgar.

Pigou, A.C. (1929) *The Economics of Welfare*, London: Macmillan.

Pigou, A.C. (1947) *Socialism vs. Capitalism*, London: Macmillan.

Plehwe, D. (2009) 'Introduction', in Mirowski, P. and Plehwe, D. (eds.), *The Road from Mont Pèlerin: The Making of the Neoliberal Thought Collective*, Cambridge, MA and London: Harvard University Press.

Rorty, R. (1984) 'The historiography of philosophy: four genres', in Rorty, R., Schneewind, J.B. and Skinner, Q. (eds.), *Philosophy in History*, Cambridge: Cambridge University Press.

Rutherford, M. (2010) 'Chicago economics and institutionalism', in Emmett, R.B. (ed.), *The Elgar Companion to the Chicago School of Economics*, Cheltenham: Edward Elgar.

Rutherford, M. (2011) *The Institutionalist Movement in American Economics, 1918-1947*, Cambridge: Cambridge University Press.

Shute, L. (1997) *John Maurice Clark: A Social Economics for the 21st Century*, London: Macmillan.

Stigler, G.J. (1941) *Production and Distribution Theories*, New York: Macmillan.

Stigler, G.J. (1943) 'The new welfare economics', *American Economic Review*, 33: 355-559.

Stigler, G.J. (1966) *The Theory of Price*, 3rd edition, London and New York: Macmillan.

Stigler, G.J. and Boulding, K.E. (eds.) (1952) *Readings in Price Theory*, Chicago: Richard D. Irwin.

Tool, M. (1978) 'Review: economics in institutional perspective, memorial essays in honor of K. William Kapp', *Journal of Economic Issues*, 12(4): 891-901.

Van Horn, R. (2009) 'Reinventing monopoly and the role of corporations: the roots of Chicago law and economics', in Mirowski, P. and Plehwe, D. (eds.), *The Road from Mont Pèlerin: The Making of the Neoliberal Thought Collective*, Cambridge, MA and London: Harvard University Press.

Van Horn, R. and Mirowski, P. (2009) 'The rise of the Chicago School of economics and the birth of neoliberalism', in Mirowski, P. and Plehwe, D. (eds.), *The Road from Mont Pèlerin: The Making of the Neoliberal Thought Collective*, Cambridge, MA and London: Harvard University Press.

Van Horn, R. and Mirowski, P. (2010) 'Neoliberalism and Chicago', in Emmett, R.B. (ed.), *The Elgar Companion to the Chicago School of Economics*, Cheltenham: Edward Elgar.

Veblen, T.B. (1904) *The Theory of Business Enterprise*, New York: Charles Scribner's Sons.

Veblen, T.B. (1921) *Engineers and the Price System*, New York: B.W. Huebsch.

5
Kapp's 'Social Costs', Clark's 'Cost Shifting' and Neoliberalism

5.1 Introduction

While most economists feel at ease to identify the boundaries of the discourse on social costs with the views of Pigou and Coase (see, for example, Aslanbeigui and Medema 1998), the distinct institutional argument developed by John Maurice Clark and Karl William Kapp has been largely eclipsed from the discourse (for efforts to revitalize this argument, see Berger 2012; Elsner, Frigato, and Ramazzotti 2012; Berger and Steppacher 2011; Gerber and Steppacher 2011). Therefore, this article has two main aims. Firstly, it reconstructs the making of the institutional argument based on unexplored archival materials, that is, the unpublished correspondence on social costs between Clark and Kapp. The aim is to analyze for the first time their important collaboration, and the development and relation of their arguments. This reveals and corrects imprecisions in the existing literature concerning their use of the term 'social costs,' sheds new light on how Clark influenced Kapp, and highlights the uniqueness of their institutional argument as a full-fledged theory of social costs. Secondly, this article provides important evidence that the discourse on social costs can only be fully understood as an interaction between neoclassical, neoliberal, and institutional argument.[62] That is, the institutional argument on social costs was developed not only as a critique of neoclassical economics, but also as a reply to the rise of post-WWII 'neo'-liberalism, exemplified in the works of F. A. Hayek and L. Mises. The analysis illustrates how the reaction of leading members of the 'neoliberal thought-collective' (see Mirowski and Plehwe 2009 for a sociology of this movement) contributed to the eclipse of the institutional argument on social costs. Thus, the article contributes an important detail to the account of the gradual demise of institutional economics in the period of the great neoliberal transformation of economics (Lee 2009; Rutherford 2011; Mirowski and Plehwe 2009). By reconstructing (Rorty 1984) the making of the institutional argument of social costs in the context of the social costs discourse with members of the 'neoliberal thought-collective,' this article contributes to the recent sociology of economic knowledge.

5.2 The Kapp-Clark Correspondence in Context

The Kapp-Clark correspondence on social costs is situated within the larger context of the demise of institutional economics as the dominant economic theory. Institutional economics is both a critique of neoclassical economics and a full-fledged and influential movement within economics (see Rutherford 2011; Kapp 2011; Dugger 2012). According to Rutherford, between 1926 and 1957 Clark was the leading institutional economist at Columbia, which was the center of institutional economics until the latter's eventual demise. The institutionalist complement that emerged there during the 1920s was given a major boost by the hiring of Clark as Research Professor in Economics. Clark described his work as 'social-institutional-dynamic theory,' developing a 'realist economics' and an approach to social-liberal planning. Before coming to Columbia, he had already critiqued neoclassical theory and called for a more properly scientific economics that was relevant to the issues of its time. The year he arrived at Columbia, he published *Social Control of Business* (1926), which further developed ideas first expressed in *Overhead Cost* ([1923] 1931). His book discussed a large number of market failures that called for additional social controls. Market failure and regulation were key areas of institutional economics at Columbia. Clark agreed with legal realists in viewing law as a key instrument of social control to improve economic outcomes. Clark even co-taught a seminar on law and economics in the 1924 and 1925 terms. Until the late 1930s the institutional program at Columbia was well established. According to Kenneth Arrow, the Veblenian influence was still present at Columbia in the early 1940s; however, things had begun to change and the research program fissured into such a variety of approaches that by the late 1930s, even the leading institutionalists W. Mitchell and Clark would no longer acknowledge a distinct and coherent institutionalism. As elsewhere, the significance of mathematical economics grew and was symbolized by the hiring of George Stigler in 1947. By the early 1950s the department was divided between the prewar institutionalists, such as Clark, and the postwar neoclassical economists, such as Stigler. Clark retired in 1953 (for more details of this account of the situation at Columbia, see Rutherford 2011; for details concerning the development of Clark's economics, see Shute 1997).

Kapp had been a research assistant at the Institute for Social Research at Columbia and an instructor of economics at Columbia between 1937 and 1945 (for a brief biography, see Berger and Steppacher 2011), when institutional economics was still dominant but had entered into its declining stage. When Columbia's postwar hiring strategy favored neoclassical economists, Kapp left for Wesleyan University (CT) (see the accounts of Lee 2003 and Rutherford 2011 on the suppression and demise of institutional economics). The tremendous influence of Clark's work on overhead costs and social economics is acknowledged in Kapp's preface to *Social Costs of Private Enterprise* (1950). Its second – revised and enlarged – edition was entitled 'Social Costs of Business Enterprise' (1963), signaling that the core of the institutional argument on social costs had already been stated by Veblen's *Theory of Business Enterprise* (1904). Kapp's work was widely reviewed and translated into many languages worldwide and made a significant impact on such events in the environmental movement in the 1970s as the 1972 UN Conference on Environment and Development, the formation of Ignacy Sachs' Center for Environment and Development, and the Socialist Environment and Resource Association (SERA). Friedrich Pollock – a leading member of the Frankfurt School and close friend of Kapp – invited Kapp to participate in the newly constituted Institut für Sozialforschung in Frankfurt. Kapp's major project, however, to initiate an international association of institutional economists in collaboration with Gunnar Myrdal, eventually failed in the late 1960s due to a lack of funding.[63] After reaching its pinnacle of influence on the social costs discourse in the early 1970s, Kapp's institutional argument on social costs (see below) has gradually been eclipsed from the discourse.

5.3 J. M. Clark's Theory of Overhead Costs and Cost Shifting

The following section shows how Clark derived the concept of cost shifting from his argument on overhead costs. This provides the intellectual context for the correspondence on Kapp's institutional theory of the social costs of private enterprise, as it is based on Clark's notion of cost shifting.[64] Clark's earliest letter in the Kapp Archives is dated Feb. 6, 1941 and is a reply to Kapp:

> Dear Dr. Kapp, Your outline and sample chapters are very interesting; and I am naturally interested in your project of developing and applying some of my ideas. [...] Needless to say, I shall be interested in how your study develops.

What was the nature of these 'ideas'? Clark developed his ideas mainly in 'Overhead Costs' (1931), arguing that 'overhead costs' refer to an

> entire family of ideas, but they have one essential thing in common [...] they refer to costs that cannot be traced home and attributed to particular units of business [...] most of the real problems involve one other fact; namely that an

increase or decrease in output does not involve a proportionate increase or decrease in cost. [...] the causes are real world complexities [...] unused productive capacity [...] 'idle overhead' [...] unused powers of production. (Clark 1931: 1)

We have a considerable body of economic generalizations, bearing on the facts that overhead costs are decidedly at variance with the assumptions and conclusions of that type of economics which searches for the conditions of a perfect equilibrium of supply and demand. (Clark 1931 in Gruchy 1967: 364)

Clark argued that the development of the forces of production in the 20th century, characterized by large amounts of fixed capital equipment, a specialized workforce, and disequilibrium, required a corresponding theory of costs (Gruchy 1967: 365-366). Reviewing the conceptual history of costs, Clark concluded that '[t]he entire idea of expenses of production is [...] a rather recent one' (Clark 1931: 1) and that the neoclassical theory of costs was modeled on a long bygone economic reality where 'virtually every element which economists now think of as an expense of production was paid for in such a fashion that each item could be directly charged to an item of product' (Clark 1931: 2). Neoclassical cost theory only held true under unique circumstances in which 'expenses were virtually all traceable directly to units of product, and overhead costs were virtually non-existent' (Clark 1931: 2). Clark concluded that the 'prevalent ideas on expenses of production date back to the domestic system and are not really appropriate to any later stage of industrial development' (Clark 1931: 2). Yet Clark argued that a proper theory of costs was crucial because 'the backbone of the science of economics is the balancing of value against cost' (Clark 1931: 17). Clark asked the crucial question how the costs of producing an additional unit of output are determined:

> Is the carload of lumber worth carrying if it covers all the costs that can be attributed to that single carload? [...] Shall we count the costs that would keep on even if the railroad shut down entirely? (Clark 1931: 19)

Clark concluded

> Evidently, 'cost' is an ambiguous term and [...] requires a thorough re-examination. (Clark 1931: 19)

> There is no natural system of prices in the old sense. Cost prices do not mean anything definite anymore. (Clark 1931: 32)

What is counted as 'costs' is thus a 'convention' with 'latitude' (Shute 1997: 60). This definition is fully in the tradition of institutional economics that focuses on the effects of habits of thought and institutions in the cumulative causation of the economic process. Clark used the concept of 'shifting and conversion of overhead costs' of human labor in the business cycle[65] to elaborate this aspect of institutional theory of costs (Clark 1931: 25-27):

> The cost to society of supporting a group of laborers does not vary with their output, for this cost goes on even though the laborers produce nothing, as is the case in periods of enforced idleness, which comes in the depression phase of the business cycle. (Gruchy 1967: 360)

Clark also extended the concept of overhead costs to mining and farming and called it 'an ultimate fact' of human cost that must be maintained in depressions (Gruchy: 361-362). He determined the problem to be that business enterprises did not treat their costs as overhead but as variable costs. The converting of constant overhead costs into variable costs determined the process by which producers judged the profitability of production. Clark observed this, for example, in the business cycle when slowing sales trigger quantity adjustments by the laying off of workers (Clark 1931: 27-30). Clark introduced the terms 'shifting and conversion of overhead costs' to describe how businesses make the workers responsible for their own maintenance, or throw the burden on society. These business measures create what Clark called the 'accelerator effect' of laying off workers and further reducing purchasing power, leading to a deterioration of productive facilities, i.e., a kind of social damage accelerator. Clark described this in a metaphor: 'All of which irresistibly suggests a man on a rock, jumping into the water for fear the tide will rise and wet him' (Clark 1931: 29). According to Clark, this reflected the conflict between social and private interests, since the former required capacity output while the latter sought to maximize revenue over variable costs (Clark 1931: 28-29).

This idea of cost shifting in the conflicting relationship between individual and social interests was a restatement of Veblen's source theme that portrayed social waste as a consequence of the fact that business enterprise did not channel economic activity in ways consistent with public interests (Rutherford 2011: 36). Veblen's pioneering analysis of institutions (including property rights, business-like and finance-like control of industry; see Gerber and Steppacher 2011) focused on social waste and damages. Veblen argued that capital resides in the continuity of ownership and that in a system of business enterprise and absentee ownership the 'strong arm intervenes' to shuffle property rights so as to control and increase private pecuniary returns, which includes a subreptitious and predatory shifting of costs and thereby an avoidance of responsibility. Moreover, Veblen argued that this process of realignment of property rights via subreption and predation not only failed to guarantee, but systematically disregarded, the maintenance and efficient use of the material funds of production. Veblen's examples included natural resource depletion – timber-lands, fur-bearing animals, oil fields – next to sabotage of industrial and workers' efficiency, causing unnecessary social waste (Krall and Gowdy 2011).

The rethinking of the notion of costs led Clark to reformulate the notions of efficiency and accounting (Gruchy 1967: 365-367). Clark argued that estimating the efficiency of the total economy could not be undertaken by using data from private accounting because it did not account for all the costs of production. Clark proposed a new form of accounting that would indicate the discrepancies between commercial and community measures of efficiency. He supported a social cost keeping as a 'form of economic reckoning which cuts through the sophisms of private financial accountancy and calls social waste by its true name'[66] (Gruchy 1967: 369). This new social accounting would be an effective device for judging the efficiency of the modern economy as a creator of 'human values.' According to Clark, it was the duty of economists to reveal the shifted and neglected costs of operating our industrial system that were left unpaid by businesses, such as idle men and machinery, destruction of utilities through fashion, waste resulting from competitive advertisement, and private business secrecy. Clark viewed this as a problem of bringing this information to the public's attention and of putting an end to unpaid costs (Gruchy 1967: 369-370). Clark hoped that once it was understood how the legal and institutional matrix produced market values, the discrepancies between market and social valuation could be reduced (Gruchy 1967: 368).

> A knowledge of the laws of overhead costs [...] opens many doors and is one of the indispensable avenues [...] overhead costs are not exceptions to a general economic law: they are the general law. (Clark 1931: 479)

In conclusion, Clark's argument on overhead costs and cost shifting constitute a further development of Veblen's ideas on social waste with a view to justify increasing social controls. In this institutional economics theory, the legal and institutional structure determines the extent to which firms have to pay the costs of production, so that prices based on costs including 'mark-up' (Lee 1999) are a function of the institutional framework of society. Without proper legal restrictions and social controls, the latter remains a system of cost shifting, a vicious circle of accelerating social damages. This theory of the institutional causes of cost shifting and social damages was developed by Kapp into the institutional theory of social costs, which is the subject matter of the following correspondence with Clark.

5.4 The Kapp-Clark Correspondence on Social Costs[67]

How far did Clark influence Kapp in developing the institutional theory of social costs as a critique of the system of business enterprise and as an argument for social accounting and controls? What was the nature of their interactions? In the above cited letter (February 6, 1941), Clark raised his 'chief concern [...] of balancing the emphasis on the negative and the positive side of the critique.' Clark contrasted the setting in which 'Overhead Costs' was written to the setting of the 1940s:

> [my early work was in a] setting characterized by detail attempts to correct particular defects in the system of private enterprise, involving no serious threat to the evolutionary continuance of the 'institution' itself [...] the present setting is different, in that breakdown and radical transformation, which are not intended by the majority of the population and for which we are not prepared, are really threatened.

Clark warned Kapp of the danger of systemic breakdown, reminding him to be aware of his responsibility in writing his book on the social costs of private enterprise:

> therefore, it seems to me particularly necessary at present to do justice to the elements of positive value in the institution [private enterprise] – in short to give a balanced presentation. [...] [Your] study seems to judge the system by ideal standards. And the use of ideal standards seems to me justifiable, if one keeps in mind the fact that they are unattainable, and that any actual alternative scheme would have its own imperfections to balance against the ones the existing system reveals. [...] If one of the alternatives is a thoroughgoing transformation to a collectivist system, its imperfections are necessarily conjectural, but might be quite serious; and they need to be recognized.

Additionally, Clark raised serious doubts whether a collectivist system would be inclined to institutionalize a 'system of social accountancy,' fearing that the imperfections would simply be shifted from the 'machinery of the markets' to the 'political machinery.' This criticism is also the core of the last documented intellectual interaction between Clark and Kapp, via Clark's book review of 'Social Costs of Private Enterprise' in the Yale Review entitled 'The New Economic Community.' In it Clark praised the systematic elaboration of the idea that an "enterprise" should reckon with all the costs it occasions, including those the business unit can shift to other members of society.' And with regard to neoclassical economics: 'if one man's gnat is another man's camel [...] Kapp presents theorists with evidence of the size of the camels they have been swallowing [...]' However, Clark also raised questions: 'has [Kapp] at certain points, charged as costs of private enterprise things that are really costs of modern methods of production under any form of organization [?] [...] is there a sound basis for presuming that a socialist government would treat these matters more justly than they are treated by a state which combines 'private enterprise' with many sided welfare policies? Is a municipality more likely to abolish the smoke nuisance from its own plant than to order a private plant to do the like?' Clark concluded that while questions remained, Kapp's book was important because it brought together ample empirical evidence for the existence of social costs, suggesting the scope and magnitude of the problem (Clark 1950: 173-174).

Both documents show not only that Kapp's critique of private enterprise was too unbalanced for Clark's taste, but also that Clark's own views on the role of private enterprise had changed since the 1920s. Since the draft of the manuscript reviewed by Clark is not available, we do not know in how far Kapp modified his critique. In this context it is of interest that Kapp's letter to Clark on December 12, 1945 referred to a working title that differs from the later book publication: 'I am very grateful to you for having read parts of my manuscript on Social Costs and Returns which I submitted to you.' We do not know whether Clark's influence was decisive on Kapp's decision not to publish roughly half of his original book manuscript, which contained a discussion of planning for social returns of 'utilities which diffuse themselves among all members of society, [...] that are to a large extent inappropriable by individual producers and cannot always be appraised in monetary terms'[68] (Kapp, unpublished ms. III). Kapp had originally developed the interconnected themes of social costs and returns in his dissertation (Kapp 1936). In the unpublished manuscript, Kapp discussed social returns

> derived from the gratification of collective needs; from international economic policies designed to achieve a balanced economy [...] and from the improvement of transportation facilities [...] scientific research, multiple purpose projects (such as TVA), and the maintenance of a social minimum with respect to essential foodstuffs, medical care, housing, and education. (Kapp, unpublished ms. III)

While the issues of social costs and planning for social returns are intimately related, the 'returns' portion was not published and remains in the Kapp Archives. Clark's warnings may have caused Kapp to improve and balance his argument on social returns, an improvement evident in his later work. For example, he published the article 'Social Costs and Social Benefits–A Contribution to Normative Economics' (1963) in the same year as *Social Costs of Business Enterprise*. This article, as well as various others from the late 1950s and early 1960s, resulted from research on the social costs and social benefits in development projects in India and the Philippines, and addressed the social costs and lack of planning for social returns by ineffective public administrations (Kapp 1959a, 1959b, 1960, 1961). These articles display Kapp's openness to balancing his argument, criticizing social costs regardless of whether they were created by private or public entities. Yet, Kapp also maintained that planning for social returns and the minimization of social costs were important goals of economic development policy and that important improvements were achieved. Starting from the interconnected problems of social costs and social returns, Kapp developed a full-fledged theoretical framework of democratic controls of science and technology, socioecological indicators, and social minima (see below for more details; for a full elaboration, see Kapp 2011).

The second half of Clark's letter (February 6, 1941) asked Kapp to consider the question of freedom. Clark saw 'value in the device of imagining the setting up of a new community, with our present knowledge.' But he asked Kapp to consider

> what sphere would be left to the market process, and what imperfections in that sphere would be tolerated in the interest of minimising central regimentation and preserving the prerequisites of liberty, both of thought and expression as well as of consumption and production?

It seems that Clark perceived Kapp's critique not only as too unbalanced, but also with too little focus on the questions of the shortcomings of alternative modes of organization, such as socialism, and the prerequisites of 'liberty.' Curiously, this criticism is similar to the one levied against Kapp in a book review by the Chicago liberal economist Frank Knight, who had institutional leanings (Knight 1951; Berger 2012; Rutherford 2010: 30-32; Emmett 2010: 282). As an exile from Nazi Germany, an affiliate of the Frankfurt School, and a student of the poet and teacher Ernst Wiechert, Kapp took the issue of integrating freedom with the alleviation of human suffering very seriously. Perhaps due to Clark's criticisms, Kapp published 'Economic Planning and Freedom'

(1950) the same year as his *Social Costs of Private Enterprise*, in which he argued for a substantive understanding of freedom that included planning for social returns. Clark's letter finished on a friendly note: 'needless to say, I shall be interested to see how your study develops.'

Four years later, on December 4, 1945, Clark wrote down his detailed comments regarding the overall scope of Kapp's draft, as well as its specific arguments. His letter consists of four densely typewritten pages, showing Clark's efforts to further influence and aid in the development of Kapp's institutional theory of social costs. As in the previous reply, the draft upon which the comments were based is not available, so that the basis for interpretation is missing. Yet the letter provides Clark's more general comments as well:

> It is interesting that you are reviving the discussion of extra-market values and costs and putting content into it, with some approach to measurement.

Importantly, Clark addressed the semantic differences of Kapp's concept of 'social costs':

> [your definition of] 'social' values and costs differs from mine in applying to non-market quantities only, where mine [Clark's] included also the quantities the market 'measures'.

This shows that Clark defined social costs as nonmarket plus market costs in the neoclassical tradition of Arthur C. Pigou (1929). This may reflect Clark's attempt to improve neoclassical theory rather than repudiate it (Lee 2009: 33), which had led him to dedicate his theory of overhead costs as 'a very small contribution toward realizing his [that is, his father's neoclassical] conception of a dynamic economics' (Clark in Gruchy 1967: 357). Throughout his work Kapp roundly rejected neoclassical economics and its conceptual framework in its entirety, criticizing its ineffective and overly conservative reform proposals. Kapp noted in *Social Costs of Business Enterprise* (1963) that Pigou had radicalized his political-economic conclusions by the late 1940s when Pigou (1947) had argued that the social inefficiencies had reached a level that justifies the socialization of the means of production. Yet Kapp maintained that Pigou's neoclassical concept of external costs was imbued with the limitations of the neoclassical theories of price and value, as well as its closed system and equilibrium preconceptions that preclude an adequate understanding of the circular cumulative causation underlying the problem of social costs and its complex value dimensions, as well as its open system character (Kapp 1963, 1976; Berger 2009).

Instead, Kapp distinguished private costs from social costs (social losses, damages, inefficiencies) to emphasize that businesses privatize profits and socialize as many costs as they can. Kapp defined social costs as that part of the costs of production that businesses shift to society to increase their profits, thus avoiding responsibility. According to Kapp, adding social to private costs results in total costs. In the literature, this important difference between Kapp's and Clark's definition of the concept of social costs has been obscured. This may be due to the fact that both agreed on the notion of cost shifting but disagreed on what to call the shifted costs (see Prasch 2005). Thus, it is Kapp's contribution to have elevated the concept of social costs to a stylized fact for a critique of capitalism, the system of business or private enterprise, and formal rationality, further mending and bringing into the open ideas of Marx, Veblen, and Weber.[69] In *The Social Costs of Private Enterprise* (1950) Kapp provides a chapter on the conceptual history of social costs, showing his commitment to engage and acknowledge the large variety of previous contributions and arguments on social costs and returns. It is also Kapp's contribution to have clearly articulated how the institutional theory of social costs differs from neoclassical (see above) and neoliberal approaches (see below).

The significance of Clark's comments is acknowledged by Kapp in his subsequent letter (December 12, 1945):

> Dear Professor Clark: I am very grateful to you for having read parts of my manuscript on Social Costs and Social Returns which I submitted to you. [...] I have studied your comments very carefully and I found them most pertinent [...] I feel that you have called my attention to serious weaknesses in the formulation of my ideas, and in most instances I have found it possible to reformulate my conclusions in a more careful and more satisfactory manner.

However, Kapp's handwritten remarks on the margins of Clark's letter indicate that he did not agree with all of his comments, leading him to reply to Clark:

> The following is a brief reformulation of my ideas – a reformulation which I owe to your challenge and which I shall incorporate in the introductory chapter. [...] The thesis of this book is briefly that the orthodox appraisal and interpretation of the economic process in the unplanned market economy is invalidated by various obstacles to rational conduct and the phenomenon of social costs and social returns.

Clark's remark that the problem of social costs had already been successfully addressed by Oskar Lange and Abba Lerner and that Kapp was 'beating a straw-man' challenged Kapp to clarify his aims with regard to developments in economics:

> The presuppositions of classical and neoclassical equilibrium economics continue to determine both the methods and the scope of modern value theory as can be easily ascertained [...] [by] the more recent system of economics which is based upon Keynes' General Theory [...] modern text-books [...] the works of such intransigent economic liberals as Professor F.A. Hayek, L. Mises, and L. Robbins [...] [even] some socialists of the 20th century have so accustomed themselves to the methods of thinking of neoclassical equilibrium analysis that they answer Mises' challenge of socialist planning by proclaiming that the socialist economy would solve the problem of allocating scarce resources among competing ends with the aid of the price mechanism and the competitive calculus. There is no hint that in order to solve the economic problem a planned economy is likely to base its economic decisions upon a social evaluation of total outlays and total benefits which [...] will have to take into account social costs and social returns. In other words, I am not aware of the fact that O. Lange and Professor Lerner have any fundamental quarrel with traditional equilibrium theory, and I have the impression that there is no room in the conceptual system of these writers for the phenomena of social cost and social returns. [...] I am also aware that value theory continues to be confined to the search for levels of equilibrium 'of the exchange value sort,' and not in terms of social value despite the fact that [...] economic decisions of the greatest importance are based on social choices and preferences.

This shows that Kapp aimed at a critique of all economic theories – even the progressive ones by Lange and Lerner – insofar as they adopted core elements of neoclassical economics and ignore the question of social valuation:

> When I said that the search for levels of equilibrium ought to be abandoned, I meant actually that the exclusive preoccupation [...] with problems of exchange value requires supplementation by a study of social value. [...] I like to hope that in the light of this letter there is perhaps a greater area of agreement between your 'Preface to Social Economics' and my 'Social Costs and Social Returns' than it appeared to you after reading the manuscript. With renewed thanks for your kindness of reading the manuscript, I am Very Sincerely Yours K. William Kapp

Kapp clearly tried to convince Clark that their works were in agreement concerning the importance of social valuation in economic decision making. In the same vein Kapp explains in the unpublished draft versions of the introduction to *The Social Costs of Private Enterprise* that he aimed at a critique of social costs under capitalism, and of neoclassical and neoliberalism theories that do not capture these realities:

> As an analysis of the social inefficiency of the unplanned market economy the study was bound to assume the character of a critique not only of capitalism but also of traditional equilibrium economics. (Kapp, unpublished manuscript I)

> the re-orientation of economics; [...] [exploration of] the possibilities for the setting up of valid criteria for economic planning and the formulation for economic policy, and perhaps to prepare the way for the elaboration of a positive theory of social value are the chief ultimate purposes of this inquiry. (Kapp, unpublished manuscript II)

The final words of Kapp's letter and the unpublished versions confirm that Kapp identified with Clark's project of *Preface to Social Economics* (1936), for which he saw the argument on social costs to be only a preliminary step. Kapp actively pursued this social economics or institutional 'foundations project' for the rest of his life (Berger and Steppacher 2011).

5.5 Institutionalism vs. Neoliberalism: The Discourse on Social Costs

The above letter to Clark also shows that Kapp was among the economists in the institutional movement who directed his work against the 'intransigent' liberalism of Friedrich A. Hayek. Moreover, the unpublished draft version of the preface to 'Social Costs of Private Enterprise' (1950) states that the core thesis of the book is directed against a revival of liberalism reflected by the success of Hayek's and Mises's works (for details, see Berger 2012). Unlike Clark's contribution on overhead cost, Kapp's social costs argument emerged less as a critique of neoclassical economics than as a late reply to von Mises's argument in the European socialist accounting debate of the 1920s. Kapp's dissertation *The Planned Economy and International Trade* (1936) developed the social costs argument as a socialist 'countervailing impossibility thesis' against Mises's famous neoliberal impossibility thesis. That is, according to Kapp, an accounting system based on market values cannot account for the social value of damages because the latter cannot find 'value expression' in exchanges between isolated individuals (Kapp 1936; Berger 2012). Therefore, Kapp concluded, allocation in a pure market economy cannot be rational. Thus, Kapp's theory on social costs was originally motivated by the emerging Austrian neoliberalism in Geneva (Plehwe 2009). At this time, Kapp was also closely affiliated with and influenced by the Frankfurt School, exiled – like Kapp – in Geneva, so that the initial development of his argument on social costs can be seen also as a contribution to the Frankfurt School's post-Weberian project, which Foucault identified as trying to show the 'irrational rationality of capitalism' (Foucault 1979: 106).

In this context it is of interest that Clark's book title *Alternative to Serfdom* (ATS) (1948) is a clear reference to Hayek's *Road to Serfdom* (RTS) (1944), and that Kapp's copy of ATS shows intense underlining and three handwritten pages of notes, indicating his agreement with Clark's arguments, in particular the beneficial role of unions and the need to focus economic inquiry on human needs. Kapp's copy of Hayek's RTS likewise shows 10 marks in the margins, including pages 37-39 on social costs and social returns, and contains six newspaper clippings from the debate stirred by Hayek's RTS and Mises's *Bureaucracy* (1944). Hayek's views on social costs evolved after RTS, and his mature point of view on social costs was diametrically opposed to Kapp's. This became especially evident in Hayek's justification of the social costs of Pinochet's dictatorship, which Hayek considered 'a necessary evil' in implementing the (neo-)liberal agenda (see Farrant, McPhail, and Berger 2012: 530). Like Hayek, Kapp also contributed to a newspaper debate following the installment of Pinochet's dictatorship. In his article, which the editor of the Swiss newspaper 'National-Zeitung' had solicited, Kapp warned of a new 'right-wing extremism that puts on the costume of liberalism' (Kapp 1974: 6). Yet Kapp mentioned no names in this article, nor did he direct his final manuscript of 'Social Costs of Private Enterprise' or any of his articles against Hayek or Mises. The most probable explanation is that Kapp hoped for a genuine dialogue on the substance of the issue by avoiding an unbalanced ad hominem attack.[70] Kapp's intellectual engagement with neoliberal economics is also evidenced by a book review that critically assessed Eucken's posthumous work on economic policy (Kapp 1953). Kapp noticed the distinct constructivist element in Eucken's work, which, according to Mirowski (Mirowski 2009), is the hallmark of neoliberalism and distinguishes it from laissez-faire neoclassical economics. Kapp's main criticism was that this approach excluded evidence that is contrary to its preconceptions, that is, that Eucken considered social costs as minor exceptions rather than systemic problems that require more substantive controls. Kapp also noted that Eucken's 'idealtype' of the exchange economy is too abstract, with no allowance for 'less harmonious' facts of economic life, such as systemic social costs.

It is important to note that Kapp's social minima proposal for minimizing social costs (Kapp 2011) is a substantivist reply to minima proposals developed by (neo-)liberal economists, that is, the minima proposal of Walter Eucken (Foucault 1979: 141, 204-206) and Hayek's 'non-discretionary rules' argument (for a discussion of Hayek's argument, see Burczak 2011). The difference lies in the extent to which Kapp wanted social minima to control the economic process. That is, he proposed a full-fledged democratic governance of science and technology decisions, including socioecological indicators, to guarantee the maintenance of social minima (Kapp 2011). Contrary to neoliberalism, Kapp's approach endorses a social and democratic dynamic centered on universal and scientifically objectifiable human needs, and the absolute value of human life in the Kantian tradition. The neoliberal approach that turns human life and needs into a means to an end is rejected by Kapp, so that social costs cannot be justified as a 'necessary evil' to achieve economic growth, profitable exchanges, or some neoliberal notion of purely formal economic freedom. Kapp dubbed his approach 'new rational humanism' (Kapp 1985) based on a theory of integrated social knowledge centered on and derived from a scientific biocultural concept of the human being. In this, Kapp pulled together research on human needs from various humanist scientists and psychologists, for example, Abraham Maslow and Erich Fromm. Kapp placed this approach in the tradition of European substantivist arguments made by Carl Menger and Karl Polanyi (Berger 2008) but also American biocultural approaches of Thorstein Veblen and John Dewey (Kapp 1961; Gerber and Steppacher 2011; Kapp 2011).[71] In sum, Kapp's institutional theory of social costs was part of his larger intellectual project of a new rational humanism and an attempt to counter neoliberal arguments.

The success of Kapp's institutional theory of social costs during the 1950s led various key figures of the 'neoliberal thought-collective' to respond or comment directly, for example, Frank Knight (1951), Guido Calabresi (1961), James Buchanan (1962), and Wilfred Beckerman (1972) (for details, see Berger 2012). Post-WWII developments in economics need to be seen as a reaction to institutional economics, with the Chicago School sharply at ideological odds with institutionalism (Rutherford 2011: 351; Mirowski and Plehwe 2009; Van Horn et al. 2011). As Rutherford has pointed out, Chicago economists often modified or reworked existing institutional economics' ideas (Rutherford 2010: 36). In the discourse on social costs, this is best demonstrated by how Coase (1960) and Stigler (1966) contributed to the discourse on social costs. Both remained conspicuously silent on previous institutional arguments and celebrated their argument on the institution of property rights as a 'scientific discovery.' Stigler's 'Coase Theorem' shifted the discourse from the problem of 'social costs' to a problem of 'transaction costs,' corresponding with his lack of interest in actual social damages (see Medema 2011). Instead of seeking ways to prevent social costs ex ante, which was the primary concern of Kapp's theory of social costs, Stigler focused on constructing ex post market-based solutions by minimizing transaction costs and assigning property rights. Stigler did not engage previous institutional arguments concerning the predatory and subreptitious aspects involved in assigning property rights and the impossibility of adequately reflecting social and ecological values in individual market exchanges.

It seems likely that Stigler's contribution to the discourse on social costs was part of his many 'demolition derbies' against institutional economics, which he hated: 'Institutional economics is dying out at a fantastic rate – though still not fast enough to suit me' (Stigler, in Rutherford 2011: 328).[72] Due to his overt dislike for institutional economics, it seems reasonable to presume that his silence on Clark's and Kapp's well-known arguments on social costs was not an innocent oversight. Clark's work was so prominent that he had received the Francis A. Walker medal by the American Economic Association in 1952, 'given to that living American economist who [...] has made over the course of his life the most distinguished contribution to economics' (Shute 1997). Instead of seeking a discourse with institutional economists, Stigler promoted Knight's 'Some Fallacies in the Interpretation of Social Costs' (1924) in his publications on price theory (Stigler and Boulding 1952) and in his 'Coase Theorem' (1966). Additionally, Stigler was among the 'commentators' who encouraged Coase to write 'The Problem of Social Costs' (Coase 1960, fn 1; see the 'Eureka' event in Medema 2011). Coase refers to Stigler's argument that the problem of social costs should be conceived of as purely 'reciprocal nature' (Coase 1960: 2), rather than social or systemic. Much like Stigler, Coase adopted a very disparaging attitude towards institutional economics, describing it as 'a mass of descriptive material waiting for a theory, or a fire' (Coase in Rutherford 2010: 25), and also remaining silent on Clark's and Kapp's arguments on social costs.

5.6 Conclusion

This article demonstrates that the dominant narrative about the discourse on social costs is incomplete. The findings show that the discourse includes Clark's and Kapp's institutional theory of cost shifting and social costs. The latter reflects a distinct and clearly distinguishable institutional argument on social costs, which further develops earlier ideas by Veblen and Marx. Thus, the institutional theory of social costs is a clearly distinguishable alternative to neoclassical and neoliberal arguments. The Kapp-Clark correspondence shows that Clark was influential in the development of Kapp's institutional theory of social costs and social returns. Throughout their works, both economists harnessed the enormous power of their argument on cost shifting as a rationale for increasing social controls of the economy and the development of a genuine social economics. Yet the archival materials also illustrate that both economists differed on the definition of social costs, and that Clark encouraged Kapp to balance his critique and to consider improving certain weaknesses of his argument. Their correspondence provides further important documentation that Kapp developed the institutional theory on social costs to counter 'intransigent [neo-]liberalism,' and that leading neoliberal economists sought strategies to undermine and eclipse the institutional argument. Thus, the discourse on social costs cannot be fully understood without appreciating the role of the institutional argument on social costs. This account differs markedly from other recent accounts, ending the hermeneutic 'stop play' strategy that fails to acknowledge institutional theories. Thereby, this article contributes to the important advancement of understanding social costs via the 'ethics of play' (Vilhauer 2010; Samuels 1990; Arrington 1990).

References

Arrington, E. C. (1990). 'Comment to Raymond Benton Jr.'s 'A Hermeneutic Approach to Economics: If Economics is Not Science, and if it is Not Merely Mathematics, Then What Could it Be?' In *Economics as Discourse – An Analysis of the Language of Economists*. Ed. Warren J. Samuels, pp. 90-101. Boston/Dordrecht/London: Kluwer Academic Publishers.

Aslanbeigui, N., and S. G. Medema. (1998). 'Beyond the Dark Clouds: Pigou and Coase on Social Costs.' *History of Political Economy* 30(4): 601-625.

Beckerman, W. (1972). 'Environmental Policy and the Challenge to Economic Theory.' *Social Science Information* 11(1): 7-15.

Berger, S. (2008). 'Karl Polanyi's and Karl William Kapp's Substantive Economics: Important Insights from the Kapp-Polanyi Correspondence.' *Review of Social Economy* 66(3): 381-396.

(ed.) (2009). *The Foundations of Non-Equilibrium Economics*. London and New York: Routledge.

(2012). 'The Discourse on Social Costs–Kapp's Impossibility Thesis vs. Neoliberalism.' In *Social Costs Today–Institutional Analyses of the Present Crisis*. Eds. Wolfram Elsner, Pietro Frigato, and Paolo Ramazzotti, pp. 96-112.

London and New York: Routledge.

Berger, S., and R. Steppacher. (2011). 'Editorial Introduction.' In *The Foundations of Institutional Economics*, by K. William Kapp, pp. 1-13. London and New York: Routledge.

Buchanan, J. M. (1962). 'Politics, Policy and the Pigovian Margins.' *Economica* 29(113): 17-28.

Burczak, T. (2011). 'A Socialist Spontaneous Order.' In *Hayek, Mill, and the Liberal Tradition*. Ed. Andrew Farrant, pp. 130-147. London and New York: Routledge.

Calabresi, G. (1961). 'Some Thoughts on Risk Distribution and the Law of Torts.' *Yale Law Journal* 70(4): 499-553.

Clark, J. M. ([1923] 1931). *Studies in the Economics of Overhead Costs*. Chicago: University of Chicago Press.

(1926). *Social Control of Business*. Chicago: University of Chicago Press.

(1936). *Preface to Social Economics: Essays on Economic Theory and Social Problems*. New York: Farrar & Rinehart.

(1948). *Alternative to Serfdom*. New York: Alfred A. Knopf.

(1950). 'The New Economic Community.' *Yale Review* 40(1): 171-174.

Coase, R. (1960). 'The Problem of Social Costs.' *Journal of Law and Economics* 3: 1-44.

Dugger, W. M. (2012). 'Book Review–The Foundations of Institutional Economics by Karl William Kapp, edited by S. Berger and R. Steppacher.' *Journal of Economic Issues* 46(3): 817-819.

Elsner, W., P. Frigato, and P. Ramazzotti (eds). (2012). *Social Costs Today–Institutional Analyses of the Present Crisis*. London and New York: Routledge.

Emmett, R. B. (2010). 'Frank H. Knight.' In *The Elgar Companion to the Chicago School of Economics*. Ed. Ross B. Emmett, pp. 280-286. Cheltenham and Northampton: Edward Elgar.

Farrant, A., E. McPhail, and S. E. Berger. (2012). 'Preventing the 'Abuses' of Democracy: Hayek, the 'Military Ursurper' and Transitional Dictatorship in Chile.' *American Journal of Economics and Sociology* 71(3): 513-538.

Foster, J. B. (2000). *Marx's Ecology: Materialism and Nature*. New York: Monthly Review Press.

(2010). *The Ecological Rift: Capitalism's War on Earth*. New York: Monthly Review Press.

Foucault, M. (1979). *The Birth of Biopolitics*. Palgrave-Macmillan.

Franzini, M. (2006). 'Social Costs, Social Rights and the Limits of Free Market Capitalism: A Re-Reading of Kapp.' In *Social Costs and Public Action in Modern Capitalism – Essays Inspired by Karl William Kapp's Theory of Social Costs*. Eds. Elsner Wolfram et al., pp. 56-71. London and New York: Routledge.

Gerber, J., and R. Steppacher. (2011). *Towards an Integrated Paradigm in Heterodox Economics–Alternative Approaches to the Current Eco-Social Crises*. London: Palgrave-Macmillan.

Gruchy, A. G. ([1947] 1967). *Modern Economic Thought–The American Contribution*. New York: A.M. Kelly.

Hayek, F. A. (1944). *Road to Serfdom.* Chicago: University of Chicago Press.
Kapp, K. W. (1936). *Planwirtschaft und Aussenhandel.* Genf: Georg & Cie.
— (1943). 'Rational Human Conduct and Modern Industrial Society.' *Southern Economic Journal* X (2): 136-150.
— (1950). *The Social Costs of Private Enterprise.* Cambridge, MA: Harvard University Press.
— (1950). 'Economic Planning and Freedom' *Weltwirtschaftliches Archiv* 64: 29-54.
— (1953), 'Eucken's Posthumous Work on Economics Policy.' *Kyklos* 6(2): 165-169.
— (1959a). 'River Valley Development Projects: Problems of Evaluation and Social Costs.' *Kyklos* 12(4): 589-604.
— (1959b). 'River Valley Projects in India: Their Direct Benefits.' *Economic Development and Cultural Change* 7(1): 24-47.
— (1960). 'Economic Development, National Planning and Public Administration.' *Kyklos* 13(2): 172-204.
— (1961). 'The Transition from a Bullock to a Tractor Economy in India: Some Indirect Effects and Benefits (with P. N. Mathur).' *Weltwirtschaftliches Archiv* 87: 333-350.
— (1961). *Toward a Science of Man in Society—A Positive Approach to the Integration of Social Knowledge.* The Hague: Martinus Nijhoff.
— (1963a). *The Social Costs of Business Enterprise.* London: Asia Publishing House.
— (1963b). 'Social Costs and Social Benefits—A Contribution to Normative Economics.' In *Probleme der normativen Ökonomik und der wirtschaftspolitischen Beratung.* Eds. E. V. Beckerath and H. Giersch, pp. 183-210. Berlin: Duncker & Humblot.
— ([1967] 1985). 'Economics and Rational Humanism.' In *The Humanization of the Social Sciences.* Eds. J. E. Ullmann and R. Preiswerk, pp. 99-120. Lanham and London: University Press of America.
— (1974). 'Environmental Indicators as Indicators of Social Use Value.' Published as 'Substantive vs. Formal Rationality.' In *The Foundations of Institutional Economics.* Eds. Sebastian Berger and Rolf Steppacher, pp. 159-169. London and New York: Routledge.
— (1974). 'Die Zentrale Frage' ['The Central Question']. *National-Zeitung,* October 5: 6.
— ([1975] 2011). 'Science and Technology in the Light of Institutional Analysis.' In *The Foundations of Institutional Economics.* Eds. Sebastian Berger and Rolf Steppacher, pp. 203-244. London and New York: Routledge.
— (1976). 'Economics in the Future: The Open System Character of the Economy and its Implications.' In *Economics in the Future: Towards a New Paradigm.* Ed. Kurt Dopfer, pp. 90-105. London: MacMillan.
— (undated). Introduction to book manuscript 'Social Costs of Private Enterprise' (draft). Unpublished.
— (undated). Introduction II to book manuscript 'Social Costs of Private Enterprise' (draft). Unpublished.

(undated). Introduction III to book manuscript 'Social Costs of Private Enterprise' (draft). Unpublished.

Knight, F. (1951). 'Review—The Social Costs of Private Enterprise.' *Annals of the American Academy of Political and Social Science* (273): 233- 234.

([1924] 1952). 'Some Fallacies in the Interpretation of Social Costs.' In *Readings in Price Theory*. Eds. George J. Stigler and Kenneth E. Boulding, pp. 160-179. Chicago: Homewood, Illinois.

Krall, L., and J. Gowdy. (2011). 'An Institutional and Evolutionary Critique of Natural Capital.' In *Towards an Integrated Paradigm in Heterodox Economics—Alternative Approaches to the Current Eco-Social Crises*. Eds. Julien-Francois Gerber and Rolf Steppacher, pp. 127-146. Palgrave-Macmillan.

Lee, F. S. (1999). *Post-Keynesian Price Theory*. Cambridge: Cambridge University Press.

(2009). *A History of Heterodox Economics—Challenging the Mainstream in the 20th Century*. London and New York: Routledge.

Martinez-Alier, J. (2002). *Environmentalism of the Poor—A Study of Ecological Conflicts and Valuation*. Cheltenham: Edward Elgar.

Medema, S. G. (2011). 'A Case of Mistaken Identity: George Stigler, 'The Problem of Social Costs,' and the Coase Theorem.' In *European Journal of Law and Economics*.

Mirowski, P. (2009). 'Postface: Defining Neoliberalism.' In *The Road from Mont Pèlerin – The Making of the Neoliberal Thought Collective*. Eds. Philip Mirowski and Dieter Plehwe, pp. 417-456. Cambridge and London: Harvard University Press.

Mirowski, P., and D. Plehwe. (eds). (2009), *The Road from Mont Pèlerin—The Making of the Neoliberal Thought Collective*. Cambridge and London: Harvard University Press.

Mises, L. (1944). *Bureaucracy*. New Haven: Yale University Press.

Nik-Khah, E. (2011). 'George Stigler, The Graduate School of Business, and the Pillars of the Chicago School.' In *Building Chicago Economics— New Perspectives on the History of America's Most Powerful Economics Program*. Eds. Robert Van Horn et al., pp. 116-150. Cambridge: Cambridge University Press.

Pigou, A. C. (1929). *The Economics of Welfare*. London: Macmillan & Co.

(1947). *Socialism vs. Capitalism*. London: Macmillan.

Plehwe, D. (2009). 'Introduction.' In *The Road from Mont Pèlerin—The Making of the Neoliberal Thought Collective*. Eds. Philip Mirowski and Dieter Plehwe, pp. 1-44. Cambridge and London: Harvard University Press.

Prasch, R. (2005). 'The Social Costs of Labor.' *Journal of Economic Issues* 39(2): 439-445.

Rorty, R. (1984). 'The Historiography of Philosophy: Four Genres.' In *Philosophy in History*. Eds. Richard Rorty et al., pp. 49-76. Cambridge: Cambridge University Press.

Rutherford, M. (2010). 'Chicago Economics and Institutionalism.' In *The Elgar Companion to the Chicago School of Economics*. Ed. Ross B. Emmett, pp. 25-39.

Cheltenham and Northampton: Edward Elgar.
(2011). *The Institutionalist Movement in American Economics, 1918-1947*. Cambridge: Cambridge University Press.

Samuels, W. J. (1990). 'Introduction.' In *Economics as Discourse—An Analysis of the Language of Economists*. Ed. Warren J. Samuels, pp. 1-14. Boston/Dordrecht/London: Kluwer Academic Publishers.

Samuelson, P. A. (1954). 'The Pure Theory of Public Expenditure.' *Review of Economics and Statistics* 36(4): 387-389.

Sherman, H. J., E. K. Hunt, R. F. Nesiba, and P. A. O'Hara. (eds.) (2007). *Economics: An Introduction to Traditional and Progressive Views*. Armonk and London: M.E. Sharpe.

Shute, L. (1997). *John Maurice Clark—A Social Economics for the 21st Century*. London: Macmillan.

Stigler, G. J. (1966). *The Theory of Price (3rd edition)*. New York and London: Macmillan Company and Collier-Macmillan Ltd.

Stigler, G. J., and K. E. Boulding. (1952). *Readings in Price Theory*. Chicago: Homewood, Illinois.

Swaney, J. A. (2006). 'Policy for Social Costs: Kapp vs. Neo-classical Economics.' In *Social Costs and Public Action in Modern Capitalism—Essays Inspired by Karl William Kapp's Theory of Social Costs*. Eds. W. Elsner, P. Frigato, and P. Ramazzotti, pp. 106-125. London and New York: Routledge.

Swaney, J. A., and M. A. Evers. (1989). 'The Social Cost Concepts of Kapp and Polanyi.' *Journal of Economic Issues* 23: 7-34.

Van Horn, R., P. Mirowski, and T. Stapleford. (eds). (2011). *Building Chicago Economics— New Perspectives on the History of America's Most Powerful Economics Program*. Cambridge: Cambridge University Press.

Veblen, T. B. (1904). *The Theory of Business Enterprise*. New York: Charles Scribner's Sons.

Vilhauer, Monica. (2010). *Gadamer's Ethics of Play—Hermeneutics and the Other*. Lanham: Lexington Books.

6
Kapp and Polanyi on Substantive vs. Formal Economics

6.1 Introduction

On the basis of the Kapp-Polanyi correspondence, this paper analyzes the relationship between the two economists, and the meaning and origin of substantive economics. This paper provides further insights into the origin of substantive economics and its full potential based on the Kapp-Polanyi correspondence,[73] adding to previous work on the similarities between Kapp and Polanyi (Swaney and Evers 1989; Heidenreich 1998; Cangiani 2006).

The distinction between the formal and the substantive meaning of 'economic' is one of the key concepts of heterodox economics. Substantive economics is usually associated with Karl Polanyi and much has been written about its meaning (Stanfield 1989a: 718; 1989b: 266; Cangiani 2003) and its relevance for modern institutional political economy (O'Hara 2000: 128-134). In fact, since the substantive-formal distinction runs like a thread through the works of several European economists, such as Karl William Kapp, Karl Mannheim, Carl Menger, and Max Weber, it may be considered a distinct European contribution to institutionalism. Some important similarities to Veblenian institutionalism regarding, e.g., social psychology (Tilman 2004) have already been pointed out.

The Kapp-Polanyi correspondence shows that both economists influenced each other in their understanding of the substantive economy and further evidences the surprising importance of Carl Menger's posthumous and untranslated second edition of the *Grundsätze der Volkswirtschaftslehre* (*Principles of Economics*) (1923) for the development of Polanyi's and Kapp's 'substantive' economics. The analysis of the Polanyi-Kapp correspondence also supports the view that the similarities between Kapp's and Polanyi's substantive economics are rooted in the 'planning debate' of the 1920s and 1930s (Cangiani 2006: 26-30). In addition, the analysis throws new light on Kapp's political economy which integrates Polanyi's understanding of the substantive economy with a theory of human needs that can be traced back to Menger's differentiation of needs according to their urgency. This allows Kapp to develop his social minima approach, i.e. substantive rationality in the tradition of Max Weber. By integrating these three different 'substantive' strands, Kapp actualizes the full potential of substantive economics.

6.2 Biographical Parallels

Kapp and Polanyi have important biographical similarities which begin during the 1920s and 1930s, when the rising power of fascism in Europe threatened and expelled thousands of intellectuals (Krohn 1993). Kapp escaped in 1933, together with his later wife Lore Masur, from Nazi Germany to Geneva, Switzerland. At the Geneva Institute of International Studies, Kapp wrote his doctoral dissertation on *Planwirtschaft und Aussenhandel* (1936) (*Economic Planning and Foreign Trade*).[74] The dissertation already contained the concern of his later work, such as a critique of an economic calculus based on market prices, and a discussion of human needs that he later developed into his bio-psycho-cultural concept of the human being (Kapp 1961; Steppacher 1994; Steppacher et al. 1977) In 1935 Kapp conducted research at the London School of Economics and it is likely that his critique of Arthur C. Pigou's neoclassical definition of externalities goes back to this period. Kapp's dissertation contributed to the 'planning debate' by elaborating solutions to the problem of fitting decisions about foreign trade with the requirements of a coherently planned internal economy. The work disputes the popular view that a planned economy requires self-sufficiency for its existence and develops ways of dealing with valuation problems that arise. Since Kapp's focus is on the Soviet Union, it is not surprising that F. Pollock, the economist of the Frankfurt School (Krohn 1993) temporarily located in Geneva was a source of inspiration because he had already worked and published on this issue earlier. Among others, Kapp's dissertation was reviewed by Gerhard Colm, a prominent member of the German émigré economists at the New School for Social Research (Colm 1938: 275-276), indicating that considerable relevance was attributed to Kapp's research.

Shortly after the publication of his dissertation, Kapp received a scholarship from the Frankfurt School, now called the Institute of Social Research and associated with Columbia University in New York City. This allowed him to participate in the stimulating and open intellectual process unfolding between the former and the New School for Social Research, where many of the German reform economists were forming the new graduate faculty.[75] His escape to the United States of America eventually allowed him to get a position first as instructor and later as professor of economics at Columbia University. It was here, at the working place of John Maurice Clark, with whom he corresponded on the issue of social costs (Kapp-Clark Correspondence, Kapp Archive), that Kapp published *The Social Costs of Private Enterprise* (1978 [1950]).

Relative to Kapp, much more has been written on the origin of Polanyi's economics. (Stanfield 1986; Cangiani 2006) For our purposes, only the following aspects deserve attention. Polanyi participated in the debate on possible forms of socialism in Vienna in the 1920s. In his 1922 essay 'Sozialistische Rechnungslegung' (*Socialist Accounting*) he takes on Mises' argument about the impossibility of a centralized socialist organization, and outlines the traits of 'rationally' planned economic production and exchange that is guided by social and democratic decision making. (Cangiani 2006: 25; Polanyi 1922). In the 1930s, Polanyi escaped to London and eventually to the United States where he worked at Columbia University and published *The Great Transformation* (1944).

6.3 The context of Polanyi's influence on Kapp's two integral projects

Kapp and Polanyi met at Columbia probably in the 1950s. In spite of the lack of evidence of direct intellectual contact in the 1940s, many similarities concerning the critique of the disruptive effects of the market system on nature and humans exist between *The Great Transformation* (1944) and *The Social Costs of Private Enterprise* (1950). The latter integrates Kapp's dissertational critique of the market economy with American institutionalism, especially the works of T.B. Veblen and J.M. Clark, demonstrating the compatibility of what may be called the distinct European institutionalist tradition.[76]

In the introduction, Kapp writes that the socio-economic history of the 19th century can be written as 'the revolt of large masses of people' against social costs (Kapp 1977 [1963] [1950]: 15). This is similar to Polanyi's *Great Transformation* which can be read as an account of social costs (Swaney and Evers 1989). In particular, Polanyi's concept of 'double movement' is a key concept of institutional economics (Caroll and Stanfield 2003: 400) linking European with American Institutionalism (Mayhew 1989), and with Marx and Lukacs (Brown 1987). According to this concept, the enforcement of the market system and commodification of land and labor leads to devastating effects, which elicit a 'double-movement', i.e. protective reaction, of the victimized to limit the market mechanism in the realm of these fictitious commodities (Polanyi 1944: 76, 138).

Kapp primarily focuses on the system of business enterprise as an institutionalized allocative decision-making process, which is exclusively based on an individual economic calculus in terms of market values, and hence takes insufficient account of socio-ecological effects (Polanyi would call this 'disembedded') and encourages maximizing profits by means of deliberate cost shifting:

> [...] the system of business enterprise must be regarded as an economy of unpaid costs, 'unpaid' insofar as a substantial proportion of the actual costs of production remain unaccounted for in entrepreneurial outlays; instead this part of the costs of production is shifted to, and ultimately born by third persons or by the community at large. (Kapp 1978 [1963]: 268)

In fact, these social costs are a 'secondary distribution' happening behind the back of people who usually cannot escape them. This harms the weakest members of society most who typically either lack sufficient means to protect themselves or are disproportionately exposed to them. According to Kapp, this constitutes circular causation of a cumulative process in the form of a vicious circle that tends to increase social inequalities at an increasing rate.

However, Kapp's work of the 1940s and 1950s goes beyond a critique of socializing costs. Essentially, two related threads may be distinguished: (1) a science of man in society; and (2) a modern institutional political economics. A brief introduction to Kapp's theoretical interests and development during this time helps to better understand the context of Polanyi's influence.

Regarding *Towards a Science of Man in Society* (Kapp 1961), it is relevant to know that at this time, Kapp was also a member of the interdisciplinary staff of the contemporary civilization course at Columbia University and of the editorial committee of the two volumes *Introduction to Contemporary Civilization in the West* (1946). Kapp used his gained historical understanding to publish *Readings in Economics* (1949), that later became *History of Economic Thought* (1956) seeing five editions. Alongside he worked on modern behavioral theory, cultural anthropology, biology, systems theory, publishing the 'Rational Human Conduct and Modern Industrial Society' (1943), 'Economics and the Behavioural Sciences' (1954) and 'Approaches to the Integration of Social Inquiry: A Critical Evaluation' (1957).

Regarding Kapp's political economy his continuing work on planning issues is relevant: 'Economic Planning and Freedom' (1950) among others (1939, 1941, 1942), and the closing chapter of *Social Costs of Private*

Enterprise (1978 [1950]) entitled 'Toward a New Science of Political Economy'. Here Kapp calls for the reformulation of the basic concepts, the broadening of the scope of economic investigation, and agrees with Max Horkheimer 'that economic analysis must transcend what has been called 'the horizon of contemporary society' (Kapp 1978 [1963] [1950]: 282). Kapp's political economy is based on his social minima approach that is rooted in the bio-psycho-cultural concept of the human being. The latter integrates research on the composition of human needs and the harmful effects resulting from their insufficient satisfaction, such as the social costs of human destructiveness and psychopathological consumerism (Kapp 1961; Fromm 1973).

Kapp's first reference to Polanyi's substantive approach has to be seen within this context:

> In order to be relevant for the interpretation of actual relationships and sequences of events under concrete historical and institutional conditions economics must be 'substantive' in the sense of taking its departure from man's actual needs and his dependence upon and interaction with his natural and social environment (K. Polanyi). Such a 'substantive' empirical science of economics must utilize the findings of the behavioural sciences in the formation of its basic premises. (Kapp 1954: 4)

It is noteworthy that the reference dates from before the publication of *Trade and Market in the Early Empires* (1957) in which Polanyi explicitly defines the substantive meaning of the economy. The correspondence supports the assumption that Kapp and Polanyi knew each other before. The quote shows that Kapp realized the relevance of Polanyi's substantive economics and economic anthropology for his own project of broadening the scope of analysis and of arriving at adequate concepts of humans and cultures.

6.4 The Kapp-Polanyi correspondence and Kapp's two integrated projects

Before analyzing the Kapp-Polanyi correspondence, it is important to take a look at Polanyi's definition of the substantive meaning of the economy (Polanyi 1957) because Kapp refers to this definition in his first letter to Polanyi:

> [...] in referring to human activities the term economic is a compound of two meanings that have independent roots. We will call them the substantive and the formal meaning. The substantive meaning of economic derives from man's dependence for his living upon nature and his fellows. It refers to the

interchange with his natural and social environment, in so far as this results in supplying him with the means of material want satisfaction. The substantive meaning implies neither choice nor insufficiency of means; man's livelihood may or may not involve the necessity of choice and, if choice there be, it need not be induced by the limiting effect of a 'scarcity' of means. (Polanyi 1957: 243)

It is our proposition that only the substantive meaning of 'economic' is capable of yielding the concepts that are required by the social sciences for an investigation of all the empirical economies of the past and present. Menger alone in his posthumous work criticized the term, but neither he nor Max Weber, nor Talcott Parsons after him, apprehended the significance of the distinction for sociological analysis. (Polanyi 1957: 244)

The fount of the substantive concept is the empirical economy. It can be briefly [...] defined as an instituted process of interaction between man and his environment, which results in a continuous supply of want satisfying material means. (Polanyi 1957: 248)

As his first letter shows, Kapp expresses his full agreement to Polanyi regarding his work on the substantive meaning of 'economic,' which Polanyi had apparently sent to Kapp prior to publication:

Dear Professor Polanyi, Many thanks for sending me the outline of the book with the text of the introduction [...] Both the outline and the introduction make an excellent impression [...] Again, as I indicated in our previous discussion, I feel that there is no fundamental gap between your position and mine. I am not trying to reorient formal economic theory; instead I am looking toward a broader conceptual framework based upon a theory of man and culture, in terms of which it will be possible to study the structure and functions of the economy as a component part of society and thus to make intelligible what seemed to be now only disparate empirical data. [...] Another question which we apparently never resolved seems to be the contribution which the holistic economists since Veblen either have made or could make to the new framework of substantive analysis. I have no doubt that your book will prove the fruitfulness of joint research project and I am looking forward to its early publication. (Kapp to Polanyi, 22 February 1956)

The quote indicates the relation between Polanyi's economic anthropology and Kapp's project of '*a broader conceptual framework based upon a theory of man and culture.*' However, Kapp's integrative framework for the analysis of the substantive economy has been largely overlooked by institutionalists. This cannot be easily explained, especially since Kapp integrated European substantive economics and the American 'holistic' tradition of Veblen, which should have been of considerable interest.

Polanyi's following letter to Kapp basically confirms that both were working on a framework for the analysis of the '*place occupied by the economy in society.*'

> Dear Professor Kapp [...] I feel I should equip myself a bit for an active support of your endeavours since they run so very much in the lines of what I believe in myself, and may well prove a channel through which further important information might be gained on the place occupied by the economies in the different societies. (Polanyi to Kapp, 14 December 1956)

The next letter was written four years later by Kapp and clarifies important points:

> Dear Karl, [...] I have always felt that our work converges in all important respects. I think your emphasis and detailed studies of markets and trade in earlier empires is much more in the tradition of Veblen's institutionalism than is usually realized. In my new book I am referring to your work—especially to your distinction of formal and substantive. (Kapp to Polanyi, 4 November 1960)

In addition to perceiving their works to be 'converged in all important respects,' Kapp emphasizes that Polanyi's substantive economics is 'in the tradition of Veblen's institutionalism.' Kapp also explicitly mentions that he refers to Polanyi's 'distinction of formal and substantive in his new book' (meaning: *Towards a Science of Man in Society*, 1961). Hence it can be inferred that Kapp considered his work to be an integration of Polanyi's and Veblen's *substantive* institutionalism. In *Towards a Science of Man in Society*, Kapp also elaborates the methodological implications of Polanyi's substantive economics, which he saw in line with Arthur Spiethoff's method of 'realtypes' and P. Tillich's critique of applying exclusively the formal function of reasoning. Kapp also integrates this European methodology with insights from Dewey's 'pragmatist' philosophy and psychology. The analysis of Kapp's letter to Polanyi thus underlines the importance of Kapp's work for the integration of European and American institutional analysis.

Polanyi's reply reveals the surprising significance of Menger's second edition of the *Grundsätze* for Polanyi's definition of the substantive economy and also throws new light on Menger's influence on Kapp's work on human needs.

> Dear Ted,[77] [...] On the matter itself we have concluded that short of a new foundation for theoretical economics, it is hardly possible to break the logical straight jacket of economic analysis. [...] Personally I keep to the redefinition: The economy as an instituted process. But the concept of an economic process takes us back again to the minimum elements required for the concept of an

economy. The key to this is Menger's Principles 2nd edition 1923 (the 'posthumous Menger'). The still untranslated Menger! (Polanyi to Kapp, 8 November 1960)

Defining '*the economy as an instituted process*,' Polanyi laid the foundation for substantive economics. Polanyi makes this point more explicit in his posthumously published article 'Carl Menger's two Meanings of "Economic" (Polanyi 1971; Cangiani 2006). A footnote explains that this article was written between 1958 and 1960 (p. 24), the time when Polanyi sent Kapp the above letter. Polanyi translates the crucial parts of Menger's text into English and finds the substantive meaning of the economy in Menger an important distinction of the 'two elemental directions of the human economy.' Menger also distinguishes between the subjective and the objective side of the economy. (Menger 1923: 60, 77; Polanyi: 23) Polanyi emphasized that Menger noticed that the scarcity meaning of economic 'could not be universalized so as to cover the phenomenon of human livelihood' (p. 22). According to Polanyi, Menger 'extended the range of inquiry so as to comprise the facts of anthropology, sociology and economic history' (p. 22). Polanyi states that Menger's expansion of the *Grundsätze* was made to make room for a theory of wants and needs, for the distinctive determination of modes of production, and for the purpose of providing a definition of the economy which would 'satisfy the requirements of the social sciences dealing with the economy in general' (p. 22). Polanyi credits Menger for his precise work, creating a concept of the human economy, 'which can be consistently applied in all social sciences that treat of the economy including economic analysis itself' (p. 23).

Polanyi also credits F. Hayek for having ignored Menger's important second edition and F. Knight for having deliberately rejected a translation of this second edition in favor of the first edition because 'it was the first edition that influenced the development of economics and the second contained much irrelevant material.' Polanyi also notes that this was against Menger's will, who had denied a translation and reprint of the first edition during 50 years of being in search of a more general theory (p. 21).

This re-evaluation of Menger's second edition of the *Grundsätze* also sheds new light on Kapp's substantive economics. In his above quoted 1954 reference to Polanyi's substantive economics Kapp raises questions pertaining to human needs. This theme goes back to his dissertational chapter on the critique of an economic calculus in terms of market values (Kapp 1936). In addition to Erich Böhm-Bawerk and Beatrice and Sydney Webb, Kapp refers to Menger's second edition of the *Grundsätze*.

Menger had criticized market-price-based accounting for its failure to account for and consider the needs of those members of society who could not participate in market transactions because they were lacking purchasing power (Kapp 1936: 37; Menger 1923: 49). Kapp quotes the following passage from Menger's chapter on 'social exigencies':

> [...] the latter [the business community] consider the smallest desire of individuals with purchasing power, and disregard the most urgent needs of humans suffering in despair. Not the actual, only the solvent and purchase-willing demand of the people are the object of the active pursuit of the business community in our society. (Menger 1923: 49, author's translation)

Menger argues that social exigencies must be differentiated from those of isolated individuals, and that the leaders of a 'real economy' (*wahre Volkswirtschaft*) have to explore the needs of all members of society (pp. 48-49). Kapp then goes on to analyze – also on the basis of Menger – how the individual's perception of his or her own needs is usually flawed by ignorance, error, and passion. In the tradition of Menger, Kapp argues that individuals are not always capable of consciously realizing their needs because awareness depends on their economic situation. Kapp criticizes that the monetary accounting in terms of market prices rests on the tacit assumption that the individual's perception of his or her own needs is sufficient and not to be questioned or subjected to further inquiry (Kapp 1936: 38; Menger 1923: 3-4). This way Kapp integrated his dissertational theme inspired by Menger's work on needs (Kapp 1936: 37-40) and Polanyi's substantive economics (Polanyi 1957) that was itself inspired by Menger's two meanings of 'economic.'

In addition to his work on a science of man in society, in his political economics Kapp continues to refer to Menger's 'laudable attempt' to distinguish between human needs according to their urgency (Kapp 1983 [1971]: 65). In fact, the editor of Menger's second edition of the *Grundsätze* explains that Chapter 3 on the 'Measure of Human Needs and Goods' is as such not contained in the first edition and constitutes a considerable extension of Menger's earlier position. The reader is informed that Menger had already originally included two pages on human needs in the first edition but had taken them out again shortly before its publication because 'he may have felt not erudite enough in natural sciences' (Menger 1923: XII–XIII). Twenty-five years after the publication of the first edition, Menger picked up the work on human needs again and 'threw himself into studying biology and physiology' (Menger 1923: IX). This resulted in the important third chapter, in which

Menger distinguishes between needs of first order and those of higher order, i.e. a differentiation according to urgency (Menger 1923: 32-56).

> Our needs are rooted in our nature and are thus [...] independent of our will. [...] Our immediate needs manifest themselves independent of our will and of our capability to satisfy them.[78] (Menger 1923: 34-35)

Menger speaks further of the 'objective' determination of needs of first order and sees no principle problem in specifying them qualitatively and quantitatively in greater detail in the context of concrete social circumstances (Menger 1923: 36-40). Menger's ideas may be regarded as the forerunner of Kapp's analysis of human needs which turns into the social minima approach of his political economy.

This demonstrates how the two threads of Kapp's work are interwoven. On the one hand, Kapp worked on an integrated framework for an understanding of the diverse cultural actualizations of the potential of the substantive economy in past and present societies. He also worked on an understanding of the requirements for the satisfaction of universal human needs and an understanding of the harmful consequences, i.e. social costs, of their non-satisfaction. On the other hand, Kapp uses both to develop a modern institutional political economy. Kapp's work traces out the problem of institutionalized decision making in a society. He argues that investment decisions and allocation have to be 'institutionalized' within a more comprehensive calculus taking account of socio-ecological effects and social minima rooted in objectified existential human needs (Kapp 1965a, 1965b). This requires societal evaluations of alternative costs and benefits, political decisions, and public controls. In fact, starting from a clear definition of social minima the mediation between conflicting interests in these processes may be made easier, or at least guarantees the gratification of the most urgent needs. Aiming at reducing social costs, Kapp applies this approach in the context of his development economics, as well as technological and environmental planning. As a conceptual framework for this approach, Kapp applies Weber's concept of substantive rationality which overlaps to a certain degree with Menger's and Polanyi's substantive economy (Kapp 1963, 1965a; Berger 2006). In this context, Kapp also explicitly refers to Adolph Lowe's political economics and instrumental analysis to point out the general direction of his political institutional economy (Kapp 1976; Berger and Forstater 2007). Hence, Kapp integrates several European 'substantive' approaches for his political institutional economics.

Kapp's subsequent letter to Polanyi illustrates how he aimed to further develop their common understanding of the 'economy as an instituted process.' The letter shows Kapp's intellectual process 'in the making,' leading eventually to *Towards a Science of Man in Society* (1961) that contains the theoretical and conceptual foundation for a dynamic and holistic substantive economics.

> Dear Karl [...] Your remark about process, if I interpret it correctly, seems to raise the question of our attitudes toward social dynamics. Does the fact that we view the economy as an instituted system not place greater emphasis on the need to study process and interacting cumulative causation? I believe that structure and system should always be so formulated as to include dynamic change. Ultimately the strength of theoretical institutionalism would seem to depend upon the extent to which we are able to transcend the economic statics of [...] neo-classical search for levels of equilibrium. [...] Myrdal's recent work on economic growth and development seems to me the best proof, if such proof were needed, that the notion of the economy as an institutionalized process not only does not preclude but rather opens the way for a substantive study of social dynamics. I am discussing some of these issues in my new book. (Kapp to Polanyi, 15 November 1960)

The quote highlights that Kapp's *Towards a Science of Man in Society* integrates key concepts of American institutionalism, in particular Veblen's concept of 'cumulative causation,' and European contributions, i.e. Myrdal's concept of 'circular cumulative causation.' Both concepts have distinct meanings (Berger *et al.* 2007) and are both important to explain the cumulatively changing place of the economy in the social system and the notion of an open economic system in circular causation with the social and physical environment. By integrating different strands of institutional economics, Kapp actualizes the full potential embodied in Polanyi's initial definition of the economy as an instituted process.

In his next letter, Polanyi once more underlines his deep appreciation for Kapp's work.

> Dear Ted [...] Your total approach, esp. in the theory-empiry range seems to me full of promise. From all my heart I wish your work success. (Polanyi to Kapp, 26 May 1961)

Kapp responds to Polanyi's letter upon returning from his second research stay in a developing country where he had applied the theory of social costs to development problems (Kapp 1959), laying the foundations for what is known as 'sustainable development.' Kapp's letter is the last documented piece of the correspondence and acknowledges Polanyi's influence:

Dear Karl [...] I found your letter of July 21 1961 [...] after our return from India. [...] Did I ever mention that your early article in reply to Mises' thesis has been very helpful to me then [!] I did my dissertation on planning and foreign trade with Mises at the Postgraduate Institute of International Studies in Geneva in the early thirties. I thought you ought to know this and that it may please you. (Kapp to Polanyi, 18 October 1962)

Kapp is clearly referring to Polanyi's 1922 article about the possibilities of socialist accounting (see above). This throws some new light on Kapp's dissertation on economic planning and foreign exchange, which neither cites nor refers to Polanyi but must now be regarded as being influenced by him. Instead of citing Polanyi, Kapp's dissertational chapter on socialist accounting cites the works of O. von Neurath, A. Tschajanov, and F. Weil. In the preface of his dissertation, Kapp thanks L. v. Mises for having taken 'friendly interest' in his work. This is truly remarkable, taking in account that Kapp's dissertation thoroughly criticizes the very economic calculus and allocation based on market prizes, which Mises considers the only 'rational' method of allocation. Kapp's political economics later proposes socio-ecological indicators, input-output models, societal evaluations, and public controls as an alternative to an accounting and allocation based on market values.

In addition to the correspondence with Karl Polanyi, it may be of interest that Kapp corresponded about the completion of a translation of *The Great Transformation* into German with Polanyi's wife, Ilona, in Vienna in 1966. This demonstrates that Kapp undertook continuous effort for Polanyi's and his common project of developing and spreading substantive economics.

6.5 Conclusion

The Kapp–Polanyi correspondence evidences the crucial role of Menger's second edition of the *Grundsätze* (1923) for Polanyi's substantive economics and for Kapp's attempt to differentiate human needs according to their urgency. On the basis of these insights, and contrary to the mainstream interpretation, Menger can be considered one of the 'fathers' of substantive economics. The Kapp–Polanyi correspondence also provides important insights into how Polanyi's substantive economics influenced Kapp's seminal work *Towards a Science of Man in Society* (1961) and his institutional political economy. The analysis also demonstrates Kapp's unique integration of European substantive economics in the tradition of Menger, Weber, Myrdal, and Polanyi, and American institutionalism in the tradition of Veblen.

References

Berger, S. (2006) 'K. William Kapp's Application of Substantive Rationality in Tradition of M. Weber as a Framework for Modern Political Institutional Economics,' paper presented at the annual meeting of AFIT 2006, Phoenix, USA.

Berger, S. and Forstater, M. (2007) 'Towards Political Institutional Economics: Kapp's Social Costs, Lowe's Instrumental Analysis, and the European Institutionalist Approach to Environmental Policy,' *Journal of Economic Issues* 41(2): 539-546.

Berger, S., Forstater, M. and Elsner, W. (2007) 'European Contributions to Evolutionary Institutional Economics: The Cases of 'Circular Cumulative Causation' and 'Open System Approach.' Some Methodological and Policy Implications,' *Journal of Economic Issues* 41(2): 529-537.

Brown, D. (1987) 'A Hungarian Connection: Karl Polanyi's Influence on the Budapest School,' *Journal of Economic Issues* 21(1): 339-347.

Cangiani, M. (2003) 'The Forgotten Institution,' *International Review of Sociology* 13(2): 327-341.

Cangiani, M. (2006) 'Freedom to Plan,' in W. Elsner, P. Frigato and P. Ramazzotti (eds) *Social Costs and Public Action in Modern Capitalism-Essays Inspired by K. William Kapp's Theory of Social Costs*, London, New York: Routledge, pp. 15-40.

Carroll, M. C. and Stanfield, J. R. (2003) 'Social Capital, Karl Polanyi, and American Social and Institutional Economics,' *Journal of Economic Issues* 37(2): 397-404.

Colm, G. (1938) 'Planwirtschaft und Aussenhandel,' *The Journal of Political Economy* 46(2): 275-276.

Fromm, E. (1973) *The Anatomy of Human Destructiveness*, New York: Holt, Rinehart and Winston.

Heidenreich, R. (1994) *Ökonomie und Institutionen—Eine Rekonstruktion des wirtschafts— und sozialwissenschaftlichen Werks von K.W. Kapp*, Frankfurt, Main: Peter Lang Verlag.

Heidenreich, R. (1998) 'The Socioeconomic Approach of K. William Kapp,' *Journal of Economic Issues* 32: 965-984.

Kapp, K. W. (1936) *Planwirtschaft und Aussenhandel*, Geneva: Georg und Cie, S.A.

Kapp, K. W. (1939) 'Economic Regulation and Economic Planning: A Theoretical Classification of Different Types of Economic Control' *American Economic Review* 29: 760-773.

Kapp, K. W. (1941) 'The League of Nations and Raw Material, 1919-1939,' *Geneva Studies* 12(3).

Kapp, K. W. (1942) 'Postwar Problems of Industrial Demobilization,' in E. Stein and J. Backman (eds) *War Economics*, New York: Farrar & Rinehart, pp. 417-443.

Kapp, K. W. (1943) 'Rational Human Conduct and Modern Industrial Society,' *The Southern Economic Journal* 10(2): 136-150.

Kapp, K. W. (1946) *Introduction to Contemporary Civilisation in the West. A Source*

Book, vols 1 & 2, New York: Columbia University Press.
Kapp, K. W. (1950) 'Economic Planning and Freedom,' *Weltwirtschaftliches Archiv* 64: 29-54.
Kapp, K. W. (1954) 'Economics and the Behavioral Sciences' in John E. Ullmann and Roy Preiswerk (eds) *The Humanization of the Social Sciences*, London: University Press of America 1985, pp. 1-20.
Kapp, K. W. (1957) 'Approaches to the Integration of Social Inquiry: A Critical Evaluation,' *Kyklos* 10(4): 373-400.
Kapp, K. W. (1959) 'River Valley Development Projects: Problems of Evaluation and Social Costs,' *Kyklos* 12(4): 589-604.
Kapp, K. W. (1961) *Towards a Science of Man in Society – A Positive Approach to the Integration of Social Knowledge,* The Hague: Martinus Nijhoff.
Kapp, K. W. (1963) 'Social Costs and Social Benefits – A Contribution to Normative Economics,' in E. V. Beckerath and H. Giersch (eds) *Probleme der normativen Ökonomik und der wirtschaftspolitischen Beratung*. Verein für Sozialpolitik, Berlin: Duncker & Humblot, pp. 183-210.
Kapp, K. W. (1965a) 'Economic Development in a New Perspective: Existential Minima and Substantive Rationality,' *Kyklos* 17(1): 49-79.
Kapp, K. W. (1965b) 'Social Economics and Social Welfare Minima,' in T. K. N. Unnithan et al. (eds) *Toward a Sociology of Culture in India, Essays in Honor of Dr Mukerji*, New Dehli: Prentice Hall, pp. 1-12.
Kapp, K. W. (1976) 'The Open-system Character of the Economy and its Implications,' in K. Dopfer (ed.) *Economics in the Future*, London: The Macmillan Press Ltd.
Kapp, K. W. (1978) [1963] [1950] *The Social Costs of Business Enterprise* (2nd revised and enlarged edition of *Social Costs of Private Enterprise* (1950)), Nottingham: Spokesman University Paperback.
Kapp, K. W. (1983) [1971] 'Environmental Disruption as an Economic and Political Problem,' in J. E. Ullmann (ed.) *Social Costs, Economic Development and Environmental Disruption*, Lanham, NY, London, University of America Press, pp. 56-70.
Kapp, K. W. and Kapp, L. L. (1949) *Readings in Economics*, New York: Barnes & Noble.
Kapp, K. W. and Kapp, L. L. (1956) *History of Economic Thought – A Book of Readings*, New York: Barnes & Noble.
Krohn, C. D. (1993) *Intellectuals in Exile–Refugee Scholars and the New School for Social Research*, Amherst, MA: The University of Massachusetts Press.
Mayhew, A. 'Polanyi's Double Movement and Veblen on the Army of the Commonweal,' *Journal of Economic Issues* 23(2): 555-562.
Menger, C. (1923) *Grundsätze der Volkswirtschaftslehre*, 2nd edition, Wien/Leipzig: Hölder-Pichler-Tempsky A.G./G. Freytag GmbH.
O Hara, P. A. (2000) *Marx, Veblen and Contemporary Institutional Political Economy, Principles and Unstable Dynamics of Capitalism*, Northampton: Edward Elgar.
Polanyi, K. (1922) 'Sozialistische Rechnungslegung', *Archiv für Sozialwissenschaft*

und Sozialpolitik 49: 377-420.

Polanyi, K. (1944) *The Great Transformation*, New York and Toronto: Farrar and Rinehart, inc.

Polanyi, K. (1957) 'The Economy as an Instituted Process,' in K. Polanyi, C. M. Arensberg and H. W. Pearson (eds) *Trade and Market in the Early Empires— Economies in History and Theory*, Glencoe, Illinois: The Free Press, pp. 243-270.

Polanyi, K. (1971) 'Carl Menger's Two Meanings of 'Economic',' in G. Dalton (ed.) *Studies in Economic Anthropology*, Washington, DC: American Anthropological Association, pp. 16-24.

Polanyi, K., Arensberg, C. M. and Pearson, H. W. (eds) (1957) *Trade and Market in the Early Empires – Economies in History and Theory*, Glencoe: Free Press.

Stanfield, J. R. (1986) *The Economic Thought of Karl Polanyi: Lives and Livelihood*, London: Macmillan Press.

Stanfield, J. R. (1989a) 'Veblenian and Neo-Marxian Perspectives on the Cultural Crisis of Late Capitalism,' *Journal of Economic Issues* 23(2): 717-734.

Stanfield, J. R. (1989b) 'Karl Polanyi and Contemporary Economic Thought,' *Review of Social Economy*, 47(3): 266-279.

Steppacher, R. (1994) 'Kapp, K. William,' in G. M. Hodgson, W. J. Samuels and M. R. Tool (eds) *The Elgar Companion to Institutional and Evolutionary Economics*, Aldershot, Brookfield, VT: E. Elgar, pp. 435-441.

Steppacher, R. Zogg-Walz, B. and Hatzfeld, H. (1977) 'K. William Kapp's Contribution to Economic and Social Science,' in R. Steppacher, B. Zogg-Walz and H. Hatzfeld (eds) *Economics in Institutional Perspective-Memorial Essays in Honor of K. William Kapp*, Lexington, MA: Lexington Books, pp. xv-xxiii.

Swaney, J. A. and Evers, M. A. (1989) 'The Social Cost Concepts of Kapp and Polanyi,' *Journal of Economic Issues* 23: 7-34.

Tilman, R. (2004) 'Karl Mannheim, Max Weber, and the Problem of Social Rationality in Thorstein Veblen,' *Journal of Economic Issues* 3(1): 155-172.

Veblen, T. B. (1904) *The Theory of Business Enterprise*, New York: Charles Scribner's Sons.

Winthrop, H. (1961) 'Waste as an Index of Social Pathology,' *The American Behavioral Scientist* 5(2): 18-22.

7

Kapp's Theory of Social Costs and Ernst Wiechert's Poetry

> [O]nly experience [...] can entitle us to participate in the discussion of such higher questions of rank[.]
> –Friedrich Nietzsche (2000, 311)

7.1 Introduction

In the first part of this article, I analyze the phenomenon of the 'double truth' in economics (Mirowski 2013), which suppresses experiential knowledge and leads to the destruction of the natural environment, community, and human civility (Kanth 1997; Marglin 2008). Subsequently, I explore the positive effects of opening economics to the creative, esthetic, and ethical potential of experiential knowledge, including works of art. In the second part of the article, I showcase the way the economist K. William Kapp was inspired by the renowned German novelist, poet, educator, intellectual, and concentration-camp survivor Ernst Wiechert. Wiechert was Kapp's teacher in high school, the Hufgymnasium in Königsberg, during the Weimar Republic. I investigate the unpublished and unexplored Kapp-Wiechert correspondence, as well as analyze some (published and unpublished) foreign language essays written by Kapp and his wife Lore Kapp. This analysis reveals how Kapp's economics drew lasting inspiration from Wiechert's art philosophy, pedagogy, novels, and poetry. This is a case study of a poetic economics that is open to experiential knowledge that makes it more humane, edifying, serene, and sensitive to the natural and social environment.

7.2 On Economic 'Double Truth'

The great financial crisis of 2008 triggered an unprecedented level of criticism of the economics profession for its failure to predict, prevent, or resolve the crisis. The main conundrum today is that nothing of significance has changed in economics, despite the fact that economists and their theories were the leading architects of the economic system that collapsed. One of the possible explanations for this situation is the 'double truth' – that is, the parallel existence of an exoteric and an esoteric truth. While the former purports and officially signals intellectual freedom, the latter is the hardcore practice of policing deviations from pro-market and pro-financial sector ideology, allowing only 'faux disputes' within narrow parameters. On one hand, the economics curriculum outside the hardcore neoclassical curriculum purports the exoteric truth of freedom to incorporate trends from the natural science (neuroeconomics, experimental and behavioral economics). On the other hand, the esoteric truth is that these are intellectually harmless alternatives because they do not threaten the core belief about markets and finance, while all truly dissenting paradigms – such as institutional, Marxist, post-Keynesian, and feminist, as well as historical and philosophical approaches to economics – are excommunicated as blasphemy (Mirowski 2013). On a cognitive level, the double truth allows the simultaneous feeling of being rebellious and subversive, while avoiding the true 'cognitive dissonance' of overcoming previously held core beliefs. This double truth is expressed in the cognitive capture of the university by a theory of knowledge that essentially holds that knowledge and truth are that for which there is market demand. On a material level, the cognitive capture corresponds to the university's capture by the financial sector (Mirowski 2011, 2013).

These insights are not altogether new. For example, Thorstein Veblen analyzed science in terms of its cultural context and intuited that economists would become intolerant partisans of business, who do not allow any argument to gain traction that is not business friendly (Veblen 1925). Nicholas Georgescu-Roegen (1966), too, alluded to the possibility that science might become subservient to business interests. Historians of economic thought have shown in great detail how the transformation of economics since the 1950s really did usher in the end of pluralism and tolerance (Morgan and Rutherford 1998). Sociologies of economics evidence that the status quo of the profession is a kind of *Gleichschaltung*, or the mainstreaming of textbooks, journals, and the core economics curriculum via the suppression of dissent (Lee 2009).

Several procedures exist to police what is taught in the economics core curriculum. The notions that students should be empowered to critically assess neoclassical economics or to question a neoclassical economist are institutionally strongly discouraged. The main rationalizations are that 'students would get too confused,' or 'there is not enough time to do everything,' or 'this is not what they need in graduate school,' or 'you must not use students as guinea pigs,' or 'this would offend the business department,' or 'you have to provide the vocational training needed for the job of an economist.' Instead, instructors are told that economics has to be taught consistently across all sections of a given course, so that the range of acceptable textbooks and course materials is a priori defined by lists of approved books. This is often coupled with the argument that the adopted textbooks have to be the ones that are adopted by higher ranked institutions as this is looked upon favorably in ranking and assessment exercises. This leads to a complete *Gleichschaltung* of class materials as higher ranked departments are, as a rule, already neoclassically mainstreamed. Additionally, instructors are presented with the argument to think of economics as a foreign language, and to teach it with emphasis on the uncritical memorization of specific vocabulary, so that students 'learn how to think like an economist.' This is linked with the argument that courses have been designated to serve the fulfillment of quantitative reasoning requirements according to 'best practice' educational requirements and assessment procedures. The emphasis is thus on conducting a great number of mathematical take-home and in-class exercises.

It is anybody's guess what happens to instructors who do not toe the line, and are daring enough to call attention to and resist the double truth involved in these procedures. Being denied tenure is, of course, not the same as having a gun put to one's head (McCloskey 2001). In a society, however, where a job is the precondition for survival – mortgage, kids, healthcare, among others – these options, for many, boil down to the same thing. The dirty secret is that the system of double truth is, at its root, held together by existential fears since very few on the inside have the courage to call it into question.

7.3 The Double Truth as a Set of Avoidable Tragedies

The double truth, and the crises into which it is implicated, can be interpreted as an avoidable tragedy (Mirowski 2013). The purging of courses in the history of economic thought, economic methodology, and philosophy of economics leaves a void at the core of understanding economics as part of culture. Most students of neoclassical economics are not told that economics never developed its own model of science, and was instead born out of a dubious imitation of energetics, still imitating all manner of trends from the natural sciences within the limits set by the double-truth doctrine. The resulting self-contradictory, fragmented, and bottomless body of theory is only held together by double truth. The resulting destabilization and fragmentation of the 'self' of young economists has been likened to the tragic fate of Metis who was consumed by Zeus (Mirowski 2013).

Another way to interpret the tragedy of science and knowledge becoming subservient to the money economy is through Johann Wolfgang Goethe's *Faust – Part 2* (Binswanger 1994). According to Hans Christoph Binswanger's interpretation, Goethe teaches that the money economy is the human quest to become master over time – that is, over transitoriness and death. The subordination of science to the accumulation of money is the path taken by Faust into a cultural and ecological disaster (Binswanger 1994).

Alternatively, the tragic role of an economics that has been 'rigorously' mathematized has been likened to that of Latin in the pre-Reformation era – that is, as a mechanism of control and exclusion. Under the guise of amoral calculation, economics infuses social institutions with greed and materialism, debases personal relations, and turns the arts of life into 'dreary avenues for pecuniary advancement' (Kanth 1997). One of the most brilliant mathematical economists of the twentieth century dubbed the over-mathematization of economics 'arithmomania,' or a disease of the mind that blinds economists to qualitative changes (Georgescu-Roegen 1979):

> Said he: If the wandering course of the moon
> By Algebra can be predicted,
> The female affections must yield to it soon.
> But the lady ran off with a dashing dragoon,
> And left him amazed and afflicted.
> –(William Rankine in Georgescu-Roegen 1979, 326)

Over-mathematizing economics has resulted in producing young economists who are brilliant, but experientially immature and ill-prepared to create powerful visions resulting from meaning and validity (Dyer 1993). In Alan Dyer's (1993, 576) words, '[their] heart can never awaken a spark in heart [and their] experiences are so meager that they are unable to say anything true, meaningful, and consequential to others. […] [Economics] starves the poetic sensibility of its children.'

7.4 Opening Economics to the Creative, Esthetic, and Ethical Potential of Experiential Knowledge

The tragedies described above are avoidable if viewed as a failure of imagination, the lack of courage to overcome previously held core beliefs, and unwillingness to defend the nurturing of human wisdom and the well-integrated self (Mirowski 2013). Remedying these failures requires, above all, the reintegration of experiential knowledge (Marglin 2008), because it opens economics to the potentials of creativity, esthetics, and ethics.

Veblen was first and most thorough in elaborating how scientific creativity is rooted in the human propensity for idle curiosity and the instinct of play (Georgescu-Roegen 1966, 5, 14; 1971, 333). He expounded the view that 'science' is the name that western civilization has given the realm, in which it lives out its proclivity for play and idle curiosity (Dyer 1986). Following the philosophy of science of Charles S. Peirce, Veblen taught economists to appreciate their capacity for creative thought by adopting the method of abduction. This conception of science involves 'musement' and pure play, including modifications in the esthetic view taken toward economic phenomena. Abduction is like a process of searching and guessing, and includes creative insights relying on imagination. The latter is of supreme importance in the formulation of a novel hypothesis because it is the only phase of inquiry that contributes something new to the structure of knowledge. It is the feeling as to how things should fit together that bears out novel hypotheses concerning complex phenomena. The process is like a creative probe into the unknown based on one's feel for the situation and one's sense of appropriateness, more divination than mathematics and quite fallible and imaginative (Dyer 1986). Relying on Albert Einstein and Max Planck's intimations, Georgescu-Roegen seconded this view, arguing that the qualities of the cognitive process that are of primary importance for economics are personal intuition, a sympathetic understanding of experience, and consummate intellectual fantasy. Of course, logic and reality's truth tests are necessary to trace out mistakes in the results of this creative process, but crucially they cannot help formulate thoughts (Georgescu-Roegen 1966).

Imagination also needs to consult with esthetics and ethics to avoid dilettantism. The purpose of ethics is to introduce high virtues into self-controlled thoughts that are needed in order to choose the truth over self-interest and to do something worthwhile in science. The purpose of esthetics is to judge hypotheses as good when they embrace one's own sense impulse, encompass a wide range of facts, and enable one to discern higher levels of order in one's sense impressions (Dyer 1986). Citing Alfred Marshall, Georgescu-Roegen argued that a sympathetic understanding of experience and a delicacy and sensitivity of touch inform one's imagination and creativity (Georgescu-Roegen 1966). Esthetics allows the scientist to create theories that are beautiful:

> The construction of intellectual signs [...] requires an artist's mentality. [...] Construction begins with [...] an artist's struggle over form and content. [...] an esthetic process through which the scientist sculpts a meaningful form from a formless body of information. [...] A beautiful theory is a sign that simultaneously signifies the surrender of our senses to and the capture by our intellects of an experience. (Dyer 1988, 160)

7.5 How the Experiential Knowledge of Art and Poetry Can Inspire Economics

Creativity, esthetics, and ethics are at the heart of an economics that is open to experiential knowledge. This openness to experiential knowledge finds a suitable analog in the experience of art. According to John Dewey, the richness and completeness of this experience can enhance the subtlety of perception, which is a crucial component of careful scientific inquiry and deliberation (Dewey in Sturgeon 1992, 356): 'The more finely we can polish the looking glass, the better will be our perception of self and society and the more humane the conviction that emerges from experience.' The experience of art engages emotions – such as beauty, enjoyment, and dignity – which puts an end to the culturally tragic separation of cold intelligence and warm emotions. It also provides more complete criteria for judging the desirability of material goods, and prevents moral and economic stagnation (Sturgeon 1992). An economist, relying on his capacity for artful experience, is:

> sensitive to complex situations, does justice to all facts, entertains competing hypotheses, is responsive to unique or different situations, has the patience and persistence to make sure the problem has been identified correctly, possesses the creative imagination to envision new possibilities, recognizes a bias toward objectivity and the ability to discount one's own prejudices, and has the courage to revise one's beliefs in light of new experience. (Sturgeon 1992, 363)

In economics, such an approach must rely on reasoning with words rather than numbers to capture the penumbra of meanings (Georgescu-Roegen 1966, 336-337). Therefore, economists should embrace a poetic spirit to wield their power (Shackle 1953, 1966), and help understand the world in a more encompassing and humane way (Dyer 1993). The economist's work needs to be edifying and healing, and his/her ideas should be honest, serious, and communicable. 'The fundamental task of an economist is to create understanding about the meanings of experiences and ideas' (Dyer 1993, 576). Such a poetic economist employs language that renders abstract and general hypotheses meaningful, triggering the curiosity of their audience and 'kindling the flame' of unconventional perspectives. The practice of humility and honesty about the changeability of economic truths are preconditions for a poetic economics. Since the development of these faculties takes time, personal experience, and maturity, economists should be instructed in the practice of patience and creative solitude (Dyer 1993).

7.6 The Economist Kapp and the Poet Wiechert: A Case Study of an Inspirational Friendship

Following the above insights, in this section I provide a case study of how the poet Ernst Wiechert inspired the economics of K. William Kapp. Before delving into these matters, however, it seems in order to introduce readers unfamiliar with German literary history or Kapp's economics to the relevant biographical background. Wiechert is one of the most prominent German novelists of the early twentieth century who was also a poet and educator. Kapp, for his part, is considered a leading mid-twentieth century institutional economist. Wiechert's post-WWII memoirs, *Jahre und Zeiten* (*Years and Times*) (Wiechert 1949) describes the humanist-socialist circles he travelled in Königsberg in the 1920s, including the family of K. William Kapp. The friendship between Wiechert and Kapp was deepened by the fact that Wiechert gave German and English lessons to Kapp at the Staatliches Hufengymnasium in Königsberg between 1924 and 1929. While Wiechert chose to stay in Germany to contribute his share to the opposition movement against the Nazis, Kapp moved to Switzerland with his future German-Jewish wife L. Lore Masur in 1933. The Kapps emigrated to the United States in 1937. When Wiechert's moving *Message for the Living* ([1945] 1946) was published in the German language newspaper, *New Yorker Staatszeitung und Herold,* Kapp initiated an extensive correspondence with his former teacher that would last until the latter's death in 1950. The mutual appreciation is best reflected in the first exchange of letters:

> You cannot imagine how glad I was that the first letter from the United States came from you [...] During all these bitter years I have always reminded [!] your person and your home. [...] I have stood it through, prison, and concentration camp, silence and loneliness, and all other things. (Wiechert to Kapp, April 26, 1946)

> It is difficult for me to express in words how much virtually every one of your books and now the message have meant to me in the now almost 13 years I have spent outside of Germany. In each of these books I found something of the ideas and thoughts of the days when I was a student of yours in Königsberg. (Kapp to Wiechert, March 6, 1946)

The opportunity for a reunion in 1949 was nearly missed when – after delivering speeches at Oberlin College in Ohio and at Stanford University – Wiechert's lecture at Kapp's work place, Wesleyan University in Middleton (CT), did not materialize. They managed to meet briefly for a reunion in New York City before Wiechert's return to Europe and his death in 1950. Coincidentally or not, during the time period of this correspondence, Kapp developed and published his reform proposals for the German educational system and for teaching economics (Kapp 1946a, 1947b, 1948, 1951). This work is also reflected in his leading role as author and co-editor of the source book of Columbia University's *Introduction to Contemporary Civilization in the West* (1946b) and his 1947 tenure as chairman of the Subcommittee of Visual Aids of the Committee on the Undergraduate Teaching of Economics and the Training of Economists of the American Economic Association (AEA).

7.7 Wiechert's Poetic Pedagogy: The Spiritual Bond Between the Artist and the Young

Commissioned for a memorial volume on the poet's sixtieth birthday, 'Wiechert als Erzieher' ('Wiechert as Educator') most directly and openly showcases the deep and lasting inspiration Kapp (1947a) received from his teacher about the great significance of art for education. The article reflects on Wiechert's renowned 1929 commencement address. The former student states his conviction that every piece of art exerts educative influence by virtue of being the bearer of an esthetic, ethic, or intellectual message. 'Every artist is at the same time an educator' (Kapp 1947a, 12, author's translation). He finds the embodiment of this view in Wiechert's comparison between the spirit of the poet and the youth:

> [Both possess] the playful as well as the fanatic, the darkly driven as well as the relentless creating, the eagle-like advancing as well as the despairing of the genius. It [youth] relives the history of the people and of humankind again. It has the paradise, the play, the first art, the first gods, the first love, the first ecstasies. It rebuilds all towers of Babylon and all altars. It destroys gods and resurrects them. It prays in the gardens of Gethsemane, goes to Golgotha and lifts the stone from its grave. It has the entire smile of humankind and all its tears. (Wiechert in Kapp 1947a, 14, author's translation)

In other words, Kapp found that the main value of the artist as educator is his/her forever young poetic spirit, which is radically open to life furthering and transformative experiences that enable a process of renewal and allow the possibility of new beginnings.

7.8 The Importance of Courage and a Free Heart

Kapp also learned from Wiechert that the purpose of poetic pedagogy is to alleviate the youth from a curse: namely, the fear of authority and unconscious attachment to traditions because they inhibit the actualization of potentials inherent in every person:

> I tried to take away from you the most horrible thing that one can carry into the wide lonesome lands: fear. The fear of people, of terms, of conventions, of authorities, of gods and devils, of ridicule and tears, of fame and disgrace, of sin and despair, of failure and death […] [I]t is the fear of the slaves. But you should go without chains and with a raised head. (Wiechert in Kapp 1947a, 15, author's translation)

Kapp recollected that one of the ways in which Wiechert had emancipated students from these fears was to openly and critically discuss the politics of the day. He believed that a person's heart needed to be freed from the narrowness of dogma, intolerance, and the prejudices of the past and present. Wiechert explicitly encouraged his students to be brave enough to prefer truth to power:

> I do not say 'be well' […] but 'be brave'! Because 'what is good? Being brave is good!' My friends, I do not say 'be well!' but I say 'be prophets!' (Wiechert 1929, 9, author's translation)

This message is also perceived by Kapp to be the leading theme in Wiechert's two famous *Speeches to the German Youth* at the University of Munich in 1933 and 1935, in which he warned against the dangers of fear and cowardice for a person's development: '[Never] be mislead […] and never […] be part of the army of the thousands and thousands who are afraid … because nothing destroys the spine of a person more than cowardice' (Wiechert in Kapp 1967, 8, author's translation).

This theme is poetically reenacted in *Message for the Living* (Wiechert [1945] 1946) which quotes Goethe's *Des Epimenides Erwachen* (*The Awakening of Epimenides*) ([1815] 2013) to emphasize the supreme importance of a 'free heart':

> Komm wir wollen Dir versprechen
> Rettung aus dem tiefsten Schmerz …
> Säulen, Pfeiler kann man brechen,
> aber nicht ein freies Herz.
> – (Goethe [1815] 2013 in Wiechert [1945] 1946, 23)

> Come, we promise rescue ...
> From suffering's deepest part
> Columns and pillars give way,
> But not a freeborn heart.[79]
> – (Goethe [1815] 2013 in Wiechert [1945] 1946, 23)

In her unpublished essay, 'The German Poet Ernst Wiechert,' Lore Kapp argues that Wiechert himself demonstrated courage by defying the Nazis in two public speeches and in a letter that protested the abuse and incarceration of Pastor Niemöller, the leader of the oppositional Confessional Church in Germany (Lore Kapp, not dated).[80] Wiechert also endured a prison term in Buchenwald between May and August 1938. Another example of Wiechert's courage, according to Lore Kapp, was the secret writing of fairy tales during the war. These tales had the ability to restore courage in a despairing readership by conveying a firm belief in the final victory of good over evil. That is, 'the world of that great and ultimate justice of which children and people of all times have dreamed' (Wiechert in Lore Kapp, not dated, 8). Wiechert's autobiographical novel *Totenwald* (*Forest of the Dead*) (Wiechert [1946] 2008) narrates the importance of courage for maintaining a person's self-respect which, for Wiechert, was so radical that he was determined to accept even the most severe personal consequences. '[T]here are situations in life in which it is necessary for one's own self-respect to be rather among the persecuted or the dead than among the victors – where survival is no longer important' (Wiechert, in Lore Kapp, not dated).

7.9 Enduring Ideals and Islands of Comfort vs. the Danger of Careerism

Yet, Kapp also learned from Wiechert that an important goal of education is to prevent the rise of cultural barbarisms by bringing the youth in touch with enduring ideals: 'truth, justice, freedom and above all love for all suffering creatures [...] [the] unconditional quest for a better, more just, and precious world, the pious reverence before altars, the chivalrous attitude towards the weak, [and] the suffering and the beaten down' (Kapp 1947a, 17, author's translation).

Wiechert derived his views from Goethe's message: 'Man should be noble, helpful and good!' ('Edel sei der Mensch, hilfreich und gut!' Goethe in Kapp 1947a, 18). This Wiechert viewed as the enduring contribution of the German *Geist* to the history of humankind. According to Kapp, the heroes of Wiechert's literary works were the bearers of this proud and lasting heritage of humankind. This poetic pedagogy is diametrically opposed to an education that inclines students to careerism and commercialism (Kapp 1947a).

Yet, on the occasion of the eightieth anniversary of Wiechert's birthday, Kapp published his views on their correspondence between 1946 and 1949. In it, Wiechert confided that his outlook on education had changed since 1929:

> We like to lie to ourselves about our ability to change the world. [...]How many students was I able to prevent from committing crimes. If it was 3 out of 50 I can be content. It will never work to sway the masses to the good. We might be able to sway them to become the state's obedient subjects, thieves, or soldiers. But never to the good. (Wiechert in Kapp 1967, 5, author's translation)

> My doubts concerning the 'human substance' grow deeper every year, and the promises of Christianity have long ago ceased to provide grounds for me. Only one thing has remained: 'But love is the greatest among them.' And the essence of life, of effort, and work is solely this: not to be a prophet but to do one's day job quietly and to create with one's life and work a quiet glow of comfort for two, three people. Only via such small islands can very slowly emerge a small world of human beings with good will, but one must never forget that it will always remain small. (Wiechert to Kapp, December 12, 1946, author's translation)

7.10 Kapp's Reform Proposals for Education and Teaching Economics

Despite the more pessimistic outlook of Wiechert's later years, his poetic pedagogy resonates in Kapp's reform proposals for the future of education in Germany and for economics. The former is a call for a truly liberating education and one that conveys that 'the struggle for greater freedom from unreasonable authority is a permanent one' (Kapp 1948, 395). The necessary reforms should favor a 'truly democratic relationship between teacher and student' (1948, 394-395). Moreover, education should foster well-integrated personalities by combining general education and specialized training. After all, it was narrow specialized education, a one-sided half-education, and arid specialism that characterized large parts of the German educational system which made people susceptible to totalitarian habits of thought (Kapp 1948, 395). These proposals echo in *Teaching of Economics: A New Approach* (Kapp 1946a), which identifies the primary danger in the fact that the teaching of economics contributes to fostering disintegrated personalities due to overly arid specialism and fragmentation of knowledge without a unifying agent. The highly abstract and unduly technical principles of economics courses also fail to arouse the interests and curiosity of students (Kapp 1946a, 382-383). As a remedy, Kapp proposed that, from the start, students should be introduced to the basic unity of the social sciences in terms of their intellectual roots:

> Since 1938 I have been a teacher myself; I have specialized in economics. I have recently devoted much time to a course which is designed to give our students a broad foundation from which to specialize. It is a course which attempts a synthesis of the methods and insights of philosophy, history, political science and economics. It reflects the conviction that we are not truly civilized if we do not know the origin and development of the fundamental ideas and institutions which together constitute contemporary western civilization. (Kapp to Wiechert, March 6, 1946, author's translation)

This historical approach relates the economic and non-economic factors, so that economic problems are understood as part of the civilization within which they occur. Kapp deemed this a broad cultural synthesis that would give the students an 'understanding of the mutual interdependence among the various aspects of life' (Kapp 1946a, 379), and would eliminate the danger of fostering narrow specialization (Kapp 1946a, 383). This emphasis on the importance of understanding the economic system as a whole and its dynamic interrelationship with society from the start is also one of the main arguments for the use of visual presentations in teaching economics (Kapp 1947b, 1951), and for Kapp's efforts to develop the extensive source materials for Columbia University's *Introduction to Contemporary Civilization in the West* (Kapp 1946b). The specialization in courses, such as public finance, should build on this 'balanced general education' (Kapp 1946a, 379), but with a view to make students understand the bearing of the special topic for the analysis of the economic process as a whole (1946a, 381). The final step of the economics curriculum should be a capstone course that acts as a 'final unification of knowledge,' exploring the purpose and meaning of theoretical knowledge and the social sciences (1946a, 381-382). In sum, Kapp's reform proposals for economics education are permeated by insights derived from Wiechert's poetic pedagogy. Both aim at fostering well-integrated personalities via an integrative, balanced, and liberating educational experience that leads out of the dead end of dogma, narrow specialization, opportunism, and careerism.

7.11 Wiechert's Romanticism, or Nature, Religion, and the Simple Life as Lasting Sources of Inspiration

Lore Kapp's essay describes the main 'moving forces' of Wiechert's writings as the relationship between humans and nature, humanitarianism, and a non-sectarian Christianity. His attitude toward Christianity is best expressed in the statement: 'I regard one creed just as good [as] another. It is like the difference between writing in Gothic or Roman letters' (Wiechert in Lore Kapp, not dated, 4).

Next to religion, Lore Kapp identified nature as the most immediate sources of Wiechert's inspiration since his childhood during which Wiechert nursed an orphan crane in his home:

> It was good for me that I began my life barefoot and looked after the cows. Because I began in quietness, I could never fall completely a victim to the noisy. Because as a child I saw the forests in their silence and growth, I could always have a quiet smile for the excited bustle with which people build their transitory dwellings [...] I could never again fall out of the world of nature. (Wiechert in Lore Kapp, not dated, 2)

In her essay, Lore Kapp praised Wiechert's unique ability to portray the close interrelation between human life and nature's landscape, and to convey that nature is an important part of human existence and a very significant source of inspiration and joy. However, Wiechert's 'return to nature' is not to be mistaken as a proposal for a primitive life. Rather, it should be understood as a revolt against the barbarism of modern commercialized society. His insistence that meaningful work is the key to human happiness was the reason why Lore Kapp placed Wiechert in the tradition of Thomas Carlyle, Ralph Waldo Emerson, and Henry David Thoreau. Yet, Wiechert's ideal was not asceticism, but included time for leisure which he viewed as an important prerequisite for creativity and the development of individuality. This philosophical core manifested itself in the utterances by the hero in *The Simple Life* (Wiechert 1939): 'We don't need possessions, we need work, poverty and a little time' (Wiechert in Lore Kapp, not dated, 9). It is also expressed by the hero of *The Jeromin-Children* (*'Die Jeromin Kinder,'* Wiechert [1947] 2013) who renounced a brilliant career to 'find satisfaction and happiness in devoting himself to the relief and spiritual guidance of his fellow villagers' (Lore Kapp, not dated, 9). In sum, according to Lore Kapp, one can say that the betterment of the human character was the primary concern of Wiechert, so much so that he expressed skepticism about a too exclusive reliance on institutional change as the guarantee for human improvement (Lore Kapp, not dated).

7.12 The Political Consequences of Wiechert's Romanticism

The importance of the romantic aspect of Wiechert's work should, according to K. William Kapp, not be underestimated because the underlying ethical values, ideals, and philosophical concepts provide the foundation for political programs and a better society. 'My friends, it is not necessary that there be more money in the world, more fast trains, more parties, more associations, more worldviews. […] But it is necessary, that there be less tears in this world, less injustice, less violence, less pain' (Kapp 1947a, 21, author's translation).

In Kapp's interpretation, Wiechert's romanticist-humanitarian ethics is compatible with the political aspirations of the most progressive circles in all countries because it depicts a political order based on the consent of the people, with fewer tears, less pain, and in which the poorest can participate in the spiritual, political, and economic emancipation of humankind. The essence of Wiechert's message were love and humanitarianism, the living proof of which Wiechert found during his persecution and imprisonment among the poor, suffering, and outlawed, rather than among the rich and safe. The only social systems that, according to Kapp, do not meet these exigencies are the totalitarian state and the laissez-faire market economy because they always turn into a paradise for the powerful and strong. The political consequence of Wiechert's message is described by Kapp as being neither socialist, nor democrat, nor egalitarian in the sense of the enlightenment ideals. Rather, it is the persistent questioning of the relationship between morals and politics, justice and power, humanitarianism and society (Kapp 1947a).

Critics often accused Wiechert of being too detached from political reality and too exclusively focused on the inner human condition, i.e., too much of a romantic. However, Kapp pleaded in defense of his teacher that even the Nazis understood the political element of his work when they imprisoned him as a political enemy for undermining the totalitarian aspirations of the dictatorship. '[H]e was not a man of politics [,] […] but he responded to the political problems of his time with political activism and in his unique poetic language [.] […] [H]is personal transformation after WWI was evident in … his criticism of the emperor [,] […] his rejection of violence and war, his criticism of the boundless quest for money and career [,] and his attitude towards Goethe' (Kapp 1967, 1-2).

Wiechert also fought the disintegration of culture by the cash nexus. '[T]he emphasis on cash and commercialism undermines the feeling of humanity and fairness [and] [...] the struggle for money destroys all the good instincts and isolates the individual from his fellow-men, thereby preparing him mentally and emotionally for all those acts and thoughts which ultimately lead to hatred, intolerance and injustice' (Lore Kapp, not dated, 5). Wiechert viewed himself as a writer who wields power by providing support to troubled souls, quoting from *Über Kunst und Künstler* (*On Art and Artists*) (Wiechert 1946): '[A] writer must not withdraw from the life of his fellow-men, must not live in an enchanted aesthetic dream-world of his own. More than ever before suffering men and women are demanding that the writer give them light and comfort and help' (Wiechert 1946, in Lore Kapp, translation by Lore Kapp). Wiechert openly critiqued the separation of morals from politics as a form of moral anarchy, as the deep cause of violence, and a sign of decay. Thus, Wiechert warned students in his speech at the University of Munich in 1935 that when a people ceased to distinguish between good and evil, it 'is already on a slippery slope and [...] on the wall will appear the hand that writes letters with fire' (Wiechert in Kapp 1967, 6, author's translation).

7.13 Kapp's Economics, or the Humanization and Integration of Social Knowledge

The foregoing analysis makes clear how profoundly not only K. William Kapp, but also his wife Lore Kapp, who was the co-author and collaborator of several publications, were inspired by Wiechert. Of course, Kapp's economics was also influenced by other traditions, such as American institutionalism and the Frankfurt School (Berger 2015a). Yet, a study of Kapp's collected works reveals an astonishing oneness with Wiechert's ethics, suggesting that this is the primary and deepest source of his economics.

Kapp's early focus on environmental disruption led to his recognition as one of the founders of ecological economics. Already his dissertation, 'Planwirtschaft und Aussenhandel' ('The Planned Economy and International Trade') (Kapp 1936) addressed the issues of air pollution and resource depletion. The dissertation was developed into the core theme of his most famous book, *The Social Costs of Private Enterprise* (Kapp 1950; see also Berger 2015a). Archival research has not produced evidence that Kapp explicitly accredited his early environmental sensitivity to Wiechert's ethics. Yet, the preceding analysis does evidence that, at the time of writing *The Social Costs of Private Enterprise*, Wiechert's novels were a source of inspiration for Kapp, and that he was aware of 'nature' being a core theme. Wiechert embraced an attitude of love for all suffering creatures, including creatures of nature, such as an orphan crane, and a way of life that is sensitive to the natural environment surrounding human beings. Kapp's economics frames the topic in terms of how existential human needs can be guaranteed through socio-ecological safety standards and minima that maintain an appropriate quality of the natural *and* social environment. In this theory, human wellbeing is tied to the wellbeing of the environment. The latter depends, according to Kapp, on the organizing principles that govern the economy and are socially determined. Kapp's economics deals with the question of how to democratically resolve the power struggles involved in socially controlling science and technology decisions, so that social-ecological safety standards are not violated. In the light of these findings, it is reasonable to attribute Kapp's early sensitivity toward environmental issues to the influence of Wiechert's ethic. Kapp aimed at crafting a space for the fulfillment of existential needs as a precondition for the betterment of the human character.

Wiechert's lessons on love and care for those in need and despair are reflected in Kapp's life-long search for ways to protect the weak, society, and nature from the cost-shifting activities of businesses, and to thereby minimize human suffering (Kapp 1950). Kapp called the analysis of the systematic socializing of costs by the system of business enterprise 'the theme of my life' (Kapp in Berger 2015b). This theme clearly echoes Wiechert's critique of commercialism, the boundless quest for money, the cash nexus, and his emphasis on the 'love for all suffering creatures.' Likewise Wiechert's warning of the dangers of moral anarchy and the separation of morals from politics is reflected in Kapp's critique of the purely formal rationality of neoclassical economics and its hidden 'normative-apologetic' character, which are the roots of social damage. As a solution, Kapp proposed a rational integration of humanitarian values into economics, arguing that Weber's substantive rationality, which is explicitly normative, is a possible avenue even for science – i.e., a 'new rational humanism' (Berger 2015a).

Wiechert's ethics is permeated by a spirit of dynamic renewal through humanitarianism, love, and return to the quietness of nature so as to find what is truly essential. Struggling to transfer this spirit into the realm of economics, Kapp sought a new departure in economics and demanded a 'return to philosophy,' a 'broadening of the scope of economic investigation,' a 'reformulation and enlargement of basic concepts' in order to 'overcome the horizon of contemporary society' (Kapp 1950, 264-264). This proposal culminated in his project of the humanization and integration of social knowledge to reverse the dehumanization and fragmentation of social knowledge and social reality (Kapp 1961). Kapp's inaugural lecture *The Dehumanization of 'Pure Theory' and Social Reality* (Kapp [1967] 1985) at Basel University – one of the centers of European humanism – and his work *Economics and Rational Humanism* (Kapp [1965] 1985) spell out this project most clearly. The lecture's opening paragraph programmatically states: '[A]ll the economic and social sciences [...] remained untouched by the humanitarian and socially critical points of departure found in Goethe, Hölderlin and Nietzsche [...] the intellectual development of today has been bought all too dearly with a loss of humanity' (Kapp [1967] 1985, 74).

Thus lamenting the shunning of art, poetry, and philosophy, as well as the resulting dehumanization of economics, Kapp demonstrated his agreement with Wiechert's ethics and pedagogy. The complete dehumanization and fragmentation of economics, in Kapp's view, was an aberration from a long humanitarian tradition. 'The Schoolmen,' as well as the secularized natural law of Hugo Grotius and Samuel Pufendorf, the philosophy of the Enlightenment, and even Jeremy Bentham, maintained the classical formulation of questions with the human being as the 'measure of all things' (Kapp [1965] 1985, 101):

> Classical humanism as well as the political and economic thinking in the philosophy of antiquity rest on this [...] formulation of questions which take [...] [human beings] and [...] [their behavior] as their point of departure. This starting point in the consideration of economic problems was basically retained during the Middle Ages [...] [when] the Christian ethics t[ook] the place of the political engagement of ancient philosophy. [...] [Human beings] with [...] [their] profane and transcendental needs [...] remain[ed] thereby in the center of the debate on economic questions and facts. (Kapp [1965] 1985, 100-101)

Consequently, Kapp called for a *New Rational Humanism* because he believed it was doubtful whether a return to the earlier humanism of Greek philosophy or of the Christian ethic can do justice to contemporary problems that are separated from antiquity and the Middle Ages by the advent of modern science and technology. Kapp ([1965] 1985, 103-104) argued for 'a substantive and human formulation of questions making the human being, i.e., a scientific and empirically derived concept of human behavior and needs the starting point of economics.'

The conceptual foundation for this project was located in the experiential knowledge of the bio-cultural openness of human beings (Kapp 1961). Kapp found an open space for introducing Wiechert's humanitarian ethics into the realm of science and rationalism by allying himself with existential philosophy, critical theory, and philosophical anthropology. The integrated and humanized body of social knowledge serves to control the scientific and technological structure of the economy via precautionary socio-ecological safety standards, guaranteeing the satisfaction of existential human needs.

The conceptual innovations of social costs, socio-ecological or existential minima, socio-ecological indicators, and the open-system character of the economy are a testament to Kapp's ability to creatively craft ethically and esthetically beautiful intellectual symbols. The power of this vision was the key for inspiring the formation of various organizations, such as the Socialist Environment and Resource Association, the European Association for Evolutionary and Political Economy, and the German Association for Ecological Economics. The Kapp Prizes of the latter two organizations are a testament to the enduring influence of Kapp's ideas.

7.14 Conclusion

Through this analysis I provided the following insights: first, the economic 'double truth' is accompanied by a repression of experiential knowledge, dissent, and by a set of avoidable tragedies, such as the inability to foresee and prevent major socio-economic and ecological calamities. Second, I demonstrated the importance of experiential knowledge for a non-commodified science in terms of imagination, fantasy, a sympathetic understanding of experience, idle curiosity, sensitivity of touch, play, divination, 'musement,' beauty, and the pursuit of truth as values *sui generis*. The experience of works of art and poetry can reconnect economists with vital meanings that make economics more imaginative, true, beautiful, and humane. The inspirational friendship between the economist Kapp and the poet Wiechert is a prime example of the way economics can be inspired by art. This is a role model for an economics that embodies a vision for the reduction of human suffering via preventative safety standards, the love for all suffering creatures, the belief in the good, the simple yet meaningful life, the importance of a free heart, the importance of nature as a source of inspiration, the courage to choose the truth over power, as well as to fight authoritarianism, totalitarianism, commercialism, and careerism. The latter phenomena are causes for the fragmentation and dehumanization of social reality. The economics professor Kapp acquired from his poet teacher Wiechert a clear understanding of the factors that threaten the well-integrated 'self,' the nurturing of human wisdom, and the achievement of socio-ecological goals. This inspirational friendship between a poet and an economist shows how economics can take its lead from art and poetry, and thereby maintain its bond with *Geisteswissenschaft* and the rest of culture through experiential knowledge. Experiential knowledge is paramount to economics because it inspires the courage to pursue creative, earnest, and beautiful visions for a viable and humane economy. These conclusions are in oneness with Veblen's (1910) hope that the instinct of 'brotherly love' can sublimate the instinct of predation if the former manages to join forces with the instincts of play and workmanship.

References

Berger, Sebastian. 'K. William Kapp's Social Theory of Social Costs.' *History of Political Economy* (2015a): forthcoming.

Berger, Sebastian, ed. 'Introduction.' In *The Heterodox Theory of Social Costs*, by K. William Kapp. London: Routledge, 2015b.

Binswanger, Hans Christoph. *Money and Magic: A Critique of the Modern Economy in the Light of Faust*. Chicago, IL: Chicago University Press, 1994.

Dyer, Alan. 'Veblen and Scientific Creativity: The Influence of Charles S. Peirce.' *Journal of Economic Issues* 20, 1 (1986): 21-41.

'Economic Theory as an Art Form.' *Journal of Economic Issues* 22, 1 (1988): 157-166.

'Dudley Dillard, Vision and the Meaning of Ideas.' *Journal of Economic Issues* 27, 2 (1993): 571-578.

Georgescu-Roegen, Nicholas. *Analytical Economics*. Cambridge, MA: Harvard University Press, 1966.

The Entropy Law and the Economic Process. Cambridge, MA: Harvard University Press, 1971.

'Methods in Economic Science.' *Journal of Economic Issues* 13, 2 (1979): 317-328.

Goethe, Johann Wolfgang. *Des Epimenides Erwachen*. Germany: Createspace, [1815] 2013.

Kanth, Rajani Kannepalli. *Against Economics: Rethinking Political Economy*. London: Ashgate, 1997.

Kapp, K. William. 'Teaching of Economics: A New Approach.' *The Southern Economic Journal* 12 (1946a): 376-383.

Co-ed. *Introduction to Contemporary Civilization in the West – A Source Book.* New York, NY: Columbia University Press, 1946b.

'Wiechert als Erzieher.' ('Wiechert as Educator.') In *Bekenntnis zu Ernst Wiechert*, pp.12-23. München, Germany: Kurt Desch, 1947a.

'Methods of Visual Presentation and the Teaching of Economics.' *American Economic Review* 37, 4 (1947b): 652-654.

'The Future of German Education.' *Journal of Higher Education* 19, 8 (1948): 394-397.

The Social Costs of Private Enterprise. Cambridge, MA: Harvard University Press, 1950.

Graphic Approach to Economics – Selected Principles and Problems (with Lore L. Kapp). New York, NY: Henry & Co., 1951.

Towards a Science of Man in Society. The Hague, Netherlands: Martinus Nijhoff, 1961.

'Ernst Wiechert zum Gedächtnis.' In *Züricher Zeitung – Literaturbeilage*, pp. 1-18. May 19, 1967.

'Economics and Rational Humanism.' In *The Humanization of the Social Sciences*, edited by John E. Ullmann and Roy Preiswerk, pp. 99-120. Lanham, MD: University Press of America, [1965] 1985.

'The Dehumanization of 'Pure Theory' and Social Reality.' In *The Humanization of the Social Sciences*, edited by John E. Ullmann and Roy Preiswerk, pp. 73-98. Lanha, MD: University Press of America, [1967] 1985.

The Foundations of Institutional Economics. Edited by Sebastian Berger and Rolf Steppacher, London: Routledge, 2011.

Kapp, Lore. 'Ernst Wiechert.' Kapp Archive. University of Basel Library, not dated.

Lee, Frederic. *A History of Heterodox Economics in the 20th Century.* London: Routledge, 2009.

Marglin, Stephen. *The Dismal Science – How Thinking Like an Economist Undermines Community.* Cambridge, MA: Harvard University Press, 2008.

McCloskey, Deirdre. 'The Genealogy of Postmodernism: An Economist's Guide.' In *Postmodernism, Economics and Knowledge*, edited by Stephen Cullenberg, Jack Amariglio and David F. Ruccio, pp. 102-128. London: Routledge, 2001.

Mirowski, Philip. *Science-Mart: Privatizing American Science.* Cambridge, MA: Harvard University Press, 2011.

Never Let a Serious Crisis Go to Waste – How Neoliberalism Survived the Financial Meltdown. New York, NY: Verso, 2013.

Morgan, Mary and Malcolm Rutherford, eds. *From Interwar Pluralism to Postwar Neoclassicism: Annual Supplement to Volume 30 History of Political Economy.* Durham, NC: Duke University Press, 1998.

Nietzsche, Friedrich. 'Beyond Good and Evil.' In *Basic Writings of Nietzsche*, edited by Walter Kaufmann, pp. 179-436. New York, NY: Modern Library Classics, 2000.

Shackle, G.L.S. 'Economics and Sincerity.' *Oxford Economic Papers: New Series* 5, 1 (1953): 1-12.

'Policy, Poetry and Success.' *The Economic Journal* 76, 304 (1966): 755-767.

Sturgeon, James. 'Nature, Hammers, and Picasso.' *Journal of Economic Issues* 26, 2 (1992): 350-364.

Veblen, Thorstein. 'Christian Morals and the Competitive System.' *International Journal of Ethics* 20, 2 (1910): 168-185.

'Economics in the Calculable Future.' *American Economic Review* 15, 1 (1925): 48-55.

Wiechert, Ernst. 'Abschiedsrede an die Abiturienten.' Berlin, Germany, 1929. Available at Ernst_Wiechert_Reden/Ernst_Wiechert_Herbig_Reden_Abschiedsrede_an_die_Abiturienten.pdf. (Accessed online May 15, 2015.)

Das Einfache Leben. Hamburg, Germany: Langen Müller, 1939.

Über Kunst und Künstler. (*On Art and Artists.*) Hamburg, Germany: Langen Müller, 1946.

Message for the Living. (Originally published in Germany as *Rede an die Deutsche Jugend.*) München, Germany: Zinnen Verlag, [1945] 1946.

Jahre und Zeiten. (*Years and Times.*) Hamburg, Germany: Langen Müller, 1949.

Totenwald: Ein Bericht. (*Forest of the Dead.*) Frankfurt am Main, Germany: Suhrkamp Verlag, [1946] 2008.

Die Jeromin-Kinder. Würzburg, Germany: Rautenberg Verlag, [1947] 2013.

8
Social Costs as a Psychological Problem

8.1 Introduction

Institutional economists since Veblen have explored the circular cumulative causation[81] between material and institutional factors, including the modes of thought of neoclassical economists that lead to socio-ecological damages (Veblen, 1919, 1925; Georgescu-Roegen, 1979; Kapp, 2011). The goal of the present article is to trace the less tangible losses that occur within the psychology of neoclassical economists that give rise to more tangible losses (damages/costs) as these economists shape the world according to their habits of thought. This is an initial step towards a more elaborate psychograph of neoclassical economists, that is, persons who feel attracted by, believe in, defend, and promulgate neoclassical habits of thought as the one and only 'capital T truth' in economic matters. Neoclassical economics is here understood as an umbrella term for modes of thought that are mechanical and arithmomorphic, and are associated with the image of the economy as a cyborg (Mirowski, 2002). In the first part, the article honors Wolfram Elsner's contribution to the philosophy of economics, that is, his treatise on 'incommensurable losses' in the development of economic paradigms that serves as a rationale for recourses and reconstructions of older ideas. A brief recourse to Kapp's economics shows that an inquiry into the lacunae of modes of thought raises psychological questions. Consequently, the second part explores psychological questions that have been posed but thus far left largely unanswered by philosophical, historical, and cultural investigations of neoclassical economics. While the inquiry assesses characteristics of neoclassical modes of thought, it cannot be emphasized enough that it is not intended to be a character assassination of the neoclassical economist. This article is not about demonstrating revulsion, revealing a dirty secret, or a wholesale vilification of neoclassical economics – after all, even Veblen had something positive to say, albeit on a very basic level, about Marshall's neoclassical cause-effect analysis (Veblen, 1919). Rather, the aim is to raise awareness of psychological factors that dovetail with cultural, historical, and philosophical factors to form the mindset of neoclassical economics. The author recognizes the contextual and interested character of this investigation that results from nearly a decade of working as an academic economist.

8.2 Elsner's philosophy of economics, or: recovering what's 'lost in calculation'

The notion and meaning of 'losses' in the development of economic science is the subject matter of Wolfram Elsner's magnum opus *Economic Institutions Analysis* (1986). According to its main thesis, 'losses' exist due to discontinuities in the development of economic paradigms, which contradicts the linear 'progress' narrative told typically by neoclassical economists and their textbooks. The treatise demonstrates the unexhausted 'evolutionary potential' of institutional economics, summoning the support of Joseph Schumpeter's dictum of the 'inspirative function' of the history of economics that can influence contemporary developments in economics. The context of his contribution is the 'post-empiricist' debate in the philosophy of science (for a summary of this debate see Bernstein (1983)) as Elsner applies one of the main insights of this debate, namely, that hermeneutic recourses to and reconstructions of past economic ideas are a way to improve today's understanding. Elsner argues that in economics, however, these recourses occur primarily due to the competitive attitudes of rival economic paradigms. He refers to the notion of 'incommensurable losses' that are not objective but relative to each of the competing and incommensurable paradigms. That is, an idea constitutes a loss only when a given paradigm views it as a loss that can provide a competitive advantage. This analysis implies that the underlying purpose of paradigms is to attain a position of power, and that the recovery of losses is thus purely power-driven, lacking a hermeneutic attitude that involves a genuine interest in understanding 'the other.' This leaves open the question as to what happens to a paradigm's losses that its proponents do not recognize either because they are unwilling or because they lack the capacity for it? In trying to answer this question, this article explores the losses of neoclassical modes of thought to which its adherents turn a blind eye.

Elsner's insights have been applied by the present author to reconstruct Kapp's open system approach (Berger and Elsner, 2009) and heterodox theory of social costs (Berger, 2015a). One of the insights is that Kapp conceptualizes social costs as losses that arise due to the market calculus that has a built-in tendency to shift, externalize, or socialize as much of the costs of production as possible. Losses accrue in the form of damages to third parties, society at large, or future generations. Why does this happen? According to Kapp, social costs are a problem of a purely *formal* rationality that has lost touch with the *substantive* nature of the material conditions (socio-economic and ecological) under consideration, thus lacking substantive rationality. This means that the problem of social costs is here associated with knowledge that is lost in formal market calculations. Consequently, social costs can be understood as a problem of distinguishing and grounding knowledge or rationality (Kapp 1961, 1985). Social costs are thus reciprocally related to losses in the realm of modes of thought. Kapp conceptualizes these less tangible losses as a kind of systemic closure exercised by market calculation. This closure means 'knowledge destruction' with regards to aspects of life that do not possess monetary exchange value per se and cannot be adequately brought under the purview of the market calculus. This means that markets lose sight of states of balance of the natural and social environment, which are a prerequisite for the fulfilment of human needs. That is, markets ignore the open system character of the economy (for a similar conception of the limitations of markets see Luhman's systems theory in Valentinov (2013)). The formal rationality of markets is, according to Kapp, mirrored in the habits of thought of neoclassical economists, which causes them to lose sight of the humanitarian notion upheld since antiquity that the human being is the measure of all things. Thus, the formalism of neoclassical economics is viewed as contributing to the disintegration and dehumanization of social reality (Berger, 2015b).

8.3 Earlier calls for a psychology of neoclassical economists

But what stands in the way of recovering the losses of neoclassical habits of thought? Indeed, Kapp raises the question why neoclassical economists refuse to understand the open system character of the economy and why they remain in an 'intellectual freeze' (Kapp, 1976). Already his major and most influential work *The Social Costs of Private Enterprise* (1950) criticizes neoclassical economics by quoting Alfred N. Whitehead's philosophy of science:

> Systems, scientific and philosophic, come and go. Each method of limited understanding is at length exhausted. In its prime each system is a triumphant success; in its decay it is an obstructive nuisance. [...] No science can be more secure than the unconscious metaphysics which tacitly it presupposes [...] Without adventure civilization is in full decay. (ibid, p. xxxi)

And Kapp agrees with Whitehead that

> '[t]he transitions to new fruitfulness of understanding are achieved by recurrence to the utmost depth of intuition for the refreshment of imagination.' [...] [and that] 'if science is not to degenerate into a medley of *ad hoc*

hypotheses, it must become philosophical and must enter upon a thorough criticism of its own foundations' applies with equal force to economics' (ibid., p. 243-4).

Moreover, he refers to Thomas Kuhn and John Dewey in his belief that the new paradigm needed to effectively deal with the environmental crisis required 'destructive innovations' that would be 'forthcoming if at all only from the outside of the discipline – from men and ideas who possess a wider range of reference and possible range of application.' (Kapp, 2015: 290). Yet, a full explanation for the 'intellectual freeze' required, according to Kapp, an investigation of the social-psychological determinants of neoclassical economics:

> [T]he majority of people seem to require a justification of the social and economic systems in which they participate, quite apart from the fact that the beneficiaries of such systems have a self-regarding interest in such normative rationalizations […] we do maintain that a demand exists for biased explanations, which in turn account at least partially for the survival and popularity of particular modes of thought. […] [the] prevailing orthodoxy [i.e., neoclassical economics] […] tends to defend itself against its critics by introducing new assumptions, simplifications, and refinements whenever one of its conclusions is challenged. The relative lack of 'success' of [institutionalism is due to] its challenge to the alleged superiority and rationality of the system of business enterprise, as compared with previous and alternative forms of economic organization. Certainly the 'failure' of institutionalism has not been due to the superior relevance and generality of conventional theory – although again it must be admitted that the latter's precision and superficial plausibility, though spurious in actuality, have given it an advantage. This is particularly true among a fraternity of social scientists who share the popular quest for certainty and determinate solutions, and who have equated quantitative conclusions and mathematical symbols with science, even if those symbols and conclusions have no definable counterpart in reality. (Kapp 2011: 18)

This quote echoes the insights of notable economists and philosophers: John Maynard Keynes (1936: 32-3) (on factors lending 'intellectual prestige,' 'virtue,' 'beauty,' 'authority'), John Dewey (1960) ('quest for certainty'), Nicholas Georgescu-Roegen (1979) ('arithmomania'), Thorstein Veblen (1925) ('business-friendly ideas') and the Duhem-Quin thesis ('auxiliary hypotheses preclude falsification') (Mirowski, 2014). Furthermore, Kapp's handwritten comments reveals his central conviction that 'no culture can be adequately analyzed if one leaves its idols intact – its sacred cows' (Kapp, 2011: 276 n1). The reference to 'sacred cows' means that Kapp perceived the calling into question of neoclassical modes of thought as a calling into question society's core religious precepts, which relates to the psychology of myths and religion. The task of the remainder of the article is to continue Kapp's forays by exploring the psychology of neoclassical economists in more detail. Thereby, this article showcases the fruitfulness of the 'Elsnerian recourse' to Kapp's economics that has stimulated this new inquiry.

8.4 Open psychological questions

The more recent discourse in the philosophy of economics leaves several questions unanswered that all point towards the need for a psychological inquiry into habits of thought of neoclassical economists. Consider, for example, how Deidre McCloskey's proposal for 'storytelling' in economics is sustained by the hope that such a turn helps to foster a community of sophisticated readers willing to try other ways of reading, to persuade economists that they are not so different from poets and novelists, and to raise self-consciousness, which has the advantage for culture at large of contributing to peace of toleration, and bringing economists back into the conversation of mankind (McCloskey 2014: 73). McCloskey argues that if 'economists [...] [learn] an adult's way of being a scientist [by opening up once again to the metaphorical nature of reality], [they] could reunify the cultures of science and literature' (ibid.: 122). She also calls for an economics that admits that we cannot know the truth, but affirm that we can come to agree on some truth. All past groundings of transcendental truths since Plato are deemed fake. McCloskey urges adults to be able to recognize that their standards are not God's own, not transcendent and not a-historical, while affirming that standards are still worth discussing. Yet, this becoming an 'adult' is not a purely rational affair as McCloskey herself argues when she identifies fear as the main cause behind the adoption and persistence of the religion of modernism by neoclassical economists and she notes the discrepancies between its coercive and dogmatic practice and its self-image of truth seeking (a kind of double truth) (McCloskey, 2001).

At this point of the narrative psychological questions seem to step into the foreground: Why does somebody shy away from becoming an adult, what is she afraid of, and why does somebody operate based on double truths? It is not difficult to derive further questions of such psychological nature from the contemporary discourse in the philosophy of economics:
● What is the (psychological) function of assumptions? (Mäki, 1994)
● What desires and wishes are projected into the discipline and why does

- it remove itself from the realm of the human individual, eliminating its idiosyncrasies? (Mirowski, 1994)
- How is it possible to emphasize the virtues of competition while insisting on the monopoly of neoclassical economics? (Hands 1994)
- What gets shunted by neoclassical economists, that is, what is 'the other' that gets denied an opportunity to speak as the voice of unreason? What are the internal (psychological) elements that give a theory discursive force and create agreement amongst its self-selected followers? What makes for the self-congratulatory attitude of neoclassical economists and its attempt to insulate its practice from the scrutiny of its rules, their discursive formation, their implicit epistemological norms, and their situatedness in society and culture? (Cullenberg *et al.*, 2001)
- Why is there such a low standard of self-criticism in neoclassical economics? What elements of fantasy, desire, affect are invested in the system of neoclassical knowledge? How does the human subject experience this expert system of knowledge? How is the discipline specific habitus inculcated via a largely unconscious process of identification with hero ideals? (Steinmetz, 2005)
- What makes for the willingness of neoclassical economists merely 'to compete within a given set of rules and institutional structures' without questioning them? (Colander, in Mearman 2012: 417)

The present article follows Steinmetz's proposal (2005) to investigate such questions as a case of the 'unconscious of science' on the grounds of Sigmund Freud's notion of 'epistemophilia' (desire for knowledge), Pierre Bourdieu's 'unconscious scientific habitus', Alfred N. Whitehead's epochal 'unconscious assumptions' and Slavoj Žižek's 'hero ideals.' The unconscious is here understood as knowledge that is not accessible to conscious awareness but can pattern conscious thought and practice. This psychology of a social group is also supported by organizational research that evidences the existence of aspirational Selfs based on inculcated hero images (Thornborrow and Brown, 2009). The main claim is that fundamental intellectual alignments are generated and reproduced to some extent without the conscious agreement of participants (Steinmetz, 2005). Moreover, Mearman's work on the self-identity of economists finds psychological treatments valuable because they allow 'factors typically excluded, such as emotion, or values to be reintroduced as factors affecting the way the economist approaches questions. Fundamentally, psychological approaches capture attitude, which could shape and be shaped by their decision whether to join a group [...]' (Mearman, 2012: 417). Psychology has been assigned a prominent place also by Mirowski who assesses the 'psychological equipment' that allows neoclassical economists to remain in error and not change their theory with a 'steely self-confidence' (Mirowski, 2013).

8.5 Lost in fear: rationalization, repression, compensation, isolation, and projection

The first systematic psychology of neoclassical economists was developed by Walter Weisskopf (1949). As chairman of the economics department at Roosevelt College he had thanked Kapp for his 'extremely interesting article on 'Economics and the Behavioral Sciences' and stated 'there is hardly anything in your paper with which I do not agree wholeheartedly' (Weisskopf to Kapp, June 2 1954, unpublished manuscript). The article referred to emphasizes the need for an integrated approach to social knowledge based on cultural and philosophic anthropology as well as social-psychology. Exploring the reasons why neoclassical economists reject the changes proposed by Kapp, Weisskopf looked towards Sigmund Freud's theory and identified the fear of social exclusion as the root problem. This fear causes the psyche to isolate and repress thoughts and ideas that go against powerful real world social institutions and interests. That is, the neoclassical concept of 'perfect rationality' plays a key role in repressing the possibility of 'irrational' behavior. Reducing fear by repressing troubling thoughts is here interpreted as a defense mechanism of the ego in order to obtain a well ordered picture of economic reality. The neoclassical method of formal abstraction is viewed as a result of the psychic function of isolation, which favors elegance just as much as harmony, and abstracts from conflicting aspects of reality. Furthermore, the conflict between the ego and super-ego is resolved by projections. The (formal and perfect) rationality demand of the super-ego is simply accepted as universal truth and projected onto reality where it assumes a moral-ethical system. The goals of society are viewed as natural and identical with the goals of the individual. The perfectly rational and informed economic agent Homo Oeconomicus is projected into a world of fundamental uncertainty and irrationality. Weisskopf also sees the psychic function of compensation as working hand in hand with repression. Impulses are being repressed and the lack of need satisfaction is compensated with wishful intellectual constructs. Therefore, neoclassical economics is deemed primarily a defense mechanism used by the ego to deny facts and substitute pleasant illusions and wish dreams for an unbearable reality. Weisskopf concludes that all the above mentioned psychological functions are operational in the neoclassical complex of ideas consisting of harmony, equilibrium, perfect information, and perfect rationality. All this happens on the unconscious level and Weisskopf cautions his readers to view this process with humility and awe rather than conceit. For him, it is no coincidence that the complex of ideas parallels Western ideals (for this section compare Weisskopf (1949)).

The subsequent magnum opus *The Psychology of Economics* (Weisskopf, 1955) goes beyond the author's earlier purely Freudian interpretation of neoclassical economics by drawing on Max Weber's work and the post-Freudian social-psychology of Erich Fromm. The spirit of capitalism is viewed as a 'value complex' of largely unconscious habits of thought. The latter emerged with Protestantism and were slowly secularized and pushed into the unconscious. In this context neoclassical economics fulfills a significant social-psychological function as the bastion of rationalism in modernity. Weisskopf argues that rationalizing and repressing non-rational and unconscious impulses is necessary to endure life in an industrial society. Neoclassical economists are therefore likened to 'high priests' who induce students to believe that there are irrefutable economic laws that prove that humans are rational:

> You are as industrial society wants you to be. You are a completely rational, conscious being, whose main purpose in life is [...] to maximize utility by equalizing expenditures at the margin. The mode of life which industrial society imposes on you is what you really want. (Weisskopf, 1955: 248).

According to this perspective, neoclassical economics appears as 'valium,' which is prescribed to calm down the human being who is torn between the ideal of rationality and her other potentialities. Importantly, Weisskopf points out the paradoxical situation that this calming function seems not to be affected by the admission of neoclassical economists that the Homo Oeconomicus model is only a hypothetical construct that has been empirically disproven and that there are several developments even within neoclassical economics that contradict it (Weisskopf, 1955). The psychology of this paradox as a kind of conceptual schizophrenia will be discussed below.

8.6 Algorithm as myth and knowledge culture, or: losing experiential authority, the 'feminine,' and community

Weisskopf's psychology of neoclassical economists as priests with an unconscious Protestant value complex is positioned in the context of capitalism and Western industrial society. This emphasizes the importance of cultural myths and religion that influence the psychology of neoclassical economists. In the cultural perspective neoclassical economics is a 'cultural artifact' that contributes to constructing the world in its own image, which is confirmed by surveys showing that the study of economics leads to less cooperative, less other-regarding behavior by celebrating the self-interested calculating (rational) individual (see Marglin (2008) for this entire section). Marglin points to the emotional exhilaration felt by students of economics when they hear that, according to the 'invisible hand' theory, acting on self-interest is morally justified and even a social virtue. Neoclassical economics is viewed as encapsulating the myth of modernity because it appeals to the consciousness of a people by embodying its cultural ideals and by giving expression to deep commonly felt emotions. That is, it is a 'fiction' that forms part of the ideology of society. Marglin argues that a myth should not per se be seen as a disease but should rather be rendered conscious, differentiated and integrated:

> The first precondition of transcending the limits of our myths [...] is to recognize them for what they are [...] the foundational assumptions of [neoclassical] economics are cultural myths rather than universal truths [...]. (ibid, pp. 38-39)

The neoclassical approach to knowledge is, according to Marglin, at the core of the myth and has the following psychological characteristics. First and foremost knowledge is abstracted from its context and ontologically reduced to algorithms. Referring to Oliver Sacks's clinical histories, Marglin notes that an exclusive focus on algorithmic knowledge is associated with 'tragic distortions of human beings' (ibid.: 129). Consequently, self-development as the process of becoming oneself is excluded because it is incommensurable with the algorithmic knowledge that Homo Oeconomicus and his given preferences demand. This mode of thought is deemed incapable of thinking about the human relationships that form community because it focuses on depersonalized knowledge. The latter economizes on the higher human faculties, such as affection, community, reciprocity, personal obligation, and love. Holism as the 'feminine' map to navigate social interactions goes 'underground' because algorithmic knowledge and its exaggerated quest for certainty denies what is learned from intuition and authority, from 'touch and feel,' that is, experiential knowledge.

According to Marglin, experiential knowledge is transmitted from master to student, from parents to children valuing the reinterpretation rather than the defeat of the authority of the fathers. The rejection and acceptance of certain types of knowledge as disorderly has been entangled with conceptions of social order since ancient Greek times. According to Marglin, the rise of insecurity and social disorder are due to 'the erosion of the authority of the father.' Personal authority is central to experiential knowledge and the attraction of algorithmic knowledge is the challenge it poses to non-algorithmic authority. Algorithmic knowledge has the effect of strengthening precocious individualism and has been adopted as a Western ideal largely unconsciously since Descartes. Algorithmic knowledge imitates the form of a mathematical theorem to remedy the emerging disunity and uncertainty of modernity. Yet, the exclusive focus on algorithmic knowledge is, according to Marglin, to blame for the failure of neoclassical economics to provide workable explanations of economic phenomena. Thus, economists face the task of explaining the economy 'with one hand tied behind the collective back' (ibid.: 147) and experiential knowledge and community do not receive the nurturing and attention they require. Personal authority and convention are rooted in community, such that experiential knowledge is rooted in community. Marglin concludes that our economic knowledge and understanding are distorted by the myth of neoclassical economics, i.e. an ideology that subordinates experiential knowledge to algorithmic knowledge.

In sum, knowledge losses are located in the realm of experiential and intuitive knowledge, the higher human faculties (affection, community, reciprocity, personal obligation, and love), and knowledge of 'vices and weaknesses of markets' (ibid.: 67). This incompatibility between neoclassical economics as a knowledge culture and the rest of culture is a common theme in cultural economics (Marglin, 2009; Jackson, 2009; Davis, 2010; Throsby, 2001; Klamer, 1996; Hartman, 1977; Boulding, 2013). The remedy prescribed by Marglin is to raise the level of consciousness regarding the living neoclassical myth as the main task of a psychology of knowledge. One way to pursue this task is to explore the archetypal dynamics of knowledge cultures. This means categorizing the latter based on how they relate to the archetypal experiences. Evidencing the emotional matrix regarding experiential authority, nature, the feminine, and novelty, Marglin's account provides valuable leads for an archetypal psychology of neoclassical economics as knowledge culture.

8.7 Archetypes and complex formation, or: the lost shadows

The project of understanding economics through archetypes has been embarked upon by Integral Economics (Gerber and Steppacher, 2014, 2012; Arnsperger, 2010; Lietaer, 2005). The goal is to integrate the psychology and 'inner life' of economists into economic analysis. Archetypes are, according to the psychologist Carl Gustav Jung, the primary source of psychic energy and the psychic symbols that bind and structure this energy (Stein, 2010). Archetypes are the symbolic representations of biological instincts and belong to the spiritual rather than the biological realm. An understanding of archetypical dynamics can yield important insights into religion (including cultural myths, such as neoclassical economics) and prevent destructive consequences for human beings whose consciousness is under the control of an archetype.

> [An archetype] mobilizes philosophical and religious convictions in the very people who deemed themselves miles above any such fits of weakness. Often it drives with unexampled passion and remorseless logic towards its goal and draws the subject under its spell from which despite the most desperate resistance he is unable, and finally no longer even willing, to break free, because the experience brings with it a depth and fullness of meaning that was unthinkable before. (Jung, in Stein, 2010: 99- 100)

Pictures, symbols and ideas can through archetypes give human beings the feeling of a sense of life and the importance of their actions, thereby generating motivations and values. When in the grip of an archetype human conscience can be virtually possessed by an idea. Jung therefore describes archetypes as *spiritus rector* of the intellect, which is then being used to justify and rationalize the archetypical idea. In this case it is not the intellect but the archetype that provides the motivation for the justification of the idea. Archetypes give form and meaning to instincts and help human beings to achieve spiritual aims. They manifest themselves in ideas and dreams and it is the duty of human beings to deal with this material ethically (Stein, 2010).

In his account of the 2008 financial crisis, Peukert outlines how a Jungian archetypical psychology of neoclassical economics' ideas can become a research program for the analysis of the emotional meaning and the long-term spiritual transcendence of its 'political-financial-scientific complex' (Peukert, 2013; Berger, 2011). According to this view, the latter fails to integrate the archetypes of the ruler, the warrior and the magician. This failure shows in the actualization of a complex taking the form of the tyrant, the sadist and the hyper-rational. For example, on a linguistic level neoclassical economics is associated with terminology, such as 'rigorous,' 'hard,' 'parsimonious,' and 'discipline' that has been deemed sadistic (McCloskey, 2001), considering that the synonyms for 'rigorous' are 'austere, strict, stringent, inflexibile, severe, stern, harsh, hard, rigid, heavy-handed, ramrod, tough' (Merriam-Webster Dictionary, 2015). The human beings subjected to the power of this complex exhibit the largely unconscious behavior (shadows) of the weakling and the masochist, and arbitrary behavior. This shadow is then projected onto others, such as heterodox economists, to avoid cognitive dissonance. Archetypal psychology views the failure to effectively deal with cognitive dissonance as the root cause of the development of the ego's shadow complex (Stein, 2010: 106). As evidenced by Marglin's and Weisskopf's accounts above, neoclassical economists exhibit the seemingly contradictory combination of normality ('you are rational and well-behaved the way the economics profession and society want you to be') and exceptionalism (the algorithmic hero fighting experiential authority, the feminine etc.). Drewermann detected this contradiction in his psychograph of catholic priests and interpreted it as a turbulence that emerges when the Self is experienced as a void. The feeling of worth is derived from the 'specialness' of the hero while the right to existence is derived from one's 'normality' (Drewermann, 1989).

According to Peukert, the archetypes of the Great Mother and the lover are being completely suppressed by the neoclassical complex, so that its shadows become widely spread, namely addiction (work, drugs, sex) and insatiability, as, for example, the main behavioral assumption of Homo Oeconomicus confirms. The Great Mother is a dominant theme in the Jungian literature (see, for example, Neuman, 1989; Hauke, 2000; Walker, 2002; Hillman, 2005). It views the suppression of this archetype as creating a collective shadow that is rooted in the prohibition against the maternal body and repressed femininity, both of which lead to an impaired ability to promote life. The reasons are seen to be a feeling of inferiority vis-à-vis the creative feminine and the separation from the mother, similar to Freud's Oedipal incest prohibition (Hauke, 2000). Hillman argues that notable Western hero archetypes, such as Faust, are responsible for this development. It is primarily the problematic relationship with their mothers that leads them into the disintegration of good and evil, and antagonism towards their fathers, that is, the disintegrated *senex-puer* archetype (Hillmann, 2005). In this interpretation the Faustian bargain with the devil represents archetypally the disintegrated shadow complex (Binswanger, 2011; Stein, 2010: 108-10). The latter contributes to the killing of Philemon and Baucis, representing the elimination of a way of life in harmony with nature, which Faust's industrial and paper money-driven economy cannot replace (Binswanger, 1994). Peukert argues that heterodox economics with its sensitive-hermeneutic method and open system approach is the needed reintegration of the suppressed archetypes of the lover and the Great Mother (Peukert, 2013). This conforms to archetypal psychology, which views Sophia (wisdom) as feminine maternal wisdom that is not abstract disintegrated knowledge, but wisdom of loving participation (Walker, 2002).

8.8 'Max U.': a phallocentric hero without soul and full natural body

Archetypal analysis assigns a key role to hero archetypes (Hillman, 2005). Similarly, Otto Rank's work *Beyond Psychology* (Rank, 1941) develops a psychology of unconsciously introjected hero imagos that drive theory formation via a soul that is conceived of as a 'creative double' (Rank 1962). Rank refers to Marx's proletariat as a hero imago while Klamer's 'Max U.' aka Homo Oeconomicus can be considered as the hero imago of neoclassical economists (Klamer, 2001). Ruccio and Amariglio (2001) point out the importance of Homo Oeconomicus which is the last bastion of defense that neoclassical economists resort to when they are pushed to defend the integrity and unity of their work. Neoclassical economists take on the attributes of this hero imago, which Klamer simply describes as their 'favorite character' or a 'metaphor.' That is, the problem-solving and soulless Max U. empties the economic subject (including economists themselves) of any and every form of moral character. According to Klamer, Max U. is a silent character, not preoccupied with his ends, which are given to him. He knows everything and only assesses constraints and benefits of the best alternative. In other words, he is reducible to a constrained maximization problem. Life is turned away from natural forms and becomes more abstract as Max U. operates in an abstract system of stylized forms. In fact, Max U. is without qualities that would make a subject human. He has no history, is devoid of moral sentiment, knows no tradition, is oblivious of the uncertainties and insecurities that plague everybody who has to make a real choice. Max U. is an absent subject in a formal structure that has meanings only because of its formal properties and he cannot tell humans how to get through life or how to live. He is a dead subject because he is left without real choices, and without meaningful subjectivity.

Klamer is convinced that the resilience of Max U. rests on the conviction of the community of its creators who find meaning in the exercises that Max U. makes possible. Part of this meaning is derived from the fact that Max U. allows sustaining the meta-narrative of enlightenment and gives its manipulators a sense of control. Furthermore, it enables the application of analytical skills, that is, to set up problems, work out the algorithm, and find a solution (Klamer, 2001: 93). According to Klamer, Max U. turns economists into a new breed of technocrats who are intrigued by the intricacies of a fully articulated system in the same manner as a computer analyst is intrigued by the possibilities of a new computer (compare also Mirowski (2002) on neoclassical economics as a cyborg science). Led by their hero imago neoclassical economists desire to speak in purely technical language which requires only precision and mathematical operations (ibid.: 98). Indeed, it is possible to view Max U. as the younger brother of Robinson Crusoe, who has been the hero archetype of liberal political economy since its beginning. Already Karl Marx had critiqued the 'Robinsonites' for misconstruing Defoe's protagonist as a-historic and a-social (Whyte, 2014). It seems that Klamer's prediction is correct that the impressive mathematical apparatus of neoclassical economics will be rendered meaningless the day that the hero archetype of Max U. no longer captures the neoclassical psyche and imagination. However, Klamer does not address the possibility that Max U. might be outlived by his older and more resilient brother Robinson Crusoe. Klamer's remedy is a return to a prudent hero archetype, which he traces back to the work of Adam Smith. The prudent hero is frank and open, capable of friendship, humble modesty and equitable justice, while being correct and exquisitely beautiful in its outline.

Feminist economists have argued for some time that there is a kind of phallocentrism at work in the predominantly male neoclassical economics profession (Nelson, 2001). In fact, Homo Oeconomicus is disembodied and possesses no sexed identity (Hewitson, 2001: 228). Neoclassical economists redefine the womb as capital, such that the mother as a sexed body disappears in a one sex-model. This is a phallocentric construction, in which fetus and mother are awarded male subject positions as self-possessive individuals who enter womb contracts. The uterus as rental space mitigates the threat of integrating mothers and the specificity of the female body into economic knowledge culture. This allows the idea of purely male procreation and eliminates the mother, which has been the myth of many phallocentric cultures of the past. This myth disavows the problem of sexual difference and maintains the myth of Homo Oeconomicus as a 'universal individual.' This permits extension of neoclassical discourse into the realm of nature (Hewitson, 2001). It has further been noticed (Amariglio and Ruccio 2001: 147) that it is the absence of a full natural body that makes bodily reproduction and the laboring body disappear from economic inquiry. In this view, neoclassical economics is based on a flat body without depth. Everything that is done resides on the surface, in the form of corporeal images that are functions of bodily orders, such as consumption and investment. In this sense there are multiple Selfs that are fragmented into different orders, yielding a dispersed and fragmented map of the body.

8.9 Cognitive dissonance, cognitive capture, and double truth, or: losing history, wisdom and the care for the self

As we have seen above, it is the inability to deal with cognitive dissonance that causes the disintegration and suppression of archetypes, the rationalization of contradictory behavior, the ingestion of cultural myths via hero images, and the formation of unconscious shadow complexes that accumulate the 'lost' psychic content. Mirowski applies cognitive dissonance theory to understand neoclassical economists as a community of religious believers in Homo Oeconomicus (Mirowski, 2010, 2013). Cognitive dissonance theory was developed in the context of research into the behavior of a sect called 'The Seekers.' When faced with proof that their predictions failed to come to pass, Seekers maintained their belief by formulating ad hoc supporting hypotheses that are not individually falsifiable. The main reaction of economists to the challenge of their post-2008 critics was to defend the Homo Oeconomicus model while at the same time proposing behavioral economics as an improvement. The problem is that behavioral economics explicitly does not aim at changing the Homo Oeconomicus model, thus declaring the incommensurable A and non-A to be true at the same time, a kind of 'conceptual schizophrenia.' This approach provides the superficial feeling of change without a true change of model or mind. It avoids dealing with cognitive dissonance, maintaining Homo

Oeconomicus as a kind of icon at all costs and against all odds. Another problem is that behavioral economics boils down to the sadism of blaming the losers for their own plight (Mirowski, 2013: 18).

According to Mirowski the model of Homo Oeconomicus is also at the core of the neoclassical theory of scientific knowledge, which treats knowledge as a commodity for the sake of market governance (Mirowski, 2011). This makes for a 'treacherous quicksand' of reflexivity full of 'double truths' that lead to 'near Freudian slips' (Mirowski, 2011: 43-4). The double truth is that an economist assumes 'God-like abilities' in that

> she arrogates to herself a constitutional capacity that she denies to her little agent offspring: the ability to survey the rules and institutions of the model, to critically engage in self-reflexivity […] [Economists] pretend to glare down on the world from Mount Olympus […]. (Mirowski 2011: 335)

Yet, neoclassical economics derived its own scientific model selectively from nineteenth-century energetics (Mirowski, 2011, 1989) while ignoring other models of science. Thus, the neoclassical self-image of a superior and independent system of knowledge clearly constitutes a double truth. The double truth seems to rear its ugly head also in the fact that its physics envy did not make neoclassical economics more scientific as is evidenced by the fact that it does not practice falsification and does not have the courage to revise its knowledge like physicists. Avoiding cognitive dissonance and adopting double truths work in tandem with cognitive capture via private sector liaisons with the 'bankster-regulator-industry complex,' which itself practices a ritual of denial, secrecy and non-democracy (Mirowski, 2013).

Homo Oeconomicus is at the root of this self-image that loses sight of the less glorious truth concerning the historical development of its own model. As a consequence of double truth, the teaching of neoclassical economics is a kind of 'brain-washing' and attack by the 'walking dead' (Zombie ideas) who hold culture in thrall (Mirowski, 2013: 18). An archetypal interpretation based on ancient Greek mythology provides the image of students who are unaware that their fate is the same as that of Metis (wisdom) who was devoured by Zeus (Mirowski, 2013: 28). Due to their alignment with neoliberal epistemology neoclassical economists have lost sight of the fact that science serves higher purposes than money, that knowledge is about care for the Self, that it is possible to speak truth to power, and that false consciousness is real in the sense that people can be and are being manipulated against their best interest (Mirowski, 2013: 76). The moral quest to discover one's own and only 'true Self' is, according to Mirowski, not part of the fragmented Homo Oeconomicus. The latter lives in the double truth of having such a plastic Self that it is never an obstacle to transforming itself into whatever the market wants while at the same time professing the belief that the market gives them what they want. The fragmented personality and vanishing Self has difficulty saying who is at the helm of the agency in a culture that is obsessed with reconfiguration and dismemberment of the soul. Mirowski identifies the gambler as the new hero image in neoclassical economics contributing to a Self-image of the dare devil. Mirowski argues that neoclassical economics primarily functions as a facade (in particular its principle texts project a face of the discipline to the world) for the vacuum at the core of a fragmented economic science, which is made up of a 'pointless succession of fashions' (Mirowski, 2013: 25). His remedy is to expose double truths and to muster the courage to expose oneself to cognitive dissonance, which is a kind of (Nietzschean) strong methodology (Mirowski, 1994).

8.10 Psychology of neoclassical economists as priests

All of the above authors highlight the psychological issues involved in neoclassical economics understood as myth or religion. Hans-Christoph Binswanger interprets in greater detail this aspect of neoclassical economists as a religious community, emphasizing the role of the 'psychological weight' of the belief in Homo Oeconomicus and Smith's invisible hand. Binswanger traces these concepts back to the habits of thought of the Stoa, which had quasi-religious status and was the main ideological rival of Christianity for hundreds of years during the Roman Empire. The key idea is that the Good arrives unintentionally by the pursuit of vices. According to Binswanger, it is this quasi-religious character of neoclassical economics' habits of thought that allowed it to become a substitute for the Christian religion of the feudal era (Binswanger, 2011). In this context it is noteworthy that Giorgio Agamben's archeology of 'oikonomia' – while recognizing Smith's own account of its Stoic sources – traces the concept of the invisible hand to its biblical origin and the 'mystery of the economy' in Christian theology (Agamben, 2011: 283).

McCloskey (2001) identifies another religion with which neoclassical economists made a pact, that is, the 'religion of modernism' that represses traditions such as rhetoric and hermeneutics, inspired by the fear of ambiguity, polysemy, obscurity, mythopoeic allusion, and primitivism. The modernist elements of neoclassical economics are responsible for the self-image of a triumphant avant-guard that has defeated tradition, shook off history, transcended time and space, believes in future more than in the past or present, destroys the past, arrives at the abstract, divorces form from content, believes that form will do the job as if by machinery, and that ornament, culture, and history are mere error terms. Modernism aspires to transcendent and ineffable truth and believes in the tyranny of the lonely genius who seeks a system to impose upon us all. Modernism seeks 'crushing proof,' 'compelling demonstration,' that which cannot be doubted, by putting nature to the rack. It seeks conviction which serves to defeat others. Modernism is elitist, exclusive, regulated by lordly experts rather than common sense, distrustful of sense perception with a preference for technicality. Obscurity keeps it in the hands of trained elites. At the same time, the above characteristics of modernist neoclassical economics are, according to McCloskey, just another version of Platonism that seeks to get to the bedrock of certainty. Plato's separation of belief (mere things heard, common opinion) from transcendent truth is here viewed as responsible for the coercive religion of modernism, the worship of experts, and the coercion to obey the guardians and experts. Transcendent truth diverts effort from the search for terrestrial truth. As modernists, neoclassical economists have problems seeing that their view is a view, as well as knowing other truly contending views, and evaluating the differences to generate wisdom (for this paragraph see McCloskey, 2001).

Considering that several of the above accounts liken neoclassical economists to priests or believers it seems fitting to refer to the relevant insights of Eugen Drewermann's psychograph of catholic priests (1989). The latter is deemed a 'phenomenology of extreme ontological uncertainty' as catholic priests do not live from within the person but predominantly from the predetermined organizational structure of the institution. Drewermann asks the question how somebody can get to the point to not want to live from within one's true Self but according to some generally prescribed ideal, 'willing to play the game' of somebody else? How does the wish emerge to delegate ones existence fully into an officially mandated character mask instead of becoming oneself? How is it possible that the internalized forms of coercion and external guidance are declared the essential truths of one's own life? The answer, according to Drewermann, is that the confirmation by others eliminates the experience of a permanent feeling of doubt towards one's own being. Office and power are absolutely needed in order to be able to live and institutionalized power justifies their existence. The fear of social exclusion leads to the identification with the expectation of others which promises great rewards. The over-fulfillment of group norms out of fear of rejection becomes a way of conspicuous behavior to intimidate others. This resembles a kind of flight into generalities that represses entire regions of the psyche, the abyss of which creates anxiety and disgust with oneself. Generalities are declared as personal such that the personal becomes general, which results in a kind of non-existence of one's identity, that is, a dishonesty or lie. Those who have lost touch with their true Self take control of the Self of others in order to hide their own loss of Self. The corset of borrowed importance saves them from falling apart. Personal risks of inner faces and dreams are avoided and instead official confirmation is sought as the truth of the Self, its guarantor for the entire value of the Self. This reflects a flight from being a person. If society produces people who sense insecurity in the deep roots of their existence, then the corset of an office is the last remaining support. The path into becoming a fully accepted member of the group becomes meaningful because it avoids the pain and the fear of the Self, and the fear of others. Everything that seemed small, unimpressive, repressed and shy in one's undeveloped person now proves to be a higher calling, an expectation of love, recognition, respect, esteem. All ridicule, fears, and longings and never acknowledged expectations now receive a goal in becoming a darling of the group. Those who reject them are now the hoi polloi, disbelievers, and enemies of the cognoscenti. But, a belief as a means to repress fear begins to produce fear itself due to ontological uncertainty, such that regimentation, supervision and control become necessary. The destructiveness of religious institutions furthers the depersonalization of its recruits who try to obtain official status to escape the dilemma of personal non-existence. This results in a governance of a suppressed and fragmented Self (for this entire section compare Drewermann, 1989).

8.11 Persecuting blasphemers and losing openness

The religious character of economics is indeed viewed as the leading cause of the suppression of all the dissenting schools of thought in economics in the twentieth century. Lee (2009) draws an analogy between the elimination of heterodox economists and the death penalty imposed on blasphemers. This view is supported by anecdotal evidence from young heterodox economists on the tenure track. If they want to question neoclassical truths in the classroom by assigning appropriate teaching materials they are told that getting tenure means they need to 'lay low' for five years and that only thereafter can they perhaps start to speak their mind. They are also admonished that what they want to teach 'is not of concern to the students.' They are instructed that now it is their 'turn to suffer' and 'to do as they are being told' because their senior colleagues also had to suffer through teaching this material. Perversely, those who insist most religiously on the teaching of neoclassical economics do not want to teach this material themselves, such that courses in principles of neoclassical microeconomics get shoved around like rotten eggs to the person with least power. Lists of approved neoclassical economics textbooks are circulated and heterodox economics texts censored in obscure 'approval' processes without any kind of coherent, substantive or convincing rationale. To their dismay young heterodox economists are told that the content of their favored heterodox economics textbook 'is not economics.' They are even temporarily prohibited from teaching by their academic Dean until their syllabus mirrors exactly the table of content of leading neoclassical economics textbooks. Purely neoclassical entry and exit tests are instituted to assess student 'progress,' but in reality serve to control content and to make sure that students get thoroughly brainwashed.

Dow specifies Lee's 'blasphemy thesis' in the sense that she views heterodox thoughts as those that are being suppressed by neoclassical economists. Dow describes various communication strategies but views the potential for genuine dialogue pessimistically due to the extreme intolerance exercises by neoclassical economists. Her conclusion is that the development of heterodox economics will take place outside of economics departments (Dow, 2011). She also considers it alarming how unaware and unreflective neoclassical economists are (Dow, 1997). Some authors view the religious war of neoclassical economists against their 'other' as simply pragmatic in the sense that mainstream views are those represented at the leading universities and journals that receive most funding, and are willing to 'play the game' (Colander, 2009). Yet, Lee and Dow identify differences in ontology, methodology, and theory. They share Lawson's thesis that the ontology of the open system, which is non-dualist (order and chaos, fuzzy mathematics) is also the core of pluralist heterodox economics as opposed to the closed system view of neoclassical economics (Dow, 2011: 71). This resonates with Peukert's view that suggests that heterodox economics' sensitive hermeneutic method is the essence of the open system approach, which is the archetype of the lover that helps to integrate disintegrated archetypes. In this sense, an open system approach that still awaits full actualization in economics is the suppressed 'other' of neoclassical economics. This suppression may be the reason for Mearman's psychological findings that heterodox economists adopt a contrarian and controversialist position (forced to by neoclassical economists?), while considering themselves to be more open and tolerant than the mainstream (Mearman, 2012: 418).

8.12 Conclusion

The preceding investigation demonstrates the fruitfulness of a psychological understanding of neoclassical modes of thought. A number of psychological phenomena were identified, such as double truths, inability to deal with cognitive dissonance, cognitive capture, fear of social exclusion, rationalization, projection, repression, introjection of hero imagos, disintegrated archetypes, complexes and shadows, fragmentation of Self and bodily functions. The diagnosis is that neoclassical habits of thought are induced by the fear of ontological uncertainty and social exclusion from the economics profession, as well as the subjugation to cognitive capture and the inability to deal with cognitive dissonance. What is 'lost' from these habits of thought is externalized or socialized and shows up in the form of social damages emanating from the economic system designed by neoclassical economists. The lost content is also repressed and creates a shadow complex that is personified by heterodox economists. This latter group exhibits more 'openness' towards experiential knowledge and a greater range of ways of interpreting and communicating this knowledge. This is why heterodox economists claim to be integrating the archetypes of the Great Mother and the lover, which are suppressed by neoclassical economics' modes of thought. These characteristics turn heterodox economists into a 'hook' for a mix of psychological projections that result in scapegoating, bullying, and visceral persecution: (1) an object of fear due to the feared content in the unconscious shadow complex; (2) a cause of cognitive dissonance and ontological uncertainty that is avoided at all costs; (3) a threat to cultural norms and powerful institutions that are considered sacrosanct; and (4) the evocation of emotions related to experiences of father and mother figures that are too painful to face. Due to the entangled relationship between heterodox and neoclassical economists this inquiry also points out the need for a more detailed psychology of the modes of thought of heterodox economics that should address amongst others its 'contrarian attitude' (introjected hero archetypes: Spartacus, proletariat?), potentially disintegrated or suppressed archetypes (lover, Great Mother, *senex-puer*), the limits to and its relation with closure, its integration of experiential and algorithmic knowledge, its failure at creative imagination that has locked it into the losing shadow position, and what Amariglio and Ruccio (2001) have identified as its narrative of the 'expulsion from the Garden of Eden.' One of the benefits of psychological treatments is that here, as Mearman rightly observes, it can highlight contradictions (why are some self-classified heterodox economists less open than even neoclassical economists?) and avoids static or dualist categorizations (Mearman, 2012).

Thus the inquiry demonstrates the fruitfulness of a hermeneutic approach to understanding modes of thought, that is, archetypal psychology. Its roots in neoplatonism allow archetypal psychology to adopt the therapeutic methods of fictionalizing, mythologizing, and pathologizing experienced images (Moore 1989; Hillmann, 1994, 2005). This brand of archetypal psychology is also referred to as 'post-Jungian' so that it is not surprising to find parallels with 'postmodern' Jungian psychotherapy (see Hauke, 2000, for the following goals of therapy). The psychological inquiry is therapeutic because it deflates the artificially inflated neoclassical habits of thought. The latter are understood as part of a complex that needs to be better integrated with other parts of the psyche. Exploring and understanding the neoclassical complex is like caring for a wound that is at the same time the eye, that is the precondition for understanding anything at all about life and to affirm it in its infliction. This is an opportunity for consciousness to celebrate itself and to free especially young economists from being absorbed into the 'mass-economist' of unconscious collective projections. As such it is also a revolt against a false religion and the dictatorship of faith that is not backed experientially. Raising consciousness through therapy retrieves lost elements of humanity through lost and abandoned experiential knowledge. Because ideas are corporeal, staying safely in a fixed established position would be equivalent to psychosomatic emphysema and thus undesirable (for the material basis of mind see also Hermann-Pilath, 2013).

Archetypal psychology views the mind as having a poetic basis and therefore finds itself in agreement with the hermeneutics of Charles S. Peirce, that is, the philosophical foundations of institutional economics (Mirowski, 2014). It also provides a basis for a 'poetic economics' that is truly therapeutic (Berger, 2015b). The goal of such a therapeutic poetic economics is 'soul making' via reinstating experiential knowledge, openness towards 'the other,' the fostering of creativity, aesthetics, and ethics, the care for the Self, and the nurturing of human wisdom. The goal is not relativism or nihilism. It shares some of the aspirations of 'storytelling' in economics, that is, the attainment of higher levels of self-awareness, peace and toleration via 'deliteralizing' (McCloskey, 2014). It is also capable of incorporating the psychological phenomena of double truths, cognitive dissonance, conceptual schizophrenia, and cognitive capture (Mirowski, 2013) by looking at disintegrated and suppressed archetypes, complexes and shadow formation. And, it permits an understanding of neoclassical economists as protagonists of a drama, in which the economic system of their making produces increasing levels of social damages (see Binswanger, 2011, for this interpretation based on Goethe's Faust and Mirowski, 2013, for the interpretation of the current economic crisis as 'a set of avoidable tragedies'). The main insight for economic policy is that increasing levels of social damages can only be prevented if economists engage in therapeutic self-reflection.

References

Agamben, Giorgio (2011). *The Kingdom and the Glory – For a Theological Genealogy of Economy and Government.* Stanford (CA): Stanford University Press.

Amariglio, Jack and Ruccio, David (2001) 'From unity to dispersion: the body in modern economic discourse,' in Stephen Cullenberg, Jack Amariglio, and David F. Ruccio (eds), *Postmodernism, Economics and Knowledge.* London and New York: Routledge.

Arnsperger, Christian (2010) *Full Spectrum Economics: Towards an Inclusive and Emancipatory Social Science.* London and New York: Routledge.

Berger, Sebastian (ed.) (2009). *The Foundations of Non-Equilibrium Economics: The Principle of Circular and Cumulative Causation.* London: Routledge.

Berger, Sebastian (2011) 'Bookreview – Die große Finanzmarktkrise.' *Journal of Economic Issues*, 45 (4): 1027-9.

Berger, Sebastian (ed.) (2015a) 'Introduction,' in *The Heterodox Theory of Social Costs – by K. William Kapp.* London and New York: Routledge.

Berger, Sebastian (2015b) 'Poetic Economics and Experiential Knowledge: How the Economist K. William Kapp was inspired by the Poet Ernst Wiechert,' in *Journal of Economic Issues*, 49 (3): 730-48.

Berger, Sebastian and Elsner, Wolfram (2009) 'European contributions to evolutionary institutional economics: the cases 'open systems approach' (OSA) and 'cumulative circular causation' (CCC),' in Wolfram Elsner and Hardi Hanappi (eds), *Advances in Evolutionary Economics: Evolutionary Models, Non-Knowledge, and Strategy.* Cheltenham: Edward Elgar.

Bernstein, Richard (1983) *Beyond Objectivism and Relativism – Science, Hermeneutics, and Praxis.* Philadelphia: University of Pennsylvania Press.

Binswanger, Hans Christoph (1994) *Money and Magic – A Critique of the Modern Economy in the Light of Faust.* Chicago: Chicago University Press.

Binswanger, Hans Christoph (2011) *Die Glaubensgemeinschaft der Ökonomen – Essays zur Kultur der Wirtschaft.* Hamburg: Murmann Verlag.

Boulding, Kenneth (2013) 'Towards the development of a cultural economics,' in *Interdisciplinary Economics – Kenneth E. Boulding's Engagement in the Sciences.* London and New York: Routledge.

Colander, David (2009) 'Moving beyond the rhetoric of pluralism: suggestions for an 'inside the mainstream' heterodoxy,' in Robert Garnett, Erik Olsen and Martha Starr (eds), *Economic Pluralism.* London: Routledge, pp. 36-47.

Cullenberg, Stephen, Amariglio, Jack and Ruccio, David F. (eds) (2001). *Postmodernism, Economics and Knowledge.* London and New York: Routledge.

Davis, John B. (2010) 'Bookreview,' *Journal of Cultural Economics,* 34: 237-40.

Dewey, John (1960) *The Quest for Certainty.* New York: Capricorn Books.

Dow, Sheila C. (1997). 'Mainstream Economic Methodology,' *Cambridge Journal of Economics,* 21: 73-93.

Dow, Sheila C. (2011) 'Heterodox economics, history and prospects [review article],' *Cambridge Journal of Economics,* 5 (6): 1151-65

Drewermann, Eugen (1989). *Die Kleriker – Psychogramm eines Ideals.* Olten: Walter-Verlag AG.

Elsner, Wolfram (1986). *Economic Institutions Analysis – The Paradigmatic Development of Economics and the Relevance of a Recourse to the Economic Classics* [German: *Ökonomische Institutionenanalyse*]. Berlin: Duncker & Humblot.

Georgescu-Roegen, Nicholas (1979) 'Methods in economic science,' *Journal of Economic Issues,* 13 (2): 317-28.

Gerber, Julien-François and Steppacher, Rolf (eds) (2012) *Towards an Integrated Paradigm in Heterodox Economics – Alternative Approaches to the Current Eco-Social Crisis.* New York: Palgrave-Macmillan.

Gerber, Julien-François and Steppacher, Rolf (2014). 'Some fundamentals of integral economics,' *World Futures,* 70: 442-63.

Hands, Wade (1994). 'The sociology of scientific knowledge: some thoughts on the possibilities,' in Robert E. Backhouse (ed.), *New Directions in Economic Methodology.* London and New York: Routledge.

Hartman, L. M. (1977) 'Economics as science and as culture,' *American Journal of Agricultural Economics,* 59 (5): 925-30.

Hauke, Christopher (2000) *Jung and the Postmodern: The Interpretation of Realities.* London and New York: Routledge.

Hermann-Pillath, Carsten (2013) *Foundations of Economic Evolution – A Treatise on the Natural Philosophy of Economics.* Cheltenham and Northampton: Edward Elgar.

Hewitson, Gillian (2001) 'The disavowal of the sexed body in neoclassical economics,' in Stephen Cullenberg, Jack Amariglio, and David F. Ruccio (eds), *Postmodernism, Economics and Knowledge.* London and New York: Routledge.

Hilman, James (1994) *Healing Fiction: On Freud, Jung, Adler.* Thompson, CT: Spring Publications.

Hilman, James (2005) *Senex and Puer.* Putnam, CT: Spring Publications.

Jackson, William A. (2009) *Economics, Culture, and Social Theory*, Cheltenham: Edward Elgar.
Kapp, K. William (1950) *The Social Costs of Private Enterprise*. Cambridge (MA): Harvard University Press.
Kapp, K. William (1961) *Towards a Science of Man in Society – A Positive Approach to the Integration of Social Knowledge*. The Hague: Martin Nijhouse.
Kapp, K. William (1976) 'Economics in the future: the open system character of the economy and its implications,' in Kurt Dopfer (ed.) *Economics in the Future: Towards a New Paradigm*. London: MacMillan.
Kapp, K. William (1985) 'The humanization of the social sciences,' eds John E. Ullmann and Roy Preiswerk. Lanhman, MD, New York, and London: University of America Press.
Kapp, K. William (2011) *The Foundations of Institutional Economics*, eds Sebastian Berger and Rolf Steppacher. London and New York: Routledge.
Kapp, K. William (2015). *The Heterodox Theory of Social Costs*, ed. Sebastian Berger. London and New York: Routledge.
Keynes, John Maynard (1936) *The General Theory of Employment, Interest and Money*. London: Macmillan.
Klamer, Arjo (1996) *The Value of Culture: On the Relationship between Economics and Arts*. Amsterdam: Amsterdam University Press.
Lee, Frederic S. (2009) *A History of Heterodox Economics: Challenging the mainstream in the 20th Century*. London and New York: Routledge.
Lietaer, Bernard (2005) *An Integral View on Money and Financial Crashes*. Accessed online 2 February 2016 at http://www.lietaer.com/images/Integral_Money.pdf.
McCloskey, Deidre (2001) 'The genealogy of postmodernism: an economist's guide,' in Stephen Cullenberg, Jack Amariglio and David F. Ruccio (eds) *Postmodernism, Economics, and Knowledge*. London and New York: Routledge.
McCloskey, Donald N. (2014) 'Storytelling in economics,' in Don Lavoie (ed.) *Economics and Hermeneutics*. London and New York: Routledge.
Mäki, Uskali (1994) 'Reorienting the assumptions issue,' in Robert E. Backhouse (ed.) *New Directions in Economic Methodology*. London and New York: Routledge.
Marglin, Stephen A. (2008) *The Dismal Science – How Thinking Like an Economist Undermines Community*, Cambridge, MA: Harvard University Press.
Marglin, Stephen A. (2009) 'The culture of economics,' *Development*, 52 (3): 292-7.
Mearman, Andrew (2012) 'Heterodox economics and the problem of classification,' *Journal of Economic Methodology*, 19 (4): 407-24.
Merriam-Webster Dictionary (2015) online at: http://www.merriam-webster.com/dictionary/rigorous (accessed 15 October 2015)
Mirowski, Philip (1989) *More Heat than Light – Economics as Social Physics, Physics as Nature's Economics*. Cambridge: Cambridge University Press
Mirowski, Philip (1994) 'What are the questions?,' in Robert E. Backhouse (ed.) *New Directions in Economic Methodology*. London and New York: Routledge.
Mirowski, Philip (2002) *Machine Dreams – Economics becomes a Cyborg Science*.

Cambridge: Cambridge University Press.
Mirowski, Philip (2010) 'The great mortification: economists' responses to the crisis of 2007 – and counting,' *The Hedgehog Review*, 12 (3).
Mirowski, Philip (2011) *Science Mart – The Privatization of American Science*. Cambridge, MA: Harvard University Press.
Mirowski, Philip (2013) *Never Let a Serious Crisis go to Waste – How Neoliberalism Survived the Financial Meltdown*. London and New York: Verso.
Mirowski, Philip (2014) 'The philosophical foundations of institutional economics,' in Don Lavoie (ed.), *Economics and Hermeneutics*. Routledge: London and New York.
Moore, Thomas (1989) *The Essential James Hillmann – A Blue Fire*. London and New York: Routledge.
Nelson, Julie A. (2001) 'Feminist economics: objective, activist, and postmodern?,' in Stephen Cullenberg, Jack Amariglio and David F. Ruccio (eds), *Postmodernism, Economics and Knowledge*. London and New York: Routledge.
Neumann, Erich (1989) *Die Grosse Mutter – Eine Phänomenologie der Weiblichen Gestaltungen des Unbewussten*. Olten und Freiburg: Walter Verlag.
Peukert, Helge (2013) *Die große Finanzmarkt- und Staatsschuldenkrise – Eine kritisch-heterodoxe Untersuchung*, 5th edn. Marburg: Metropolis.
Rank, Otto (1941) *Beyond Psychology*. Philadelphia: E Hauser.
Rank, Otto (1962) *Art and Artist*. New York and London: W.W. Norton Company.
Stein, Murray (2010) *Jung's Map of the Soul – An Introduction*. Peru, IL: Open Court Publishing.
Steinmetz, George (ed.) (2005) *The Politics of Method in the Human Sciences: Positivism and Its Epistemological Others*. Durham, NC: Duke University Press.
Thornborow, Thomas and Brown, Andrew D. (2009) "Being regimented': aspiration, discipline and identity in the British Parachute Regiment,' *Organization Studies*, 30 (4): 355-76.
Throsby, David (2001) *Economics and Culture*. New York: Cambridge University Press.
Unpublished manuscript: Kapp-Weisskopf Correspondance. Kapp Archive, University of Basel, Switzerland.
Valentinov, Vladislav (2013) 'K. William Kapp's theory of social costs: a Luhmannian interpretation,' *Ecological Economics*, 97: 28-33.
Veblen, Thorstein (1919) *The Place of Science in Modern Civilization and other Essays by Thorstein Veblen*. New York: B.W. Huebsch.
Veblen, Thorstein (1925) 'Economics in the calculable future,' *American Economic Review*, 15, (1): 48-55.
Walker, Steven (2002) *Jung and the Jungian's on Myth*. London and New York: Routledge.
Weisskopf, Walter A. (1949) 'Psychological aspects of economic thought,' *Journal of Political Economy*, 57 (4): 304-14.

Weisskopf, Walter A. (1955). *The Psychology of Economics.* Chicago: University of Chicago Press.

Whyte, Jessica (2014) 'The Fortunes of natural man: Robinson Crusoe, political economy, and the Universal Declaration of Human Rights,' *Humanity: An International Journal of Human Rights, Humanitarianism, and Development,* 5 (3): 301-21.

9
Social Costs, Open Systems, and Circular Cumulative Causation

9.1 Circular Cumulative Causation (CCC)

There is widespread understanding among evolutionary institutional economists that the CCC was directly derived from *Veblen's* concept of '*cumulative change*' (e.g., Argyrous and Sethi 1996, 485) and that the two are more or less identical (e.g., Mayhew 2001, 243). In fact, approaches dealing with 'cumulative' effects were common in England, Germany and Sweden in the 1920s. Suffice to mention the work of Adolph Lowe and the 'Kiel School' on the causes of the trade cycle (e.g., Forstater 2003 309ff.) as well as Knut Wicksell's work on inflation and Myrdal's work on the dynamics of savings and investment rates (e.g., Sandelin 1991, 186ff.). Myrdal formulated the fully developed CCC for the first time in Appendix 3 of his *American Dilemma – The Negro Problem and Modern Democracy* (1944) and used it as a research hypothesis to explain the circular (reinforcing) causation between prejudices, i.e., social norms and *institutions* in general, and poverty, triggering a *vicious circle* or 'cumulative effect.' The latter is manifest in increasing inequalities, instabilities and even a major crisis of the whole socioeconomic system. Myrdal derived the concept from his earlier models in *Monetary Equilibrium* (1939) and considered Wicksell a forerunner of the CCC (Myrdal 1944, 1065, fn. B; see also Wahid 2002, 85). The two distinct elements of the CCC are *circular* (reinforcing) causation and its *cumulative* effect. Myrdal gave a clear statement of circularity and cumulation in *Asian Drama – An Inquiry into the Poverty of Nations* (1968):

> [...] circular causation will give rise to a cumulative movement only when [...] a change in one of the conditions will ultimately be followed by a feed-back of secondary impulses [...] big enough not only to sustain the primary change, but to push it further. Mere mutual causation is not enough to create this process [...] (Myrdal 1968, 1875).

Elsewhere he had formulated:

> Because of such circular causation a social process tends to become cumulative and often to gather speed at an accelerating rate (Myrdal 1957, 13).

However, without delving into the details of Veblen's '*cumulative change*,' there appears to be some difference between Veblen's and Myrdal's understandings. Veblen's definition of cumulative change has been:

> For the purpose of economic science the process of cumulative change that is to be accounted for is the sequence of change in the methods of doing things – the methods of dealing with the material means of life (1898, 387).

Veblen used the conception to stress causal inquiry that is based on factual givens and historical processes:

> The economic life history of the individual is a cumulative process of adaptation of means to ends that cumulatively change as the process goes on [...] (1898, 391).

According to Veblen, the main characteristic of an evolutionary economist is that

> he insists on an answer in terms of cause and effect [...] the notion of cumulative causation (1898, 377).

Of course, Veblen was aware of the potential *reinforcing* nature of institutions in relation to non-institutional factors, and thus the frequently self-reinforcing nature of the whole socio-economic process. However, his concept of cumulation, *per se*, does not contain the idea of a self-reinforcing positive feedback and even states that there is 'no trend' in cumulative causation (Veblen 1907, 304). This might even be the reason why Myrdal did not explicitly mention Veblen's concept in this context in his 'Remarks upon Receipt of the Veblen-Commons Award' (Myrdal 1976, 215). Thus, Myrdal's CCC cannot simply be read as a theoretical module introduced and already used by Veblen. Recent studies have stressed the difference between the two understandings as well (see Bellets and Sosthe 2006; Angresano 1997, 85).

In fact, CCC is an empirically oriented heuristic, much more specific than Veblen's 'cumulative change,' to detect and specify critical processes, vicious circles and *cumulative crises* of socioeconomic systems. Myrdal's CCC appears to be the first scientific application of the ancient idea of a vicious circle to socioeconomic problems. *Positive feedback loops* apply the idea of the CCC in more formal system dynamics models (e.g., Richardson 1991, 77) so that an integration of the two should be based on the CCC rather than Veblen's concept. This said, it nevertheless appears completely consistent with Veblen's original 'research program' for a radical, critical, evolutionary-institutional 'political economy.'

9.2 Open System Approach (OSA)

The meaning of Georgescu-Roegen's and Kapp's contributions to OSA shall also be reconsidered against the background of recent contributions that parallel OSA with the open system ideas of philosophical Critical Realism and Ludwig v. Bertalanffy's 'General System Theory' (see Hodgson 1999, 145; Mearman 2002, 573), and against the understanding that Georgescu-Roegen's 'bioeconomics' is a metaphorical approach (Hodgson 2005, 133).

9.2.1 Thermodynamics and Openness at the More Complex Level of Human Society

The OSA was built upon the biological theory of open systems developed by Ludwig v. Bertalanffy and Erwin Schrödinger in the 1930s, and showed how living organisms are thermodynamic open systems. In Kapp's words:

> [Living organisms] are open systems which maintain themselves in a steady state due to an influx and efflux of nutrients and waste materials. [...] [They] use materials from their environment for the maintenance of orderly processes [...] It is these superimposed self-regulating mechanisms which tend to restore balance [...] and give the appearance of purpose and direction not found in the inanimate closed systems [...] (Kapp 1961, 93)

The complex formation of the life process (as an open system) thus seems to be compatible with the implications of the entropy law. Therefore, from a physical viewpoint, the economic process is an *entropic* transformation because it transforms low into high entropy, which is irrevocable waste (Georgescu-Roegen 1966, 97).

However, OSA also focuses on the social *institutions* that co-determine the speed of the entropic transformation process and of socioecological degradation (e.g., Georgescu- Roegen 1966, 96, 126) and thus involves an institutional analysis of the most complex level of organization, i.e., human society. The term 'open system,' as used in thermodynamics, is distinct from its application at higher levels of organization. To understand the 'openness' of the socioeconomic system, the socioeconomist has to analyze institutions in which the open economic system is 'embedded' and the institutional changes, which it elicits in the wider cultural and societal framework.

9.2.2 The 'Biocultural Concept of Man'

Individual openness has a long-standing humanistic tradition since Erasmus and Arnold Gehlen (see for example, Kapp 1961, 1967;

Steppacher, Zogg-Walz, and Hatzfeld 1977; Steppacher 1994). In this tradition, Kapp's 'biocultural concept of man' conceptualizes behavior through the enculturation process of a uniquely 'open' and 'unfinished' biological structure. The quasi-embryonic state results in an extreme dependence of the infant, and the completion of the biological process of maturation has to take place in interaction with a highly variable environment. Man is born endowed with a little differentiated system of drives and with a high degree of plasticity. Human basic needs of cooperation and communication are the outcome of the human experience of helplessness and isolation. These experiences call for assurance that can only be established in interpersonal relationships in which man is able to affirm his self-esteem. This *interaction* is a precondition for the development of man's potentialities and he depends on a process of *enculturation* to become a human being that is unconscious in early childhood. Hence, individuals become culturally conditioned and view reality through their acquired linguistic and symbolic systems (see for example, Kapp 1961, 155ff.).

9.2.3 The Non-Metaphorical Character of the OSA

Georgescu-Roegen and Kapp considered openness to establish a causal analysis, which *directly* takes physical and institutional chains into account (e.g., Kapp 1976). Thus, the OSA is not based on analogies or metaphors from natural sciences. The idea of openness was used to deal with discontinuous nonlinear feedbacks, which characterize the dynamic interdependencies between the different subsystems, as well as of each subsystem with the composite whole. This differs from an ontological understanding of 'open systems,' of Critical Realism for instance (e.g., Lawson 1994, 220-2), because the latter assumes a reality independent of observations and the possibility of the separation of theory and object. This inevitably leads to a purely formal understanding of an open system, as a thing in itself with a high level of abstraction that is not subject to further inquiry. In the pragmatist tradition of John Dewey, Kapp warns against this skepticism concerning the validity of sensory perceptions, and the trend toward greater abstraction (Kapp 1961, 195-7). Kapp cautions against the purely *formal* use of the term 'system' and advocates the *substantive* approach in the tradition of Max Weber and Karl Polanyi (Kapp 1961, 198-9).

> [F]or the formal concept of system acquires meaning and content only by making explicit the distinguishing characteristics of specific modes of association (Kapp 1961, 103).

Despite his early interest in systems theory – documented in correspondence with William R. Ashby and Bertalanffy – Kapp distances himself from mathematical cybernetics and finds that there are too many problems in constructing a 'General System Theory' (Kapp unpublished manuscript, 190).

Thus, OSA seems to differ from (thermodynamic) analogy approaches, such as self- organization (see for example, Witt 1997), the (biological) *ontology* approach, and Universal Darwinism (Hodgson 2002). In Kapp's view, analogies from the natural sciences add confusion rather than insight since predetermined causal mechanisms taken from the natural sciences may divert attention from important inherent characteristics of the socioeconomic system (e.g., Kapp 1961, 56-60). Again, an instance may be seen in the use of the physico-chemical 'self-organization' metaphor to justify the non-interventionist worldview of Hayek's 'spontaneous order.' Kapp's 'substantive' approach, in contrast, makes use of biological and physical knowledge in a direct integration, as far as this is directly applicable to the biological open character of man and the material level of the economic process.

9.3 'Political-Economic' Institutionalism

9.3.1 Social Costs as a Result of the Open System Character and of Circular Cumulative Causation

A major field of application is involved in Kapp's lifelong preoccupation with the *Social Costs of Private Enterprise* (1950). The private firm shifts a certain share of the costs of production in the form of socio-ecological degradation to third parties, to the society at large, and, via the 'commons,' to future generations. Social costs are non-market relationships generated by the market, which illustrate the openness of the economic system toward the institutional framework that tends to give rise to increasing social costs; in all, an overall circular cumulative causation. Veblen shared this critical institutional view of the 'market' economy, analyzing the causes and detrimental effects of the pecuniary institutions in the age of the business enterprise.

In modern EIE, this critical institutional analysis of the causes and effects of social costs has often fallen outside the attention and research programs of evolutionary institutional approaches. The understanding of the open system character of the economy with its circular cumulative effects and its provoking heuristic to investigate social costs, vicious circles, socioecological degradation and socioeconomic crises has often been 'lost' out of the approaches and conceptions of modern EIE (on the conception of 'paradigmatic losses' in economics, see Elsner 1986). Note that this critical approach results from Kapp's specific application of 'openness' as a mode of abstraction on different levels of organization.

9.3.2 'Political Institutionalism'
Thus, taking the direct integration of biophysical openness of man and his socioeconomy seriously, Kapp proceeded from a radical critical analysis of the 'market' economy and its private firm to a 'political-economic' approach of collective decision-making, planning, intervention and institutional design. In an unpublished version of 'Open System Character of the Economy and its Implications' (Kapp 1976), Kapp stressed the fact that the open system character of the economy requires a new economics because economic effects on the natural environment can threaten socioeconomic reproduction.

> In short, as soon as the open character of economic systems is fully realized the formulation of social goals and objectives and the problem of collective choices can no longer be avoided. Such objectives and choices with respect to the maintenance of dynamic states of ecological and economic balance for the maintenance and improvement of the conditions of social and individual existence (quality of life) must become the point of departure of normative science of economics. [...] In short, a normative science of economics taking account of the open system character of the economy would imply a complete reversal of the analytical procedures of the discipline as heretofore practiced and applied. [...] the new task of economics would be to elucidate the manner in which collectively determined social goals and objectives could be attained in the most effective and socially least costly manner. (Kapp 1976, 18)

Thus, Kapp developed a 'Political Institutionalism' that deals with policy-making aiming at the reduction of social costs (Kapp [1971] 1983a). Kapp argued that the political process has to generate priorities in the light of defined human needs, i.e., 'quality of life.' He believed in the scientific contribution to define the fundamental requirements of human life and survival as an integral part of a constellation of societal goals. The universal values of existential needs could be objectified and transformed by scientific inquiry into social minima and maximum tolerance levels, e.g., for environmental pollution.

9.3.3 'Systemic' Policy
Ex-post measures or ad-hoc methods, however, fall short of what seems to be required to protect or improve the quality of the environment. So, he assumed a 'systemic' stance.

> Pollution effects are not minor side-issues and cannot be easily corrected by isolated *ad hoc* measures of legislative control, chosen and preferred because they are more or less compatible with the market system. [...] What has always been put in question by the phenomena of [...] social costs is the rationality of allocation and production patterns guided by market prices. (Kapp [1971] 1983a, 124)

In view of the rapid deterioration of the environment, Kapp argued that ex-ante measures will play an increasing role, as well as direct controls that stop pollution by prohibition and curtailment of production of toxic materials. He underlines that nothing is more important than the planned development of technologies designed to reduce or eliminate environmental disruption. In addition, Kapp proposes a more comprehensive economic calculus, which takes into account the short-run and long-run social costs and potential benefits of alternative patterns of resource allocation (Kapp [1974] 1983).

CCC has highlighted the fact that the components of the whole are reciprocally interlinked in uneven and complex manners – i.e., the links are in constant flux and mutually overlap. Hence, a prerequisite for setting in motion a cumulative reduction of social costs in a virtuous circle is an understanding of the interrelations between subsystems which in turn should not be changed in isolation. Effective policy requires a concerted effort in many variables, such as institutions, education, and technology. Their specific interrelatedness determines the cumulative effects.

Policy-making has to be aware that because the system is moving, the coefficients of interrelations among the various conditions in a circular causation are not known with precision because of inertia, time lags and in some periods and areas even a non-responsiveness of the system to changes (Myrdal 1968, 1870-8). Hence, the policy maker has to be aware of the complex *time* factor, as the effects on different variables of the system could be very different over time (also e.g., Myrdal 1957, 19).

9.4 Conclusion

This paper has tried to illustrate that OSA and CCC, conceived in their original meanings and implications, may become key concepts of a more 'political-economic' EIE. The latter would be concerned with the elaboration of alternative 'systemic' policies, and the elaboration of social goals as part of the processes of collective interaction. The dominant properties of original OSA and CCC seem to be that they are able to conceptualize socioeconomic and socioecological openness and change, and integrate knowledge from the natural sciences directly to comprehend the 'entropic' socioeconomic process. Hence, they avoid the dangers of potentially arbitrary utilizations of metaphors, analogies and ontologies taken from the natural sciences.

A reintegration of these conceptions into cutting-edge EIE would shift the center of attention toward dealing with direct biophysical openness of man and the socioeconomy, and, specifically, with the tendency of the system of 'markets' and private business enterprise toward cumulative crises, and its unwarranted effects, i.e., social costs in a comprehensive, systemic, and scientific understanding. Thus, it has been illustrated that the direct integration of biophysical knowledge about openness leads to a critical, radical, and 'systemic' analysis of social costs and a 'political-economic' evolutionary-institutionalist conception of policy-making and 'systemic' institutional design, which might bring modern EIE closer again to its original Veblenian impetus.

References

Angresano, James. *The Political Economy Of Gunnar Myrdal: An Institutional Basis for the Transformation Problem*, Cheltenham (UK), and Northampton (MA, USA): Edward Elgar, 1997.

Argyrous, George, and Rajiv Sethi. 'The Theory of Evolution and the Evolution of Theory: Veblen's Methodology in Contemporary Perspective.' *Cambridge Journal of Economics* 20, 4 (1996): 475-95.

Bellets, Michel, and Frank Sosthe. 'Anticipations, Institutions, and Market Process Theories: A Re-interpretation of Myrdals Institutionalism.' st.etienne.fr/creuset/www/ pubwp/WP CREUSET99 2.pdf. Accessed April 14, 2006.

Elsner, Wolfram. *Economic Institutions Analysis – The Paradigmatic Development of Economics and the Relevance of a Recourse to the Economic Classics. The Example of Institutional Analysis (German: Ökonomische Institutionenanalyse)*. Berlin: Duncker & Humblot, Volkswirtschaftliche Schriften No. 367, 1986.

Forstater, Mathew. 'Cumulative Causation à la Lowe: Radical Endogeneity, Methodology, and Human Intervention.' In *Growth, Distribution, and Effective Demand – Alternatives to Economic Orthodoxy. Essays in Honor of Edward J. Nell* edited by G. Argyrous, M. Forstater, and G. Mongiovi, 309-16. London: M. E. Sharpe, 2003.

Georgescu-Roegen, Nicholas. *Analytical Economics – Issues and Problems*. Oxford, London: Oxford University Press, 1966.

Hodgson, Geoffrey M. *Evolution and Institutions: On Evolutionary Economics and the Evolution of Economics*. Cheltenham (UK), Northampton (MA, USA): Edward Elgar, 1999.

'Darwinism in Economics: From Analogy to Ontology.' *Journal of Evolutionary Economics* 12, 3 (2002): 259-81.

'Decomposition and Growth: Biological Metaphors in Economics from the 1880s to the 1980s.' In *The Evolutionary Foundations of Economics* edited by K. Dopfer, 105-50. Cambridge (UK): Cambridge University Press, 2005.

Kapp, K. William. *The Social Costs of Business Enterprise* (2nd revised and enlarged edition of *Social Costs of Private Enterprise* (1950)). Nottingham: Spokesman University Paperback, [1950, 1963] 1977.

'General System Theory and the Integration of Social Science.' *Kapp Archive*, Basle (CH), (unpublished manuscript). Estimated date of manuscript, late 1950s.

Toward a Science of Man in Society – A Positive Approach to the Integration of Social Knowledge. The Hague: Martinus Nijhoff, 1961.

'Economics and Rational Humanism.' In *The Humanization of the Social Sciences* edited by J.E. Ullmann and R. Preiswerk, 99-120. Lanham, New York, London: University Press of America, [1967] 1985.

'Implementation of Environmental Policies. United Nations Conference on the Human Environment 1971.' In *Social Costs, Economic Development and Environmental Disruption* edited by J.E. Ullmann, 111-42. Lanham, New York, London: University of America Press, [1971] 1983a.

'Governmental Furtherance of Environmentally Sound Technology.' In *Social Costs, Economic Development and Environmental Disruption* edited by J.E. Ullmann, 143-207. Lanham, New York, London: University of America Press, [1974] 1983b.

'The Open-System Character of the Economy and its Implications.' *Kapp Archive*, Basle (CH) unpublished version of 'The Open-System Character of the Economy and its Implications.' In *Economics in the Future* edited by K. Dopfer. London: Macmillan Press, 1976.

Lawson, Tony. 'Philosophical Realism.' In *The Elgar Companion to Institutional and Evolutionary Economics*, Vol. 2 edited by Geoffrey M. Hodgson, Warren J. Samuels and Marc R. Tool, 219-25. Aldershot, Hants, England, Brookfield, VT, USA: Edward Elgar, 1994.

Mayhew, Anne. 'Human Agency, Cumulative Causation, and the State.' *Journal of Economic Issues* 35, 2 (2001): 239-50.

Mearman, Andrew. 'To What Extent is Veblen an Open-System Theorist?' *Journal of Economic Issues* 36, 2 (2002): 573-80.

Myrdal, Gunnar. *Monetary Equilibrium.* London: W. Hodge & Company, Ltd., 1939.

American Dilemma – The Negro Problem and Modern Democracy. New York and London: Harper & Row, 1944.

Economic Theory and Under-Developed Regions. London: Gerald Duckworth, 1957.

Asian Drama – An Inquiry Into the Poverty of Nations. New York: Pantheon, 1968.

'Remarks upon Receipt of the Veblen-Commons Award.' *Journal of Economic Issues* 10, 2 (1976): 215- 16.

Richardson, George P. *Feedback Thought in Social Science and Systems Theory.* Philadelphia: University of Pennsylvania Press, 1991.

Sandelin, Bo. *The History of Swedish Economic Thought.* London and New York: Routledge, 1991.

Steppacher, Rolf. 'Kapp, K. William.' In *The Elgar Companion to Institutional and Evolutionary Economics, Vol. 2* edited by Geoffrey M. Hodgson, Warren J. Samuels and Marc R. Tool, 435-441. Aldershot, Hants, England, Brookfield, VT, USA: Edward Elgar, 1994.

Steppacher, Rolf, Brigitte Zogg-Walz, and Herman Hatzfeld. 'K. William Kapp's Contribution to Economic and Social Science.' In *Economics in Institutional Perspective-Memorial Essays in Honor of K. William Kapp,* edited by Rolf Steppacher, Brigitte Zogg-Walz, Herman Hatzfeld, xv-xxiii. Lexington Mass.: Lexington Books, 1977.

Veblen, Thorstein B. 'Why is Economics not an Evolutionary Science?' *The Quarterly Journal of Economics* 12, 4 (1898): 373-97.

'The Socialist Economics of Karl Marx and His Followers.' *The Quarterly Journal of Economics* 21, 2 (1907): 299-322.

Wahid, Abu N.M. *Frontiers of Economics – Nobel Laureates of the Twentieth Century,* Westport, Conn.: Greenwood Press, 2002.

Witt, Ulrich. 'Self-organization and Economics – What is New?' *Structural Change and Economic Dynamics* 8, 4 (1997): 489-507.

10
Social Costs and Myrdal's Circular Cumulative Causation

10.1 Introduction

This paper reconstructs the CCC's original meaning, and methodology from the writings of Myrdal and Kapp to explore the unique characteristics of this *key* concept of institutional economics. Moreover, the paper demonstrates the CCC's application to minimize social costs via economic planning and its implications for *Political* Institutionalism, pursuing the research project outlined in the Journal of Economic Issues, (Berger and Forstater 2007). Incorporating new unpublished material from the Kapp Archive, namely the Myrdal-Kapp correspondence and Kapp's CCC lecture notes, the paper provides valuable insights about the cooperation between the two economists, and about Kapp's conceptual understanding of CCC. In the second part of the paper, important differences to Veblen's Cumulative Change CC^V and Kaldor's Cumulative Causation CC^K are pointed out to underline the CCC's uniqueness and significance for institutional economics.

10.2 The Origin of CCC

Myrdal formulated the CCC for the first time in Appendix 3 of *American Dilemma – The Negro Problem and Modern Democracy* (1944), using it as a research hypothesis for the circular (self-reinforcing) causation between prejudices, institutions, and poverty. This triggers a vicious circle or 'cumulative effect' of increasing inequalities, and poverty. Myrdal defined two distinct elements of the CCC, i.e., circular causation and its cumulative effect, in *Asian Drama – An Inquiry into the Poverty of Nations* (1968):

> [...] circular causation will give rise to a cumulative movement only when [...] a change in one of the conditions will ultimately be followed by a feed-back of secondary impulses [...] big enough not only to sustain the primary change, but to push it further. Mere mutual causation is not enough to create this process. (Myrdal 1968, 1875)

Elsewhere he had formulated:

> Because of such circular causation a social process tends to become cumulative and often to gather speed at an accelerating rate. (Myrdal 1957, 13)

Kapp applied CCC throughout his analyses of social costs since the 1940s, and systematically elaborated the concept's significance for the integration of the social sciences in the 1950s (Kapp [1950] [1963] 1977, 23, 25; 1961, 183, 187-8).

10.3 Meaning and Methodology

The CCC is *the* main antithesis to the mechanistic analogy and stable equilibrium of the social and economic system. As such it denies a necessary ameliorative trend in development, rejects stage theories, and anticipates the danger of poverty, and societal crisis. However, CCC is no doctrine of hopelessness because vicious circles can be broken, virtuous circles are possible, and a cumulative process also calls forth counteracting forces (Myrdal 1944, 1065; 1957, 35; 1968, 1357, 1859; Kapp, unpublished lecture notes).

As a precondition for self-reinforcing causation, CCC presupposes reciprocal causation and rejects the 'primum mobile' causation theory (Kapp 1961, 188). Thereby, the CCC takes a stand in an old philosophical debate about cause and effect. For instance, Hegel was convinced that the reciprocal relation of cause and effect is the next truth that science will discover, whereas Schopenhauer stated that an effect cannot be the cause of its cause. Also, Marx saw the development of the whole as being constituted of factors that interact with each other and with the whole. Regarding Marxian dialectics, Kapp argued that the CCC neither doubts the relevance of ideological nor material factors but that it rejects that one factor is *per se* exclusive and that the analysis can be restricted to it. Contradictions between material conditions and ideas, etc., are however, possible (Kapp, unpublished lecture notes, Kapp Archive). Myrdal rejected Marxian dialectics if they are interpreted as attributing causal potency to the economic factor alone (Myrdal 1968, 1855-1905).

> If social events and social change emerge in a process of reciprocal interaction between the elements of the system (i.e., within the inner structure), it is no longer adequate to attribute causal potency to an individual variable or impulse. Rather, the outcome (the event, the process) must be viewed as the result of the entire initial situation and the interaction process as well the basic properties of the total social structure. (Kapp 1961, 188)

Therefore, attributing causal potency to the economic factor leads to only *seemingly* clear correlations. The CCC hence focuses on *all* relevant factors and rejects working with analytically closed models. The relevant factors can, of course, only be determined empirically in a given situation. Denying the existence of a primary cause neither implies a denial of the causal principle nor renders the search for relevant factors, their interdependence, or the direction of their change futile. The economic process is part of a larger social process and has to be analyzed as such. Thus the CCC, as applied in the context of economic planning, has focused on the conditions of the following categories of the social system that are by no means exclusive: (1) output and incomes; (2) conditions of production; (3) levels of living; (4) attitudes toward life and work; (5) policies; and (6) institutions (Myrdal 1968). The CCC analysis confirmed the Veblenian account of the role of institutions (Kapp 1961; 1963b):

> [...] certainly the main resistance to change in the social system stems from attitudes and institutions. They are part of the inherited culture and are not easily or rapidly moved in either direction. Even in the very long run, attitudes and community institutions may stay much the same [...] the inertia of attitudes and institutions may be formidable [...] [and] the main reason why a 'take off' may easily be abortive [...]. (Myrdal 1968, 1872)

Kapp even applied the CCC to circular causation between the open economic system and the environment, as well as circular causation in the environment, e.g., synergetic effects of different pollutants that disrupt the human environment in a cumulative process. This approach is similar to systems thinking.[82] In light of the social system dynamics, exhibiting non-constant reciprocal interactions between the system and its parts that are often characterized by an uneven spread along the time axis, Kapp followed that the power of scientific analysis is limited and that it is doubtful whether a general theory or law can be expected of social science. Consequently, Kapp as well as Myrdal asserted that there exists no math of social change, and rejected empty formal modeling (Kapp unpublished lecture notes; 1961, 188; 1965a; Myrdal 1968, 1866).

Kapp considered the CCC to be *the* key concept of institutional economics (Kapp 1977; 1968), and writes to Myrdal:

> I read the Appendix [galley proofs of Appendix 2 of Asian Drama] with great profit; I am very much impressed [...] I think we now have a synthesis of an analysis in the sense of a theoretical framework and a system of tools for the study of the underdeveloped world. [...] your tools go much beyond the underdeveloped countries and [...] a good deal of your new framework of analysis could be fruitfully applied in the study of developed countries. (Kapp, Oct. 19, 1967. Unpublished Kapp-Myrdal Correspondence.)

Taking CCC with its emphasis on interrelatedness seriously demands inter-disciplinarity, and questions the autonomy of each social science (Kapp unpublished lecture notes; 1961). Moreover, Kapp considered the CCC to have the characteristics of a scientific 'paradigm' with its own analytical apparatus, philosophical perspective, and hypothesis. He lists its main characteristics as follows: CCC (1) frames problems, (2) brings problems closer to solution, (3) necessitates an identification of relevant causal factors, (4) necessitates a causal analysis of real interaction relationships, (5) necessitates systems view, (6) necessitates analysis of temporal processes, and (7) avoids teleology, the projection of ready-made meanings, relationships, results, and processes. To prevent the turning of CCC into a dogma, Kapp even proposed to explore if there is indeed no single determining factor (Kapp, unpublished lecture notes).

10.4 Minimizing Social Costs via Economic Planning

Applying the CCC to economic planning, Myrdal and Kapp both started from explicit value premises (Myrdal 1929; 1944, 1035-1064; 1958; Kapp 1950; 1965a; 1973a). Desirable and possible positions of the system have to be justified normatively because they are neither automatic, nor natural (Kapp, unpublished lecture notes). Both regarded it as a threat to science, when research results are deemed 'objective' while they are determined by *hidden* pre-analytical values.

The values made explicit by Myrdal are the democratic equality ideals of the enlightenment that played a major role in the radical reforms of feudalism and the implementation of democratic institutions in Europe and the United States. This led to Myrdal's concern for poverty and increasing disparities between the rich and the poor that is similar to Kapp's concern for the fulfillment of basic human needs, i.e. his social minima approach (Kapp 1965a; 1965b):

> I have long felt that we are kindred souls and I am quoting you in a big book on South Asia [...] [I want to] thank you for your most interesting and inspiring article, Social Economics and Social Welfare Minima [...]. (Myrdal Dec. 5, 1966)

Reflecting these value dispositions, the CCC serves as a conceptual tool[83] to break the vicious circle of poverty (Myrdal 1970; Kapp 1973a) that is caused by inequalities in the (a) economic (*e.g., income inequalities, including the unequal distribution of land*); (b) social (*e.g., lack of social mobility, including unequal educational opportunities*); and (c) political (*e.g., unequal participation in the political process, including qualitatively defective administration*) realms within poor countries as well as their unequal trade relations with industrialized countries. In self-reinforcing circular causation these inequalities further inequalities most in poor regions. In other words, these inequalities are the cause and effect of poverty (Kapp 1973a; Myrdal 1970).[84] Poverty as a form of insufficient satisfaction of basic human needs is a substantive indicator of social costs (Kapp 1963a).

Complementing the cause-effect analysis with a normative means-ends dimension, Kapp and Myrdal proposed 'political' economics that is concerned with economic planning in real terms to guarantee social minima, and minimize social costs (Myrdal 1960; 1968, 1879; Kapp 1965b; 1973b; Berger and Forstater 2007). Economic planning with monetary indicators usually leads to a selection of growth and maximization of profits at the expense of environmental goals. Social costs of environmental disruption jeopardize the fulfillment of basic human needs because they mostly affect the weakest that are usually more exposed or have less means to protect themselves. This is an instance of circular cumulative causation of social costs. In contrast, economic planning that aims at guaranteeing social minima, according to Kapp, needs a comprehensive system of social accounting with a diversity of heterogeneous indicators. Such indicators reflect the present state and exigencies of the socio-ecological system and its effect on the condition of human life with respect to explicit socio-ecological objectives (minimum socio-ecological standards). Due to CCC, the indicators are interrelated and the deterioration of the quality in one socio-ecological category influences other categories. The indicators, furthermore, have to reveal the actual and potential dangers for human health and well-being, and for social reproduction. Growth is understood as an improvement in the socio-ecological conditions, measured in real terms via socio-ecological indicators in terms of which development planning takes place (Myrdal 1970; Kapp 1973a, 4). Consequently, growth and the improvement in the quality of the social and ecological environment are identical goals, and there is no trade-off in this integrative view of 'eco-development' (Kapp [1976b] 1977). Kapp cautioned, however, that it is important not to conceal that vested interests are affected by implementing a comprehensive accounting system (Kapp 1973b).

CCC leads to alternative criteria for economic planning. The environment's 'revolutionary' character is that environmental values are social use values. Kapp argued that environmental policies, the evaluation of environmental goals and the establishment of priorities require substantive economic indicators in terms of social use values (politically evaluated) for which the formal calculus in monetary exchange values fails to provide a real measure. In this context, Kapp referred to Max Weber's discussion of Otto v. Neurath's 'Naturalrechnung' (accounting in material units) who had 'taken up the hint' of Marx and Engels that not exchange value but use value, i.e., 'useful effects' and free 'disposable time' are the source of real wealth and thus quality of life. Hence, the criteria for planning are the useful effects of different goods and services balanced against the required expenditure of labor (Kapp [1973b] 1974).

10.5 Differences to Veblen's and Kaldor's CC

Building on previous research (Berger and Elsner 2007), this paper furthermore argues that Veblen's concept of 'cumulative change' (CC^V) differs from Myrdal's CCC. Applying it mainly to 'the sequence of change in the methods of dealing with the material means of life' (Veblen 1898, 387), Veblen described the economic life history as a 'cumulative process of adaptation of means to ends that cumulatively change as the process goes on [...]' (Veblen 1898, 391). The main characteristic of an evolutionary economist is that 'he insists on an answer in terms of cause and effect [...] the notion of cumulative causation' (Veblen 1898, 377). Thus his concept, *per se*, does not contain the idea of a self-reinforcing (positive) feedback and even states that there is 'no trend' in cumulative causation (Veblen 1907, 304) whereas CCC explicitly refers to trends, such as increasing inequality and poverty. However, similarities exist and have been noticed by Kapp: (a) the rejection of a tendency toward equilibrium, and (b) viewing cultural and economic processes as unending, non-teleological, and moved by institutional inertia (Kapp [1950] [1963] 1977, 25).

Kaldor's principle of 'cumulative causation' (CC^K) differs substantially from the CCC in the Myrdal-Kapp tradition in terms of method, research interest, and application, which confirms Setterfield's finding of a unique Kaldorian tradition (Setterfield 2001, 109). Kaldor's interpretation of CCC is mainly based on Myrdal's *Economic Theory and Under-Developed Regions* (1957), leaving the more important later applications aside. Hence, it remains unclear how much of the CCC he agreed with. This is not to deny certain similarities (e.g., the rejection of equilibrium economics, unequal trade). The question is whether these similarities are substantial and whether they outweigh important differences.

In a subchapter called 'the principle of cumulative causation' Kaldor wrote 'what Myrdal called the principle of "circular and cumulative causation" [...] is nothing else but the existence of increasing returns to scale [...]' (Kaldor [1970] 1978, 143). In another subchapter called 'the theorem of endogenous and cumulative change,' Kaldor asserted that 'with increasing returns change becomes progressive and propagates itself in a cumulative way. Myrdal [...] called this the 'principle of circular and cumulative causation' (Kaldor [1972] 1978, 186).

It seems that because Kaldor was mostly interested in the economic mechanism of 'increasing returns' he interprets Myrdal accordingly. This is, however, a much more narrow approach than the one taken by CCC à la Myrdal-Kapp. It is true that Kaldor generally conceded the importance of non-economic factors in the development process, such as the effects of governmental intervention and training on growth (Argyrous 2001, 105; Toner 2001, 99). Unlike Myrdal and Kapp, however, in Kaldor's writings on CC^K an attempt to explain how these relevant factors of the social system are interrelated is missing. Although Kaldor's 'interrelatedness' portrayed the economy as a 'complex web of interrelations' (Argyrous 2001, 105) it focused mainly on the interdependencies of 'economic' components, such as machinery, and organizational structure (Toner 2001, 100). The fact that Kaldor's analysis of institutions was marginal and of secondary importance has also been noticed by Toner (1999, 115). On the whole it seems that Kaldor's research interest is more limited to the 'economic,' which may explain why he preferred the term 'cumulative' over 'circular causation.'

Unlike Myrdal and Kapp, Kaldor did not state his value premises and did not apply CC^K for political economics. His CC^K considered unequal development even as the outcome of a 'natural cause of events' (Kaldor [1970] 1978, 148) due to 'deep-seated causes that are unlikely to be rendered inoperative' (Kaldor [1970] 1978, 144). Kaldor also takes industrial growth measured via monetary indicators as a given end. This methodology seems different from CCC. Myrdal and Kapp saw industrial development more critically, especially when a large part of the population remains poor and when environmental disruption contributes to the vicious circle of poverty. Moreover, indicators of exchange values are, according to Kapp, arbitrary because they take asymmetries in purchasing power for granted and abstract from many relevant conditions. Hence, they neither adequately reflect the status quo of the quality of life nor the success of the development effort.

10.6 Conclusion

This paper showed how Kapp and Myrdal developed the CCC into *the* key concept of institutional economics. Moreover, it was demonstrated how both economists turned the CCC into a cornerstone of *Political Institutionalism* by applying it to economic planning to effectively minimize social costs. The comparison with Veblen's CC^V and Kaldor's CC^K validated that the CCC holds the fuller theoretical and conceptual potential for institutional economics.

References

Argyrous, George. 'Setterfield on Cumulative Causation and Interrelatedness: A Comment.' *Cambridge Journal of Economics* 25, 1 (2001): 103-106.

Berger, Sebastian and Wolfram Elsner. 'European Contributions to Evolutionary Institutional Economics: The Cases of Cumulative Circular Causation (CCC) and Open System Approach (OSA). Some Methodological and Policy Implications.' *Journal of Economic Issues* 41, 2 (2007): 529-537.

Berger, Sebastian and Matthew Forstater. 'Towards Political Institutionalist Economics. Kapp's Social Costs, Lowe's Instrumental Analysis, and the European Institutionalist Approach to Environmental Policy.' *Journal of Economic Issues* 41, 2 (2007): 539-546.

Kaldor, Nicholas. *The Case of Regional Policies, in: Further Essays in Economics.* London: Holmes and Meier Publishers [1970] 1978.

The Irrelevance of Equilibrium Economics, in: Further Essays in Economics. London: Holmes and Meier Publishers [1972] 1978.

Kapp, K. W. *The Social Costs of Business Enterprise* (2nd revised and enlarged edition of Social Costs of Private Enterprise (1950)). Nottingham: Spokesman University Paperback, [1963] 1977.

Towards a Science of Man in Society. A Positive Approach to the Integration of Social Knowledge. The Hague: Martinus Nijhoff, 1961.

'Social Costs and Social Benefits – A Contribution to Normative Economics.' In *Probleme der normativen Ökonomik und der wirtschaftspolitischen Beratung,* edited by E. v. Beckerath and H. Giersch, 183-210. Verein für Sozialpolitik. Berlin: Duncker & Humblot, 1963a.

Hindu Culture, Economic Development and Economic Planning in India. Bombay/London: Asia Publishing House, 1963b.

'Economic Development in a New Perspective: Existential Minima and Substantive Rationality.' *Kyklos* 17, 1 (1965a): 49-79.

'Social Economics and Social Welfare Minima.' In *Towards a Sociology of Culture in India, Essays in Honor of Dr. D. P. Mukerji,* edited by T.K.N. Unnithan et al., pp 1-12. New Delhi: Prentice Hall of India, 1965b.

'In Defence of Institutional Economics.' *Swedish Journal of Economics* 70, 1 (1968): 1-18.

'Entwicklungspolitik in neuer Perspektive: Bemerkungen zu Gunnar Myrdals Politisches Manifest über die Armut in der Welt.' *Blätter für deutsche und internationale Politik* 18, 3 (1973a): 1-12.

'Environmental Indicators as Indicators of Social Use Value.' In *Environmental Policies and Development Planning in Contemporary China and other Essays*, pp. 127-138. Paris/The Hague: Mouton, [1973b] 1974.

'The Open-System Character of the Economy and its Implications.' In *Economics in the Future*, edited by Kurt Dopfer, pp. 90-105. London: The Macmillan Press Ltd., 1976a.

'Development and Environment: Towards a New Approach to Socio-economic and Environmental Development.' In *Economics in Institutional Perspective – Memorial Essays in Honor of K. W. Kapp* edited by Rolf Steppacher, et al., pp. 205-218. Lexington, MA, Toronto: Lexington Books, [1976b] 1977.

'The Nature and Significance of Institutional Economics.' *Kyklos* 29, 2 (1977): 209-232.

Unpublished lecture notes on the CCC; Myrdal-Kapp Correspondence, Kapp Archive, Basle, Switzerland.

Myrdal, Gunnar. *Das politische Element in der national-ökonomischen Doktrinbildung*, Bonn-Bad Godesberg: Verlag Neue Gesellschaft, [1929] [1932] 1976.

American Dilemma: The Negro Problem and Modern Democracy. New York/London: Harper & Row, 1944.

Economic Theory and Under-Developed Regions. London: Gerald Duckworth, 1957.

Value in Social Theory – A Selection of Essays on Methodology by Gunnar Myrdal. London: Routledge & K. Paul, 1958.

Beyond the Welfare State – Economic Planning in the Welfare States and its International Implications. New Haven: Yale University Press, 1960.

Asian Drama – An Inquiry Into the Poverty of Nations, Vol. III. New York: Pantheon, 1968.

The Challenge of World Poverty, A World Anti-Poverty Program in Outline. New York: Pantheon Books, 1970.

'Remarks upon Receipt of the Veblen-Commons Award.' *Journal of Economic Issues* 10, 2 (1970): 215-216.

Setterfield, Mark. 2001. 'Cumulative Causation, Interrelatedness and the Theory of Economic Growth: A Reply to Argyrous and Toner.' *Cambridge Journal of Economics* 25 (2001): 97-102.

Toner, Philip. *Main Currents in Cumulative Causation – The Dynamics of Growth and Development*. New York: St. Martin's Press, 1999.

'History versus Equilibrium' and the Theory of Economic Growth, by Mark Setterfield: A Comment.' *Cambridge Journal of Economics* 25 (2001): 97-102.

Veblen, Thorstein B. 'Why is Economics not an Evolutionary Science?' *The Quarterly Journal of Economics* 12, 4 (1898): 373-97.

'The Socialist Economics of Karl Marx and His Followers.' *The Quarterly Journal of Economics* 21, 2 (1907): 299-322.

11
Social Costs and Lowe's Instrumental Analysis

11.1 Kapp's Theory of Social Costs

In his significantly prescient work, *The Social Costs of Private Enterprise* (1950), Kapp defines social costs as that share of the total costs of production that the individual enterprise is not held accountable for, and which it shifts to third parties, society as a whole, or future generations in the form of harmful consequences and damages (Kapp [1963] 1977, 13).

> Whenever social costs are shifted onto economically and politically weaker sections of society without compensation, a redistribution of the costs of production, hence real income is involved. (Kapp 1972b, 16)

Kapp's theory shows that social costs are to a large extent a non-market phenomenon because the relations between production, the environment, and the individual, are not voluntary market relations, but involuntary one-sided relationships forced on the individual. The individual cannot escape them and they happen 'behind his back.' Environmental pollution is synergetic with pollutants mixing in the ecosystem in a way that makes it impossible to determine responsibility. Moreover, pollution is cumulative; once thresholds are passed, the effects are out of proportion relative to their cause. Social costs originate because firms are not held responsible for the full cost of production. The profitability of many investments would cease altogether if producers had to pay the full costs. Because of asymmetric power relations, the bearers of social costs are usually too weak to defend themselves against this cost shifting.

According to Kapp, social costs reflect above all a misallocation of resources resulting from an institutionalized economic calculus that induces economic units to take inadequate account of harmful environmental effects of their investment (including location) and production decisions. This purely formal rationality in decision-making is based on the information provided by market prices together with the principle of profit maximization and cost minimization by means of cost shifting. In this instituted process, investment decisions depend on net present value, which gives an incentive to shift costs to the future to diminish their discounted present value. Kapp shows how this institutionalized economic monetary calculus leads to a path of economic growth and profit maximization via premature resource depletion rather than environmental goals. The self-reinforcing nature of economic institutions leads to cumulative, ever increasing social costs.

> They [social costs] are damages or diseconomies sustained by the economy in general, which under different institutional conditions could be avoided. [...] if these costs were inevitable under any kind of institutional arrangement they would not really present a special theoretical problem. [...] to reveal their origin, the study of social costs must always be an institutional analysis. Such an analysis raises inevitably the question of institutional reform and policy. (Kapp 1963, 186)

11.2 Linking Kapp's Approach with Lowe's Instrumental Analysis

We now take a closer look at Lowe's Instrumental Analysis in order to point out links to Kapp. In his 'Remarks' ([1980] 1987) on receiving the Veblen-Commons Award, Lowe makes his views on economic science explicit. While supporting Veblen's definition of evolutionary science ('a theory of a cumulative process of adaptation of means to ends') he advocates an evolutionary way of thinking in regard not only to the object, but also to the method of economic analysis. This is necessary due to changes in socio-psychological and institutional factors. Unlike the natural sciences, there is no invariance of the object of inquiry in economics (Lowe [1980] 1987, 228-33), because the economic system is an open system in which reciprocal interlacements and cyclical flows change socio-ecological and economic variables (Löwe 1935; Lowe 1969, 9-10). Since the publication of *On Economic Knowledge* (1965), Lowe's major theoretical concern has been the means-ends relation, which means shifting attention to the theory-practice relationship, aiming at preventing unwarranted developments through public controls (Krohn 1996, 91, 173-4).

Lowe advocates that the goal of economics should be to discover the suitable means for the attainment of previously stipulated ends. The ends are treated as known goals and are established through political decisions. Hence, according to Lowe, the first task for economics is Instrumental Analysis, which evaluates different paths by which the current state can be transformed into the terminal state (Lowe [1980] 1987, 228-33). In other words, in his 'Political Economics' the role of theory is to instrumentally devise means, such as public controls. The latter would provide a set of suitable controls to establish the context and behavioural patterns suitable to attain societal macro-goals, which are highly amenable to the incorporation of bio-physical limits (Forstater 1996, 60, 109, 116). This is important because from the late 1960s onward, Lowe incorporates environmental factors into his analysis (Forstater 2004, 19), which focused on the constant side effects of technical change and structural upheavals resulting from that change. Hence, not short-term interventions, but comprehensive long-term planning and intervention are proposed (Krohn 1993, 115). This 'working backwards' from a politically defined goal is what the subtitle *Political Economics* is all about (Krohn 1993, 153). Importantly, it has been shown that Lowe's focus on 'knowledge for goal seeking' is a version of C. S. Peirce's method of inference 'abduction' because it treats the future state of the system as known, by defining in political terms the goals to be reached, and works out a plurality of possible paths to achieve it (Forstater 2004, 25-8) By the time he finished *On Economic Knowledge*, Lowe was aware that his Instrumentalism aimed at a revision of traditional economics (Krohn 1996, 91, 173-4). It tries to reconnect the economic process with the essential components of the sociopolitical world (Krohn 1993, 154). Lowe, however, did not depart entirely from the traditional ways of argumentation because he only discussed the modal rules for a goal-adequate path, not the ethical standards for economic action (Krohn 1996, 149). This is why Lowe's Instrumentalism is not presented as totally 'new,' but incorporates new elements, identifies something implicit and unrecognized bringing it into full consciousness, elaborating its possibilities and promoting its potential contribution (Forstater 1996, 116, 118).

Lowe's Instrumental Analysis bears similarities and is highly complementary with Kapp's theoretical framework for reducing social costs. Kapp expresses his agreement with Lowe's *On Economic Knowledge* in two letters to F. Pollock dating from 1966 (Pollock Correspondence, Kapp Archive),[85] and in an unpublished version of his article 'The Open System Character of the Economy' (1976):

> the new task of economics would be to elucidate the manner in which collectively determined social goals and objectives could be attained in the most effective and socially least costly manner. [...] This brings our notion of normative economics close to that of political economics: the theory of controlled economic systems as developed by Adolf Loewe [sic] *On Economic Knowledge* [...] also R. L. Heilbronner [sic], 'On the Possibility of Political Economics.' (Kapp 1976, 20)

The Social Costs of Neoliberalism

According to Kapp, social costs show the open system character of the economy that induces physical and institutional causal chains in the form of non-market relationships and secondary distribution. The amount of social costs that is taken into account depends on the power structure of society because vested interests are affected. Therefore, social costs can only be reduced significantly in a social evaluation of the relative importance of social costs and benefits, which carries elements of political decisions as to social purposes and goals. Kapp elaborates a process that consists of different stages of societal goal formulation, conflict mediation, and democratic decision making between the affected groups of society (Kapp [1974] 1983).

In this approach, Kapp applies Dewey's pragmatic Instrumentalism to policy making, which shows how all crucial decision-making must invariably include an exploration of the goals pursued both as far as their content and their implications are concerned (Kapp 1965, 59).

> [...] the instrumental elaboration of the paths to be followed, the choice of means in its broadest sense, both belong to the rational setting of objectives and their rational achievement, i.e., rational in the light of empirically testable criteria. [...] The logic of the determination of objectives is added to the logic of the achievement of objectives by the introduction of means suited to the objectives. When political economics is oriented towards the preservation of life and providing the means of existence [...] it includes the exploration of what is necessary and possible and, in the form of political action, deals at the same time with the question of how appropriate reforms may be used to realize sets of objectives that have been recognized as necessary and found social acceptance. (Kapp [1968] 1985, 112-3)

According to Kapp's approach, policymaking requires flexibility that must guide the exploration of ends and means in their changing natures. Search for alternative possibilities and prognosis of alternative courses of action take place in interrelation with the choice of ends and the formulation of right action. These are progressively specified on the basis of comprehensive feasibility studies, i.e., scientific research efforts designed to provide information through a simulated prognosis of events. The quality of the plan depends on how well the information used in the simulation can anticipate the real outcome. Constant use of feasibility surveys is a precondition of the success of the plan. This means that the policy maker has to deal with questions as to the role and nature of modern science, technology, input mixes and production functions, which cannot be taken as given but are dependent variables (Kapp 1965, 64-73).

11.3 Implications for Environmental Policy

An integrated approach of Kapp's Theory of Social Costs and Lowe's Instrumental Analysis bears implications for environmental policy aiming at a reduction of social costs and bringing the system onto a suitable path for achieving a sustainable economy. The starting point has to be the elaboration (i.e., vision) of goals, and Kapp argues that the political process has to arrive at priorities in light of objectively defined human needs and requirements, including the quality of life. What is required is nothing less than the scientific definition of fundamental requirements of human life and survival, and ecological sustainability as integral parts of the constellation of goals. Particular aspects of the quality of the environment, such as air or water, must be an end in itself, because they are existential human needs. By subjecting them to scientific inquiry, the universal values of existential human needs (Steppacher 1994) can be objectified and transformed into social minima and maximum tolerance levels for pollution. Once they are determined, social minima allow evaluating and exploring different means and ends in light of their differing costs and benefits, their effects on the physical and social environment, and hence, their effect on the satisfaction of human needs. One way to measure social costs is in terms of existing deficiencies by comparing the actual state of pollution with the maximum permissible concentration of pollutants (per time period and within a particular geographical region). These environmental standards are arrived at by defining social minima based on a definition of human needs, such as minimum requirements for clean air.

> […] we suggest that the substantive definition of social costs and social benefits is possible in terms of objective requirements […] [because they] can be determined with a considerable degree of scientific method and objectivity. That is to say, the identification of social costs and social benefits calls for scientifically determined social minima […] (Kapp 1963, 193-4)

Obviously, the neoclassical or Pigouvian approach based on 'externalities' takes a different point of departure that relies on market prices. Kapp gives several reasons why socio-ecological values and needs cannot be adequately expressed in terms of market prices (Kapp 1972a). First, market prices are never 'objective' but reflect private economic costs and profits that are an arbitrary outcome of the asymmetric distribution in purchasing power, conflict and compromise. Reliance on market prices usually leads to the morally least desirable option; namely, that the ones with the greater purchasing power shift social costs to the poorest because it is 'cheap and easy.' Starting from initially small differences, the market mechanism initiates a vicious circle of ever increasing unequal distribution via circular cumulative causation. Second, social costs are an all-pervasive phenomenon, a kind of secondary distribution that not only concerns market actors but also the interests of society and future generations. Determining a discount rate for the social costs that are shifted to future generations clearly shows that fundamental moral issues are involved that cannot be left to markets. Third, one-dimensional market prices cannot reflect the heterogeneous processes in the ecological system. This would be necessary if market prices were to serve as an informational basis aiming at reducing social costs. Fourth, 'internalizing' them via payments of 'green' taxes does not make 'pollution' go away and cannot replace the irreversibly lost quality of the environment. Ex-post remedial measures and indirect methods fall short of what seems to be required to protect or improve the quality of the environment.

> Pollution effects are not minor side-issues and cannot be easily corrected by isolated *ad hoc* measures of legislative control, chosen and preferred because they are more or less compatible with the market system. […] What has always been put in question by the phenomena of […] social costs is the rationality of allocation and production patterns guided by market prices. (Kapp [1971] 1983, 124)

In view of the rapid deterioration of the environment, Kapp argues that *ex-ante* measures before pollution occurs will play an increasing role, as well as direct controls that stop pollution by prohibition and curtailment of the production of toxic materials. 'Cases in point would be the […] closing down of factories in selected areas with […] unacceptable rates of pollution' (Kapp [1971] 1983, 129). Kapp cautions that even direct controls are not the key answer to environmental disruption. Kapp underlines that nothing is more important than the planned development of technologies designed to reduce or eliminate environmental disruption. Technology must not be considered as an independent variable, but be defined in terms of societal goals or the satisfaction of individual and societal needs. The causal principle has to be replaced by that of the end result – a process in which explicit social norms become the starting point for environmental policy pertaining to technology. A major issue is the financing of government promotion of research ideas for green technologies. Part of governmental funds can flow into government research institutes, another part into industry's considerable research resources. The most important thing, however, is the creation of legal and institutional prerequisites. Here, direct measures such as prohibitions, regulations and environmental standards must be applied, and appropriate organizations created to control them. (Kapp [1974] 1983).

In addition, Kapp proposes a more comprehensive economic calculus, which takes into account the short and long-run social costs and potential benefits of alternative patterns of resource allocation. Kapp argues that policymaking requires a system of accounting for the socio-economic and environmental impact, a diversity of socio-ecological indicators (Kapp [1972c] 1974). These reflect the present state and exigencies of the state of the socio-ecological system as an inventory of the total situation with the actual and potential dangers for human health and well-being, for social productivity and indeed for human life and survival. Only such a comprehensive accounting serves as an adequate basis for decision making that will reduce social costs. The informational basis of environmental indicators serves to establish environmental standards, and is a tool for continuous evaluation of the effectiveness of social control. Importantly, Kapp's main tenet is that environmental and economic development must go hand in hand. Trading them off is potentially self-defeating and harms the weakest the most. Kapp underlines that this approach to policy is neither an invitation to disregard costs, nor support for a technocratic approach, or the false assertion that socialism is a remedy for social costs.

11.4 Research Project: 'Political Institutionalism'

The future research project aims at recovering the common roots of the Kapp-Lowe approach in 'European' Political Institutionalism, and its potential for the further development of modern economics. Combining Lowe's Instrumental Analysis and Kapp's Social Costs approach opens the way for a comprehensive planning process for economic and environmental sustainability. Lowe's methodological alternative provides the guidelines for mapping out blueprints of potentially sustainable paths, while Kapp's analysis can be fruitfully integrated in both the planning and execution phases. But the Kapp-Lowe approach is a general framework that may be applied to a great variety and number of policy issues. It is our intention to further explore the details of this method and to apply it to additional problems of the contemporary political economy.

References

Forstater, Mathew. *Political Economics and Instrumental Analysis: Adolph Lowe's Methodological Alternative for Economic Theory and Public Policy*. Unpublished Ph.D Dissertation, New School for Social Research, 1996.
'Visions and Scenarios: Heilbroner's Worldly Philosophy, Lowe's Political Economics, And the Methodology of Ecological Economics.' *Ecological Economics* 51 (2004): 17-30.

Kapp, K. William. *The Social Costs of Business Enterprise* (2nd revised and enlarged edition of *Social Costs of Private Enterprise* (1950)). Nottingham: Spokesman University Paperback, [1963] 1977.
'Social Costs and Social Benefits – A Contribution to Normative Economics.' In *Probleme der normativen Ökonomik und der wirtschaftspolitischen Beratung*, edited by E. v. Beckerath and H. Giersch, 183-210. Verein für Sozialpolitik. Berlin: Duncker & Humblot, 1963.
'Economic Development in a New Perspective: Existential Minima and Substantive Rationality.' *Kyklos* 18, 1 (1965): 49-79.
'Pollock Correspondence.' *Kapp Archive*, Basle (CH), 1966.
'Social Costs, Neoclassical Economics, and Environmental Planning: A Reply.' *Social Science Information* 11, 1 (1972a): 17-28.
'Environmental Disruption and Protection.' In *Socialism and the Environment*, 13-24. Nottingham: Spokesman Books, 1972b.
'Environmental Indicators as Indicators of Social Use Values.' In *Environmental Policies and Development Planning in Contemporary China and Other Essays*. Paris/The Hague: Mouton, [1972c] 1974.
'The Open-System Character of the Economy and its Implications.' *Kapp Archive*, Basle (CH) unpublished version of 'The Open-System Character of the Economy and its Implications,' in *Economics in the Future* edited by K. Dopfer. London: Macmillan Press, 1976.
'The Implementation of Environmental Policies.' In John E. Ullmann (ed.), *Social Costs, Economic Development and Environmental Disruption*, edited by John E. Ullmann, 111-142. Lanham, New York, London: University of America Press, [1971] 1983.
'Governmental Furtherance of Environmentally Sound Technology.' In *Social Costs, Economic Development and Environmental Disruption*, edited by John E. Ullmann, 143-207. Lanham, New York, London: University of America Press, [1974] 1983.
'Economics and Rational Humanism.' In *The Humanization of the Social Sciences*, edited by John E. Ullmann and Roy Preiswerk, 99-120. London: University Press of America, [1968] 1985.

Krohn, Claus-Dieter. *Intellectuals in Exile – Refugee Scholars and the New School for Social Research*. Massachusetts: The University of Massachusetts Press, 1993.
Der Philosophische Ökonom – Zur Intellektuellen Biographie Adolph Lowes. Marburg: Metropolis, 1996.

Löwe, Adolf. *Economics and Sociology – A plea for co-operation in the social sciences.* London: George Allen & Unwin Ltd. 1935.

Lowe, Adolph. *On Economic Knowledge.* Armonk: M.E. Sharpe, 1965.

'Toward a Science of Political Economics.' In *Economic Means and Social Ends – Essays in Political Economics*, edited by Robert L. Heilbroner, 1-36. Englewood Cliffs, NJ: Prentice-Hall, 1969.

'What is Evolutionary Economics?: Remarks upon the Receipt of the Veblen-Commons Award.' In *Adolph Lowe – Essays in Political Economics: Public Control in a Democratic Society*, edited by A. Oakley. Brighton: Wheatsheaf Books Ltd., [1980] 1987.

Steppacher, Rolf. 'Kapp, K. William.' In *The Elgar Companion to Institutional and Evolutionary Economics, Vol. 2* edited by Geoffrey M. Hodgson, Warren J. Samuels and Marc R. Tool, 435-441. Aldershot, Hants, England, Brookfield, VT, USA: Edward Elgar, 1994.

12

Social Costs and Hayden's Social Fabric Matrix for Policy-Making

12.1 Introduction

This article is inspired by Gregory F. Hayden's *Policymaking for A Good Society: The Social Fabric Matrix Approach to Policy Analysis and Program Evaluation* (Hayden 2006), a foundational work for policymaking that combines insights of American Institutionalism and Pragmatism into a unique methodology. Hayden calls it a 'how to' book for policy analysts and policymakers in order to design policies and programs that more efficiently and effectively solve problems.

Environmental degradation is one of the most pressing problems that modern policymakers have to grapple with particularly in the form of social costs. Rational evaluations of a situation as a means for deliberation require knowledge about social as well as private costs and benefits. An elaboration of different paths and scenarios depends on the adequate representation of alternative total costs and benefits. The three major theoretical contributions dealing with the problem of social costs are by the neoclassical economists Pigou and Coase, and the institutional economist Kapp. Since the 1950s Kapp proposed a kind of policymaking to minimize social costs that is similar to Hayden's approach in that it emphasizes working with primary and secondary criteria and the application of systems principles, such as openness, negative and positive feedbacks.

First, this chapter explores how Hayden's main concern is closely linked to problems of social costs and why he insists on the importance of primary criteria. The paper then presents Kapp's 'rational humanism' or 'normative economics' because it shows how primary and secondary criteria can be applied to evaluate social costs in a nonutilitarian way to avoid the theoretical and practical limitations of the Coasian and Pigouvian frameworks. The paper concludes that Kapp is an important precursor of Hayden's approach whose work provides important insights for policymaking to minimize social costs.

12.2 Framing Social Costs: The Need for General Systems Analysis and the Limitations of Utility Theory

Hayden refers to the problem of social costs explicitly in relation to the importance of General Systems Analysis (GSA): 'The function of GSA in evaluating government programs, social costs, public goods, and environmental policy is a tool kit of principles for understanding systems. The principles are to be used to describe and explain the working of the socioecological systems in order to allow for the evaluation of the system and its parts [...] They are theories for organizing analysis, explaining systems, and judging policies.' (Hayden 2006:51) It can thus be inferred that Hayden considers GSA useful for evaluating social costs because their systemic nature requires a systems approach.

Hayden's belief is that policymaking paradigms should be consistent with the complexity of reality. One important principle of Hayden's GSA is the open system approach: 'All real-world systems are open systems, and all open systems are non-equilibrium systems. "Open systems are those with a continuous flow of energy, information or materials from environment to system and return"' (ibid: 52). This is in the tradition of ecological institutional economists Kapp and Nicholas Georgescu-Roegen who applied institutional economics to conceptualize problems of environmental degradation (Berger and Elsner 2007). The principle of positive and negative feedbacks is another important and logically connected GSA principle. 'For policy purposes, especially with regard to the natural environment, the system concept of negative and positive feedback is very important. [...] What makes the open systems approach so vibrant from a policy standpoint is the fact that it views the environment as being an integral part of the functioning of a [...] system. Thus, external forces that affect the system need to be accounted for in the analysis of the system. [...] Positive feedback systems [...] tend to be unstable since a change in the original level of the system provides an input for further change in the same direction' (ibid: 58). This GSA principle was applied by Gunnar Myrdal and Kapp under the name of 'circular cumulative causation' to address social costs (Berger 2008) and will be dealt with in the second part of the paper.

Consequently, approaches that simplify or even distort the problem at hand are rejected: 'Ideas like utility maximization ignore culture, social beliefs, institutions, power relations, traditions, procedures, and so forth, and, therefore, are not useful with regard to real-world policy analysis and decision making' (ibid:14). Hence, Hayden concludes that 'utilitarian ideas for capturing and analyzing the real world are irrelevant to those who want reliable policy analysis' (ibid: 15). By arguing that utility maximization and utilitarian ideas are not fit to deal with the complexity of the real word, Hayden actually reiterates Kapp's argument regarding the limitations of neoclassical 'solutions' to problems of social costs, which Kapp had based in an understanding of openness and circular cumulative causation. This point will be further elaborated in the second part of the paper.

Another limitation of utilitarianism that concerns the framing of social costs is the assumption that the pecuniary prices charged by the corporation can be utilized as 'the measure of benefits and costs for the analysis of public programs and that monetary prices are to be the common denominator' (ibid: 15). Hayden argues that by adopting price as the measure of value, neoclassical policymaking concepts, such as cost–benefit analysis and the Coase theorem, endow the corporations with exaggerated legitimacy and power because its analytical apparatus becomes the dominant model of analysis. 'In terms of policy power, the selection of the corporation's criterion of success – that is in dollar flows – as the social criterion of success provides [corporations with] a definite advantage in terms of political legitimacy, standing and power' (ibid:16). Hayden calls it a category mistake to take price as a measure of social value for the purpose of a policymaking paradigm. 'The willingness to pay for a good is a subjective want. That is inconsistent with the purpose of public policy. The purpose of public policy is to provide for social beliefs through political association and public processes […] [and not] to submit to the criterion of market price' (ibid: 16). Hayden argues that neoclassical economists have selected money making as the dominant policy criterion, as narrowly focused and misguided criteria that lack a concern for multisocietalism and multiculturalism (ibid:39). This usually leads to following market rules of pecuniary enhancement so as not to have to judge consequences by society's criteria (ibid: 46). 'Our system will not be allowed to prosper if the neoclassical standard of the market is to be the scientific criterion for making judgments about ecological systems policy' (ibid: 48-49).

12.3 A Normative Matrix for Social Costs: Primary Criteria and Socioecological Indicators

Against the aforementioned background of GSA and the limitations of utilitarian criteria for analyzing and evaluating social costs, Hayden raises the important question regarding the role of primary and secondary criteria that stand between the social system and policy evaluation (ibid: 37). Hayden stresses the importance of deriving alternative norms and values, that is, primary and secondary criteria. Criteria are to be consistent with belief clusters in the relevant context which does not preclude that beliefs are sometimes the object of policymaking themselves (ibid: 40-41). Importantly, criteria also become the object of inquiry in evaluating their effects on socioecological processes: '[...] a major part of policy analysis will be to study the community structural changes that take place as a result of the application of a set of criteria and their resulting policies, and to change the criteria if they lead to undesirable consequences' (ibid: 41-42). Criteria can be modified and refined: 'The refinement of the interpretation and application of criteria is achieved through discretionary processes made up of legislative bodies, judicial proceedings, research inquiries, advocacy efforts, and so forth' (ibid: 42). What is more, Hayden denies that there is one single set of criteria and argues that a different set of criteria are needed for every context particularly if contexts overlap (ibid: 43). This matches his rejection of seeking and enforcing one unified common ground with regard to normative criteria (ibid: 43). Yet, Hayden argues that it is possible that the problem itself generates the criteria of its resolution (ibid: 36) so that, for example, the primary normative criteria for the ecological system have to be consistent with the maintenance of a particular kind of ecological systems (ibid: 19).

This is why Hayden deals with the difficult task of generating a database of information for the guidance of the policymaking process and presents a methodology for developing socioecological indicators. 'As was emphasized in the social indicator movement that began in the 1960s [cf. Kapp], all useful measures are ultimately social. They are recognized as social indicators to indicate that they are relevant to some social context, rather than as ultimate 'measures' having universal applicability' (ibid: 61-62). Hayden applies John Dewey's measurement standards for the design of indicators 'from quality to quantity,' mentioning especially site-specific ecology and consistency with the problem. In addition, Hayden underlines that the indicators must be consistent with the primary goal because operationally the indicator becomes the public policy decision criterion. Indicators as secondary criteria become *the* action criteria (ibid: 62-63). In reality, policy indicators determine the final policy result because the evaluation of alternatives depends on indicators used for their valuation. Hence, it becomes important that the indicators used to measure and value alternatives are consistent with the primary goals.

In conclusion, Hayden's approach points to the difficult task of subjecting values and criteria to the policymaking process as they are not outside the scope of science but can be evaluated in terms of their consequences. This hints at the primary task of an institutional approach to social costs, that is, to develop alternative criteria for the evaluation of social costs when utilitarian criteria are not considered. Since social costs and benefits cannot meaningfully be measured in terms of market prices, there is a need to outline alternative criteria for measurement and evaluation. The question arises as to what forms of criteria exist that are suited to measure social costs. If problems provide the criteria for their solution, as Hayden argues, then it should be possible to find a normative common ground for the problem of social costs. It is here that Kapp's approach to policymaking for the environment (social and physical) can be fruitfully incorporated into Hayden's approach. Kapp proposed the universal value of basic human needs from which context-dependent criteria (social minima) can be developed as primary criteria. The degree to which social minima are not fulfilled would then be an objective nonutilitarian measure of social costs.

12.4 Kapp's Humanist Approach to Policymaking and Social Costs

Kapp is perhaps best known as the economist who developed a theory of social costs in the tradition of American institutionalism (Veblen 1904) (Kapp 1950, [1963] 1977) and a policy approach that links Dewey's pragmatic instrumentalism (Dewey 1922) with Max Weber's substantive rationality (Weber [1925] 2005).

12.4.1 The Complexity Theory of Social Costs and the Limitations of Utilitarian Policies

According to Kapp's theory, the extent to which social costs are accounted for depends on the political structure of society requiring environmental policy and institutional reforms to minimize them. '[Social costs] are damages [...] which under different institutional conditions could be avoided. For, obviously, if these costs were inevitable under any kind of institutional arrangement they would not really present a special theoretical problem. [...] to reveal their origin the study of social costs must always be an institutional analysis. Such an analysis raises inevitably the question of institutional reform and economic policy which may eliminate or minimize the social diseconomies under discussion.' (Kapp 1963:186) 'No democratic society can and will tolerate this subordination of the social system to the dictates of formal rationality. The universal reaction of society to the neglect of social costs [...] has taken a variety of forms [...] compelling private producers to internalize [...] social costs'. (Kapp 1963:202)

Realizing the normative-political character of the problem of social costs and its problematic dependency on asymmetric power relations, Kapp sought a way of dealing with problems of social costs scientifically without resorting to formal approaches of the utilitarian kind. In fact, his divergence from Pigouvian (1924) and Coasian (1960) policy approaches does not only result from the realization of the problem's normative-political character but also from their faulty logic and practical limitations. For instance, Kapp considered it as logically faulty to define the concept more precisely than is justified: 'An element of inescapable indeterminacy may remain either due to the lack of homogeneity of the facts or of people's valuations or due to a lack of knowledge about causal interrelationships.' (Kapp [1971b] 1977:309) Kapp pointed to circular cumulative causation in the ecological system and fundamental uncertainty: 'Pollution and the disruption of the environment are the results of a complex interaction of the economic system with physical and biological systems which have their own specific regularities. Moreover, pollutants from different sources act upon one another and what counts are not only the effects of particular effluents and toxic materials but the total toxological situation. [...] Those who have studied these complex relationships know that environmental disruption can easily become cumulative with pervasive and disproportionate effects per unit of additional pollutants' (ibid: 314-315). Kapp's theory of social costs stresses 'the cumulative character and complexity of the causal sequence which gives rise to environmental disruption and social costs' (ibid: 315) and 'the delicate system of interrelationships' (Kapp [1963] 1977:94). His theory can in this sense be coined a 'complexity theory' of social costs that does not exclude less tangible effects. Kapp emphasized that social costs cannot be considered as being minor side effects in relatively isolated locations, but have to be seen as all pervasive. He even combined this with a historical hypothesis: 'as the economy becomes more complex, nonmarket interdependencies are likely to assume greater significance. For this reason social costs are bound to become increasingly important.' (Kapp [1965a] 1983:5) Under conditions of complexity and uncertainty the price mechanism that relies on individual subjective evaluations alone cannot identify a viable output position. It is largely impossible for 'the individual to ascertain the full range of short and long run benefits of environmental improvements, or for that matter, of the full impact of environmental disruption upon his health and well-being.' (Kapp [1971b] 1977:314) Likewise, it can sometimes be difficult to causally determine who is responsible for effects either because of incomplete knowledge or because effects are out of proportion to each individual cause. Referring to Myrdal, Kapp reminded us 'that statistical convenience and measurement must *not* be permitted to set limits to concept formations and thus to exclude relevant elements' (ibid: 309-310).

Kapp rejected the application of the utilitarian principle, that is, the willingness to pay or accept compensation that assigns monetary exchange values to ecological effects. This method is, according to Kapp, as arbitrary as the distributional inequality which it expresses because the 'willingness to pay' depends on the 'ability to pay' and has nothing to do with the objective and real exigencies of states of socioecological balance. 'The use of the willingness to pay as criterion of quantifying and evaluating the quality of the environment has the insidious effect of reinterpreting original human needs and requirements into a desire for money and of evaluating the relative importance of such needs in terms of criteria which reflect the existing inequalities and distortions in the price, wage and income structure' (ibid: 313). Kapp made the case that monetary criteria such as the willingness to pay are not appropriate because they do not evaluate the characteristics that define the quality of the environment and its potentially negative impact on human health, human well-being, and human survival (ibid:316). In addition to these theoretical inconsistencies, Kapp argued on practical grounds that formal approaches have the effect of neither guaranteeing the fulfillment of the requirements of socioecological balance nor the satisfaction of basic human needs because they focus on rule-following, that is, their solutions are predetermined and limited by a prescriptive formal apparatus. In addition, they remedy social costs only ex-post, which can be too late if damaging effects are irreversible, and they can be too little if the formal calculus prevents taking into account the whole range and full extent of repercussions: 'making the content and extent of the control of environmental quality dependent upon individual willingness to pay could at best lead to piecemeal measures and an ineffective formal suboptimization if it does not become the pretext for endless delays or a policy of doing too little too late' (ibid:315).

12.4.2 Rational Humanism and Primary Criteria
Kapp proposed a new rational humanism that would humanize economics by starting from a clear notion of universal human needs (Kapp [1967] 1985:99-120). According to Kapp basic human needs are

universal values and should become the basis of substantive rationality in the tradition of Max Weber (Weber [1925] 2005). 'Any substantive treatment of human needs and the resulting notion of substantive rationality is based in part on the normative axiom that human life and human development and survival are values which need no further proof or demonstration' (Kapp, unpublished manuscript, Chap. 4:11). In his unpublished manuscript 'The Foundations of Institutional Economics' Kapp argued that Marxists and Institutionalists start from the value premise of human needs (ibid:11).[86] Kapp also referred to the concept of 'social reproduction,' which was first developed by the Physiocrats and later adopted by Marx and Engels. Social reproduction is considered as a goal in itself and as a useful tool for elaborating hypotheses regarding defects and inefficiencies of the social system (Kapp 1974:132, 134-135).

Regarding values Kapp explicitly refers to, on the one hand, the Myrdalian position that value judgments always influence economic science and that they have to be made explicit in order to escape the danger of claiming value-free results (Myrdal [1929] 1954; Kapp 1968:6). On the other hand, however, Kapp seems to have gone further than Myrdal when he proposed that a substantive (value-laden) formulation of concepts with 'objective' categories that does not depend on an infinite variety of subjective values is in fact possible. For him 'objectively' ascertainable values exist and therefore a 'science of the essential being' (Wissenschaft des wahren Seins) (Blum 1982:49, 1977:51). For Kapp facts and values are not only interlinked but values, especially the universal value of human existential needs is the object of science. Regarding the interrelationship of facts and values, Kapp also adopted Marx's point of view that the analysis of facts is capable of yielding normative conclusions (Sollenspostulate), while rejecting naive empiricism (Kapp 1974:39).

To understand Kapp's rational humanism as a version of Weber's substantive rationality it is helpful to take a look at what is considered the central humanistic reference point (Blum 1977:49; Steppacher 1994:435). Kapp started from the 'uniqueness of the biological structure of the human organism' (Kapp 1961:139). His biocultural concept argues that beyond certain basic physiological needs no innate needs exist. Yet the human being has to satisfy certain universal or essential needs if he is to develop as a human being. These needs result from the fact that humans are born in a quasiembryonic state without the safety of a fixed instinct hierarchy and experience helplessness, anxiety and dependency: (1) the need for cooperation and communication, (2) the need for self-esteem, self-affirmation, and individuation, (3) the need for safety, order, and security. These needs are social in character because they can only be satisfied in society, so that humans and society are interrelated aspects of life that cannot be meaningfully separated. This constitutes the unique biological structure of humans that is 'open' and that necessitates a 'process of growth' as a condition of the actualization of latent potentialities (Kapp 1961:156). The failure to satisfy these needs may lead to various forms of stress, tension, and anxiety (ibid:174). From this Kapp concluded that human beings share universals by virtue of being human in close accordance with findings of theorists, such as Abraham Maslow and Erich Fromm. According to Blum, even depth psychology shows that there is an objectively observable and scientifically determinable 'common denominator' in humans that expresses a quality that is both uniquely and universally human (Blum 1977:50). Kapp formulated the usefulness of such an understanding of human nature: 'An empirically validated concept of man and human nature and an understanding of the impact of the enculturation process on the human personality and self-actualization may ultimately enable the social scientist to appraise [...] [the] impact [of the social and physical environment] on the individual' (Kapp 1961:178).

This background allowed Kapp to derive criteria for a rational humanism that are substantive, meaning that they are sought and found in the degree of satisfaction of human needs. This process embodies a differentiation of human needs according to their urgency into basic and higher needs. According to Kapp, it is possible to determine minimum standards in the fields of public health, medical care, education, housing, transportation, and recreation based on empirical data with greater agreement than usually assumed. Hence, human needs become operable as social minima. While remaining subject to revision in the light of new scientific research they have to become ends in themselves because they reflect basic human and social needs (Kapp [1971a] 1983:117). In this context, Kapp praised Carl Menger for having faced the difficult task in the 2nd revised edition of *Grundsätze der Volkswirtschaftslehre* of differentiating between needs of first order and those of higher order (Menger 1923:32-56; Kapp 1972:217). As criteria human needs are clearly very different from the formal subjective maximizing, undetermined utility functions, or abstract money units of formal rationality that conceal great disparities (Blum 1982:67, 69). Referring to Immanuel Kant, Kapp argued that that which cannot be exchanged has no exchange value but intrinsic absolute value. Thus, for him human life and survival are not exchangeable commodities and their evaluation in terms of market prices is in conflict with reason and human conscience (Kapp 1974:132).[87] Kapp emphasized that the door remains open for empirical validation and refutation and the possibility of disproving evaluations (Kapp 1963:188-189). Kapp applies the term 'objectivity' of norms in a pragmatic sense of a susceptibility to revision in the light of experience and the empirical test. Human needs as norms become a reference point that makes it possible to say which means and ends are 'healthy' or 'good.' Norms and values are open to scientific evaluation and guide economic policy. In this, rational humanism links Weber's concept of substantive rationality to Dewey's pragmatic instrumentalism that considered value judgments to guide theoretical and empirical analysis (Bush and Tool 2001:198-200). In elaborating rational humanism Kapp drew farther away from Weber and closer to Dewey who stated that all crucial decision making must invariably include an exploration of the objectives pursued both as far as their content and their implications are concerned (Kapp 1965b:59). Kapp also referred to Dewey's distinction between the 'manipulative' use of reason (formal rationality) and the 'constructive' use of intelligence. He favoured the latter because it is concerned with the realization of genuine opportunities, the exploration of new possibilities, and it requires the projection of the full repercussions of action under different circumstances (Kapp 1963:194-195).

Rational humanism moves beyond the limit of Weber's notion of objectivity that was tied to his version of 'scientific' instrumental reasoning that is not concerned with criteria. Building on the contribution of Dewey, Kapp found a way to treat value-related decisions as also 'objective' in a pragmatic sense. It seems that Kapp associated freely with Weber's notion of substantive rationality and it can be considered his innovation to build this orientation toward higher norms, in particular human needs, into economic reasoning and to render them operational as primary criteria. The very concepts of substantive rationality and value-related reasoning are evidence of Weber's intuition that even his scientific instrumentalism has certain limits. This is what inspired Kapp's theoretical innovation and brings into the open what Weber had only hinted at. Kapp's concept of universal human needs demonstrates that there is not an infinite amount of possible standards of value and that values are not beyond the scope of science. Yet, it is important that rational humanism does not enter into what Weber called 'ethics of conviction' with its uncritical and unconditional devotion to an absolute idea and fixed aim which leads to a neglect as to its consequences. Instead it remains within the confines of what Weber called 'ethics of responsibility' (Kapp 1963:188- 189). Kapp fully agreed with Weber by emphasizing that science must never be used to impose dogmatic value judgments (Blum 1977:51).

Kapp's rational humanism in policymaking means that fundamental requirements of human life and survival are integral parts of the constellation of goals of economic policy and social controls. For example, particular aspects of the quality of the environment such as clean air and water must be an end in itself via scientifically derived environmental norms that reflect basic human needs. Kapp's policymaking places the human being and basic needs in the centre by proposing social minima, ecological maximum tolerance levels, socioecological indicators, and social controls (Kapp [1971a] 1983, [1973] 1974, [1974] 1983). Kapp was convinced that the solution to the problem of social costs required a new *Political* Economy (Kapp 1950, [1963] 1977) or normative economics: 'the new task of [normative] economics would be to elucidate the manner in which collectively determined social goals and objectives could be attained in the most effective and socially least costly manner' (Kapp 1976:102). In elaborating his humanist approach to policymaking Kapp relied on Dewey's instrumentalism: 'the instrumental elaboration of the paths to be followed, the choice of means in its broadest sense, both belong to the rational setting of objectives and their rational achievement, i.e., rational in the light of empirically testable criteria [i.e. social minima]. [...] The logic of the determination of objectives is added to the logic of the achievement of objectives by the introduction of means suited to the objectives. When political economics is oriented towards the preservation of life and providing the means of existence [...] it includes the exploration of what is necessary and possible and, in the form of political action, deals at the same time with the question of how appropriate reforms may be used to realize sets of objectives that have been recognized as necessary and found social acceptance.' (Kapp [1967] 1985:112-113)

12.4.3 Social Minima and Socioecological Indicators for Measuring Social Costs

Rational humanism applied to policymaking aims at objectifying scientifically and making operational the value of human needs via social minima. Social minima are objective criteria – a kind of measuring rod – for the appraisal of the 'health' of the social and physical environment which enable economists to establish norms and values scientifically. Social minima can further be transformed into maximum tolerance levels. These are ecological norms, which allow evaluating and exploring different means and ends in the light of their differing costs and benefits, their effects on the physical and social environment, hence their effect on the satisfaction of human needs. Maximum tolerance levels can be used to measure social costs in terms of existing deficiencies by comparing, for example, the actual state of pollution with the maximum permissible concentration of pollutants. 'What we suggest as undeniable is the fact that as we extend the applicability of [social minima] we 'rationalize' and 'objectify' the determination of social costs and social benefits and remove their evaluation increasingly from the realm of subjective or ideological self-deceptions and distortions' (Kapp 1963:202).

At this point it becomes clear that Kapp's realization about the social nature of the problem of social costs and the importance of finding workable and scientifically sound solutions forced him to break with Weber's position on value-free instrumentalism: 'In contrast to M. Weber we suggest that the substantive definition of social costs and social benefits is possible in terms of objective requirements […] [because they] can be determined with a considerable degree of scientific method and objectivity. That is to say, the identification of social costs and social benefits calls for scientifically determined social minima' (Kapp 1963:193-194). Yet, at the same time Weber's notion of substantive rationality remained the main inspiration for his rational humanism: 'The identification of social costs and social benefits derives its objectivity from an orientation toward a substantive rationality which reflects the extent to which a given group of persons is or could be adequately provided with goods and services, or protected against unnecessary losses' (Kapp 1963:190, 193). Kapp acknowledged that social minima do not make the decision process free of conflict. 'We do not deny that the social evaluation of the relative importance of social benefits and social costs will always carry elements of political decision as to social purposes and goals. […] Admittedly this relationship [social minima] does not give rise to an unequivocal and self-evident determination of social goals and social values; but it […] facilitates the formulation of aims and priorities which are accessible to scientific interpretation and the pragmatic test' (Kapp 1963:203).

Kapp's policy approach also offers derived (secondary) criteria for environmental policy. Kapp argued that environmental policies, the evaluation of environmental goals and the establishment of priorities require a substantive economic calculus in terms of social use values (politically evaluated) for which the formal calculus in monetary exchange values fails to provide a real measure. Hence, an integral part of Kapp's policymaking is a comprehensive system of social accounting with a diversity of heterogeneous socioecological indicators that reflect the present state and exigencies of the socioecological system and its effect on the condition of human life in the light of explicitly stipulated environmental objectives (minimum environmental standards). Socioecological indicators include an inventory of the total situation, a kind of stock taking as a departure point. This inventory of the present state of the environment has to contain the actual and potential dangers for human health and well-being, to social productivity and indeed to human life and survival. Yet, Kapp cautions that it is important not to conceal that vested interests are affected by implementing a more comprehensive accounting system (Kapp [1973] 1974).

12.5 Conclusion

In conclusion, Kapp's approach fits into the framework of Hayden's Social Fabric Matrix (SFM) because both are based on the same philosophical foundation, that is, Dewey's pragmatic instrumentalism and a nonutilitarian approach to value. SFM's key system principles and components are also found in Kapp's open system approach to social costs. Thus, SFM is *the* technique that makes it possible to apply Kapp's theory of social costs in concrete problem settings to effectively resolve problems of social costs. The real advantage is SFM's graphical-formal tool box that allows the framing of the problem situation by better understanding circular cumulative causation between the open economic system and its physical and social environment. In addition, SFM's method to policymaking as a social process under the influence of different values allows for approaching social costs as Kapp did, i.e. by means of primary criteria (social minima and maximum tolerance levels) and secondary criteria (socioecological indicators).

References

Berger S (2008) Circular cumulative causation (CCC) à la Myrdal and Kapp – political institutionalism for minimizing social costs. J Econ Issues 42:357-365.

Berger S, Elsner W (2007) European contributions to evolutionary institutional economics: the cases of cumulative circular causation (CCC) and open system approach (OSA) – some methodological and policy implications. J Econ Issues 41:529-537.

Blum FJ (1977) Professor Kapp's approach to a science of man in society in the light of the emerging new consciousness and social order. In: Rolf S et al (eds) Economics in institutional perspective – memorial essays in honor of K. William Kapp. Lexington Books, Lexington, pp 47-60.

Blum FJ (1982) 'Die Bedeutung des Universalen für alternative Theorien der Gesellschaft: Max Weber und William Kapp'. In: Leipert C (ed) Konzepte einer humanen Wirtschaftslehre. Offene Welt, Frankfurt am Main, pp 41-72.

Bush PD, Tool MR (2001) The evolutionary principles of American neoinstitutional economics. In: Dopfer K (ed) Evolutionary economics: program and scope. Elsevier, Boston, pp 195-230.

Coase RH (1960) The problem of social costs. Law Econ 3:1-44.

Dewey J (1922) Human nature and conduct – an introduction to social psychology. The Modern Library, New York.

Hayden GF (2006) Policymaking for a good society: the social fabric matrix approach to policy analysis and program evaluation. Springer, Berlin.

Kapp KW (1950) *The social costs of private enterprise.* Harvard University Press, Cambridge, MA.

Kapp KW (1961) *Toward a science of man in society – a positive approach to the integration of social knowledge.* Martinus Nijhoff, The Hague.

Kapp KW [1963] 1977 The social costs of business enterprise (second enlarged edition of The social costs of private enterprise (1950)). Spokesman, Nottingham.

Kapp KW (1963) Social costs and social benefits – a contribution to normative economics. In: Beckerath EV, Giersch H (eds) Probleme der normativen Ökonomik und der wirtschaftspolitischen Beratung, Verein für Sozialpolitik. Duncker & Humblot, Berlin, pp 183-210.

Kapp KW (1965a) Social costs in economic development. In: Ullmann JE (ed) Social costs, economic development and environmental disruption. University Press of America, Lanham/ London, pp 1-38.

Kapp KW (1965b) Economic development in a new perspective: existential minima and substantive rationality. Kyklos 18:49-79.

Kapp KW [1967] 1985 Economics and rational humanism. In: Ullmann JE, Preiswerk R (eds) The humanization of the social sciences. University Press of America, Lanham/London, pp 99-120

Kapp KW (1968) In defence of institutional economics. Swed J Econ 70:1-18.

Kapp KW [1971a] 1983 Implementation of environmental policies. In: Ullmann JE (ed) Social costs, economic development and environmental disruption. University Press of America, Lanham/London, pp 111-142.

Kapp KW [1971b] 1977 Social costs, neo-classical economics, and environmental planning. In: Kapp, K. William [1963a] 1977. The social costs of business enterprise, Appendix. Spokesman, Nottingham.

Kapp KW (1972) Umweltgefährdung als ökonomisches und wirtschaftspolitisches Problem. Schweizerische Zeitschrift für Forstwesen 123:211-222.

Kapp KW [1973] 1974 Environmental indicators as indicators of social use value.

In: Kapp KW (ed) Environmental policies and development planning in Contemporary China and other essays. Mouton, Paris/The Hague.

Kapp KW (1974) Environmental policies and development planning in contemporary china and other essays. Mouton, Paris/The Hague.

Kapp KW [1974] 1983 Governmental furtherance of environmentally sound technology. In: Ullmann JE (ed) Social costs, economic development and environmental disruption. University Press of America, Lanham/London, pp 143-207.

Kapp KW (1976) The open-system character of the economy and its implications. In: Kurt Dopfer (ed) Economics in the future. The Macmillan Press, London, pp 90-105.

Kapp KW (undated) The foundations of institutional economics (unpublished manuscript). Kapp Archive, Basel.

Menger C (1923) Grundsätze der Volkswirtschaftslehre, 2nd, revised edn. Hölder-Pichler-Tempsky A.G./G. Freytag G.m.b.H, Wien and Leipzig.

Myrdal G [1929] 1954 The political element in the development of economic theory. Harvard University Press, Cambridge, MA.

O'Hara PA (2000) Marx, Veblen, and contemporary institutional political economy. Edward Elgar, Cheltenham/Northampton.

Pigou AC (1924) The economics of welfare, 2nd edn. MacMillan & Co., London.

Polanyi K [1947] 1968 Obsolete market mentality. In: Dalton G (ed) Primitive, archaic, and modern economies – essays by Karl Polanyi. Beacon Press, Boston.

Steppacher R (1994) Kapp, K. William. In: Hodgson GM, Samuels WJ, Tool MR (eds) The Elgar companion to institutional and evolutionary economics, vol 2. Edward Elgar, Aldershot, Hants and Brookfield, pp 435-441.

Veblen TB (1904) The theory of business enterprise. Charles Scribner's Sons, New York Weber M [1925] 2005 Wirtschaft und Gesellschaft. Zweitausendeinsverlag, Frankfurt am Main.

13
Social Costs of Salmon Fisheries: A circular cumulative causation analysis with policy implications

13.1 Introduction

Since the second half of the twentieth century, in particular, the Western industrialized world has experienced an unprecedented economic 'growth' that is customarily expressed in terms of GDP. Industrialization, manufacturing and growing markets have paved the way for exploiting the benefits of so-called 'increasing returns' that are at the core of CCC growth theories. In this very same economic process, however, the enormous wealth of biotic renewable resources, such as fisheries, has been reduced and exploited to an extent that has brought many of them near collapse and several species near extinction. Depletion of renewable and non-renewable resources as well as pollution are real costs that remain unaccounted for in markets. This is why an accounting in terms of market values underlying concepts such as 'economic growth' (GDP in market prices) and 'increasing returns' (in terms of exchange values) has been fundamentally criticized in the planning debate of the 1920s and 1930s, by the ecological development movement in the 1960s and 1970s, as well as by the movement for social cost accounting and green GDP in the 1980s and 1990s. In other words, the ecological context matters and economists must not turn a blind eye to the wealth-diminishing aspects of growth in manufacturing. In order to capture these important aspects, this chapter proposes Myrdal's and Kapp's CCC.

First, we identify common characteristics between Myrdal's principle of circular cumulative causation (CCC) and the pre-analytical vision of ecological economics (EE), as exemplified by its treatment of fisheries. It is argued that there is a common 'complexity perspective' that goes back to the 1940s when K. William Kapp applied the CCC to socio-ecological problems. Hereby, we demonstrate how CCC serves as a common denominator concept for institutional and EE. Second, we provide a circular cumulative causation analysis of the life cycle of salmon, and the social costs of salmon depletion and farmed salmon. Kapp's CCC-based theory of social costs captures the wealth-diminishing features of the economic system. The CCC perspective leads to a social minima approach in which states of social and ecological balance become part of economic rationality.

13.2 CCC as a methodology for fisheries

Applying CCC in the ecological context raises the question as to whether it is compatible with EE's approach to complex renewable resources, such as salmon fisheries. EE's approach to fishery depletion argues that crafting institutional frameworks for sustainable resource utilization not only requires an understanding of the interactions between economic institutions and their effects on the ecological system, but also knowledge of the complex interactions within the system of biotic resources itself.

> Variables of an action situation [...] are also affected by attributes of the biophysical and material world being acted upon and transformed. What actions are physically possible, what outcomes can be produced [...] are affected by the world being acted upon in a situation. (Ostrom 2005: 22)

'Appropriators in the field have to explore and discover the biophysical structure of a particular resource' (Ostrom 2005: 243). Thus, the attributes of resources themselves affect the sustainability of particular institutions so that the success of resource regimes depends on the characteristics of the resource. 'With improved understanding, it may become possible to diagnose resource use situations well enough to separate promising institutional forms from those unlikely to achieve desired goals' (Dietz *et al.* 2002: 25).

Realizing the importance of knowledge about the resource situation, EE comes to adopt a 'non-equilibrium' view of the ecological system in which fisheries are considered to be complex resources (Rose 2002: 241). This means that all relevant factors, such as habitat, spatial distribution of local stocks, population behaviour, spawning stock biomass, the population size of other species, such as prey fish and predators and other ecological factors have to be considered (Wilson 2002: 331). Accordingly, EE holds that scientific research about causal relationships affecting the population size of fish bears many uncertainties, often preventing precise measurement and exact quantitative foundations for decision-making (Wilson 2002: 329, 334-40). Fisheries are, furthermore, considered heterogeneous so that situational local knowledge is deemed important:

> Fishers have to know a great deal about the ecology of their inshore region including spawning areas, nursery areas, the migration routes of different species, and seasonal patterns [...] inshore fisheries that have survived [...] have learned how to maintain these critical life-cycle processes with rules controlling technology, fishing locations, and fishing times. (Ostrom 2005: 230)

Due to this complexity view, EE has serious doubts about the unproven 'primum-mobile' assertion of formal resource economists that deems the spawning stock biomass the *only* relevant factor for sustaining stocks (Wilson 2002: 329, 331). EE rejects extremely simple, formal approaches of resource utilization, such as H. S. Gordon's 'equilibrium' resource model, and their conclusions. Gordon's impact is still manifest in those approaches to fisheries that focus on the 'maximum economic yield' of a single species, showing little concern for the complexity of the ecological system. Species are treated as isolated entities, essential reciprocal interrelationships are neglected, and fundamental uncertainty is reduced to stochastic uncertainty (Dietz *et al.* 2002: 9-10; Wilson 2002: 329).

Quite similar to EE's complexity approach, Myrdal developed CCC to analyze complex socio-economic dynamics:

> The dynamics of the [...] system are determined by the fact that among all the endogenous conditions there is circular causation, implying that, if there is a change in one condition, others will change in response. [...] There is no basic factor; everything causes everything else. This implies interdependence within the whole [...] process. (Myrdal 1978: 774)

According to Myrdal, the task of CCC analysis is

> to analyze the causal inter-relations within the system itself as it moves under the influence of outside pushes and pulls and the momentum of its own internal processes. [...] The outside forces push and pull the system continuously, and at the same time change the structure of forces within the system itself. (Myrdal 1957: 18)

As a result, Myrdal argued that

> it is useless to look for one predominant factor, a 'basic factor' [...] everything is cause to everything else in an interlocking circular manner. [...] the application of this hypothesis moves any realistic study [...] far outside the boundaries of traditional economic theory. (Myrdal 1957: 19)

This shows how Myrdal designed CCC as a framework of complex *causal* analysis in the Veblenian tradition rather than as a *teleological* search for levels of equilibrium or 'primum-mobile' causation.

CCC accepts the time element and uncertainty as important characteristics of many complex dynamics: 'because the system is in constant movement [...] the coefficients of interrelations among the various conditions in a circular causation are ordinarily not known with quantitative precision' (Myrdal 1978: 774). 'The time element is of paramount importance, as the effects [...] will be spread very differently along the time axis' (Myrdal 1957: 19).

> Elements of inertia, time lags, and in extreme cases the total non-responsiveness of one or several conditions to changes in some set of other conditions are problems of great complexity [...] Consequently, our analysis [...] must often end in broad generalizations and merely plausible hypotheses, built upon limited observation, discernment and conjectural judgments. (Myrdal 1976: 83)

Myrdal defended the CCC's methodological middle ground between the exact reasoning of mathematics and naïve empiricism against mainstream critics:

> In calling the holistic approach the fundamental principle of institutional economics, I imply that our main accusation against conventional economists is that they work with 'closed models' with too few variables. [...] institutional analysis, not working with the wholesale exclusion of so much which is important, will seldom be able to argue quantitatively in such precise terms, simply because our knowledge of relevant facts and the inter-relations between those facts is not that precise. [...] we are generally more critical than conventional economists. [...] We just want our theory and models, indeed even the concepts we use, to be more adequate to the reality we are studying. (Myrdal 1976: 83-4)

Studying Veblen's and Myrdal's CCC approaches in the 1940s and 1950s, Kapp was probably the first economist to apply CCC to ecological problems (see his theory of social costs; Kapp 1950). In this context, Kapp applied the CCC as a working hypothesis, i.e. 'a guiding principle of interpretation in the light of which we look at facts in order to see whether it improves our understanding,' broadening the frame of reference and also the unit of investigation (Kapp 1965b: 6). Kapp chose the CCC because it allowed the researcher to follow the lead of the subject matter, i.e. to view the socio-economic and ecological processes as the outcome of a circular cumulative process in which a number of causes interact upon each other and with their effects. '[Economics] is necessarily concerned with processes of considerable complexity. [...] Above all [CCC] directs our attention away from the futile search for the primary cause of [...] events' (Kapp 1965b: 7). His socio-ecological indicator approach to measuring advances in development perceived the quality of life as a totality in which everything is interlinked with the quality of the human environment. For example, pollutants in water and pollutants in air interact with one another in a reciprocal and even self-reinforcing manner to impact upon the quality of life in a cumulative manner. In addition, Kapp pointed to certain critical zones or thresholds in the ecological system, beyond which a change in a variable could have disproportionate and possibly irreversible effects (Kapp [1973] 1974: 100-1).

Kapp's CCC perspective is compatible with open system theory and the implications of the entropy law (2nd law of thermodynamics) as pointed out by Georgescu-Roegen (1971). They all view the economic system as embedded in the ecological and social system from which it receives its inputs and which affect all interconnected systems. Importantly, CCC embodies the perspective that disruptive ecological effects can feed back and cause harm in the economic system (Berger and Elsner 2007). In conclusion, EE's approach to complex problems and fisheries and CCC's methodology are compatible. The CCC analysis of salmon in the following part of the paper is inspired by Kapp's proposal:

> By viewing human action as taking place within, and with repercussions on a physical and social environment with specific structures and regularities, it becomes clear that the various spheres of man's environment which are affected by his action are interdependent [...] causal analysis cannot be carried on in terms of one or the other of the compartmentalized social, physical and biological disciplines [...] we still lack such a theory and/or science which is capable of elucidating the mode and outcome of the complex interaction of several systems. [...] However, there is one important aspect we do know about the causal chain [...] in many (if not in most) instances it is a process of circular causation which has a tendency of becoming cumulative unless some deliberate action is taken to arrest or redirect it. (Kapp [1970b] 1983: 44)

13.3 A CCC-analysis of salmon's life cycle, salmon depletion, and farmed salmon

Applying the CCC to salmon's life cycle and salmon depletion, the following section demonstrates how the working hypothesis elucidates the complex reciprocal and self-reinforcing causation between salmon stocks and other species and plants in oceans, rivers, and land, as well as relations between ecosystems. Cumulative effects over time, such as the cumulative exhaustion of salmon stocks, and the likelihood of incomplete knowledge about interrelations are taken into consideration. The abundance of salmon stocks is explored not as an independent entity but with the hypothesis of being the result of circular cumulative causation, i.e. the cause and the effect of a balance in the ecological system exhibiting complexity and sensitivity. This analysis aims at providing an understanding of the ecological problem situation, setting the stage for a discussion of the social costs and underlying institutional causes of salmon depletion.

At alternate intervals of their life cycle, salmon utilize both marine and freshwater habitats, a life history strategy known as 'diadromy.' Born in lakes and streams, salmon migrate to the sea where they live for several years, then swim back upstream to spawn, and for many species to die.

- *Salmon's reciprocal interaction with the ocean system*: Young salmon arrive in the ocean after about a year of development in lakes, rivers, and streams. At this point in the salmon life cycle, the new ocean dwellers, called smolts, already eat other fish, and as they grow they hunt prey that is larger and higher up the food chain. Smolts, however, are consumed *en masse* as they reach the ocean 'by several species of marine birds and mammals, including seals, sea lions, and small whales [...] and some saltwater fishes, for example, walleye pollock [...] and Pacific herring' (Willson and Halupka 1995: 493). Those that survive live on to accumulate over 90 per cent of their adult body weight at sea, amassing a deposit of marine nutrients that proves incredibly important for inland terrestrial ecosystems. Salmon, fattened by ocean food webs, grow ripe with eggs, endure a final bulk-up and growth of secondary sex characteristics, and head inland, sometimes travelling hundreds of miles and thousands of feet in elevation to return to the streams in which they were spawned (Hildebrand *et al.* 2004: 1-2).
- *Salmon's reciprocal interaction with the stream-forest systems*: As salmon travel upstream they are killed and eaten by a broad variety of terrestrial predators that rely on them as 'a predictable, dependable, concentrated, and accessible resource high in protein and energy' (Hildebrand *et al.* 2004: 2).

Moreover, Hildebrand *et al.* argue that spawning salmon have also been important in supporting the nutrient requirements, particularly nitrogen, of periphyton, juvenile salmon, and resident fishes. Growth rates of juvenile fish in streams containing spawning coho salmon (*Oncorhynchus kisutch*) were double those that lacked returning fish, and the proportion of salmon-contributed nitrogen in the tissues of freshwater biota ranged from 17 to 30% across trophic levels. (ibid: 2)

Those salmon that die as a result of the rigours of upstream travel, or are killed and incompletely consumed both by their predators and the scavengers that follow, end up depositing their nutrients into forest flora. The impact of this deposition is extensive, and it has been observed that almost a quarter of the nitrogen embodied in the trees and shrubs within 150 meters of salmon-running streams come from marine sources. That is, a quarter of the nitrogen in some forests is left by salmon. As a result, vegetation within range of this marine nitrogen deposition is shown to achieve triple the growth rate at spawning sites relative to reference sites (Helfield and Naiman 2001: 2406). Shading by riparian vegetation moderates stream temperatures, controlling rates of embryo development. Bank stabilization by riparian roots minimizes erosion, which threatens embryo survival by restricting intragravel flow and oxygenation of redds. Litter inputs provide allochthonous organic matter supporting production of aquatic insects, which are an essential food source for juvenile salmon. Riparian forests also enhance stream habitat through the production of LWD (large woody debris). Among other functions, LWD increases the structural complexity of stream channels, thereby creating preferred habitat for spawning. Instream LWD also creates areas of low flow velocity, providing shelter from winter high flows, which is an important cause of mortality in overwintering fry and incubating embryos. Overall, the presence of LWD in spawning streams enhances production of salmonids fishes (Helfield and Naiman 2004: 2407).

Consequently, Helfield and Naiman argue that enhancing the growth of riparian trees and the production of LWD inputs to the riparian zone serves as a self-reinforcing causation in which spawning salmon help to enhance the survivorship of subsequent salmonid generations, as well as the success of terrestrial and aquatic predator species and proximal flora. It is apparent that such a system operates cumulatively; that is, salmon runs in one year affect the next, and salmon runs in that year affect runs far into the future.

This analysis of the salmon life cycle, and its cooperative integration with the surrounding ecosystems, provides the basis for illustrating the disruptive effects of unsustainable industrialization as evidenced in case studies from Maine, the Clackamas River Basin in Oregon, and the Rhine River in the Netherlands. Salmon is a valuable economic resource in the modern human economy because it is one of the largest commercial fish and one of the healthiest sources of protein and fat in the human diet (Myers and Worm 2003: 280). Fish resources, in general, are of paramount importance to the human economy because three billion people around the world currently rely on fish protein for at least 20 per cent of the animal protein in their diet (Mercer 2006: 5). However, only a few regions still produce wild salmon abundantly and some scientists even project that by 2050 there may be no commercially viable fisheries left anywhere in the world (Worm *et al.* 2006: 790).

As one of the largest salmon tributary systems in the United States, the Clackamas River Basin terrain was heavily timbered and rocky, and development in the basin was slow until the late 1800s when industrial machinery cleared the way for settlement. Salmon populations were damaged by timber harvest, road building, driving logs downstream, dam building, removal of riparian vegetation, and the destruction of side channels and wetlands. These changes contributed to dramatic losses of salmon habitat and productivity:

> the annual return of [...] salmon and trout to the Columbia River Basin has decreased from an estimated 12-16 million individuals in the 1880s to 2.5 million in the 1980s (NPPC 1987). Furthermore, Nehlson *et al.* (1991) identified 214 stocks of Pacific salmonids from California, Oregon, Idaho, and Washington that they considered to be of special concern, as they face a high or moderate risk of extinction. (Hildebrand *et al.* 2004: 5)

> Maine has the oldest and last Atlantic salmon fishery in North America. Historically, 34 rivers and streams in Maine had naturally reproducing Atlantic salmon populations. [...] Before the construction of dams in the early 1800s, the upstream migrations of salmon extended well into the headwaters of large rivers [...] vast amounts of habitat in the headwaters of the Penobscot and Kennebec Rivers were used for spawning and rearing. (Saunders *et al.* 2006: 540)

Organized fishing was accomplished mostly with the use of weirs, which contributed to the relatively rapid depletion of the fishery. By the late 1800s output peaked, and in 1948 only 40 salmon were caught. Maine's 'catch-and-release only' system was shut down in 1999 for fear of endangering the very limited salmon population (Kocik and Sheehan 2006: 3).

The Rhine River in the Netherlands has hosted salmon species probably since the retreat of the glaciers which carved the river itself. Modern fishing efforts for salmon in the Rhine were typical, steady progressions until 'the end of the 1920s witnessed a major decline in salmon catches,' and eventually, 'the Dutch salmon fishing industry effectively ceased to exist after 1933' (De Groot 2002: 213). Massive restocking programs since the 1930s have not proven successful, suggesting a failure to comprehend the particular needs of salmon – for example, '[it] is not clear whether certain smells that are characteristic of the spawning grounds are still discernible to salmon that have passed through rivers rich in detergents' (De Groot 2002: 215). Much of the continued depression of salmon abundance is also caused by a large number of locks and weirs, canalization and flood control, sand and gravel extraction, and wastewater discharges (De Groot 2002: 215).

The above case studies identify organized overexploitation of salmon and the elimination of habitat through construction as the combined causes of a cumulative disruption of the salmon life cycle and salmon depletion. As early as 1950 Kapp's understanding of CCC led him to detect the importance of maintaining states of complex ecological balance and guaranteeing sustainable rates of exploitation: 'these far-reaching and often irreversible consequences of human activities are all due to the fact that they disturb the complex and highly sensitive ecological balance' (Kapp [1950] [1963] 1977: 95). In particular, Kapp observed the vulnerability of salmon fisheries due to their breeding habits and the possibility of cumulatively diminishing stocks: 'whenever the rate of utilization exceeds the critical limit [...] the resource flow tends to decrease and the resource may finally lose its capacity to renew itself altogether' (Kapp [1950] [1963] 1977: 93).

The decline of wild salmon catches was followed by farmed salmon so that 'in only a short time, salmon have gone from abundance to depleted stocks to abundance again. What has made this possible is aquaculture' (Clay 2004: 515). 'World salmon and salmon trout supply increased more than four-fold between 1980 and 2001 and the share of North American wild salmon in total world supply fell from more than half to about one-sixth' (Knapp *et al.* 2007: xv). Today, over half of the salmon consumed in the world is farmed. Farming salmon requires huge and constant inputs of both non-renewable sources of energy and materials, and releases wastes concomitant with the scale of inputs. In their infancy, salmon are kept in heated tanks to encourage growth. Soon after they grow into smolts, they are individually vaccinated (Clay 2004: 516-18). Research into farmed animals has observed that agricultural and veterinary medicines have cumulative effects in ecosystems as they are excreted out of target animals and into local watersheds (Daughton and Terns 1999: 921).

> When the salmon finish their yolk sacs, they are fed protein pellets made from 'junk fish,' which are commercially unviable fish species, or by-catch. This diversion of food from ocean ecosystems to human enterprise not only has a negative impact on ocean food webs, but the input of fish products is two to four times the volume of fish outputs for these crops. Because of their dependence on wild-caught fish and shrimp, salmon aquaculture deplete

rather than augment fisheries resources [...] about 1.8 million tons of wild fish for feed were required to produce 644,000 metric tons of Atlantic salmon – a 2.8: 1 ratio [...] Consequently, [salmon farming] depends heavily on fishmeal imported from South America. (Naylor *et al.* 1998: 883)

As the salmon grow to maturity they are moved from freshwater ponds to saltwater pens on coasts. Here they are kept at high densities, where 'water circulation [...] washes away faeces, uneaten feed, and other wastes. At present, waste disposal costs farmers nothing' (Clay 2004: 519). While the farmers may not suffer the effects of the salmon's effluent, ocean ecosystems have long been known to be susceptible to artificial nutrient inputs, as in the case of nitrification and the Gulf of Mexico's 'dead zones.' During the adult lifespan of these salmon, cage failures and escape are not uncommon; in fact, farmed Atlantic salmon have been found as far as the South Pacific (Naylor *et al.* 1998: 883). These escapees also result in 'interaction of farm with wild salmon [which] results in lowered fitness, with repeated escapes causing cumulative fitness depression and potentially an extinction vortex in vulnerable populations' (McGinnity *et al.* 2003: 2443). Finally, farmed salmon may present a significant threat to health. Salmon raised in captivity have never been studied to explore the effects of their close-proximity lifestyle and their ability to cope with continuous exposure to concentrated faeces throughout their life cycle. There is reason to suspect that the diseases these salmon suffer as a result of aquaculture (Naylor *et al.* 1998: 883) have effects on their final consumers. A slab of farmed salmon also represents inputs of untested veterinary medicines, and there are 'health risks (based on a quantitative cancer risk assessment) associated with consumption of farmed salmon contaminated with PCBs, toxaphene, and dieldrin [which] were higher than risks associated with exposure to the same contaminants in wild salmon' (Foran *et al.* 2005: 552). The cumulative and synergetic effects of different pollutants in animals and humans are difficult to determine with exactitude but can lead to great social costs in the form of adverse health effects. As yet another example of biological cumulative effects, salmon are exposed to these chemical compounds through their natural predation, wherein top-level predators like salmon ingest contaminated prey whose life-history strategy is essentially to collect toxins through its own feeding.

The analysis of salmon depletion and subsequent farmed salmon abundance illustrates how the disruption of ecological balance is cumulative and directional, heading towards greater ecological degradation. The CCC analysis of salmon depletion shows a process in which certain economic organizing principles and modern industrial fishing techniques in circular causation disrupt the complex ecological balance of the salmon life cycle, causing salmon depletion with complex negative effects on interconnected species and plants and ecosystems. The cumulative causation of economic organizing principles and technology triggers a further downward spiral of ecological degradation via farmed salmon. In the latter the interaction between pollutants is synergetic and cumulative, there are time lags during which they accumulate in fish, humans and the environment, and there is uncertainty about the exact nature of their interrelations as well as the magnitudes of hidden effects. The heavy dependency on non-renewable energy inputs makes the production process of farmed salmon a wasteful and inefficient enterprise, certainly when compared to wild salmon. The protein inputs are imported from already relatively poor regions, further jeopardizing ecological balance in these regions and diminishing their potential to satisfy their own basic needs.[88] Moreover, the pollution of the oceans through aquacultures is an instance of ecological degradation at a rate that is higher than the natural rate of restoration and possibly irreversible.

13.4 The social costs of salmon depletion and of farmed salmon

The CCC perspective may be considered one of the main reasons why Kapp adopted a definition of social costs that is broad enough to cover not only economic costs that may be expressed in monetary terms but also effects of less tangible character, such as effects on the impairment of human health and the quality of life: 'the term 'social costs' covers all direct and indirect losses sustained by third persons or the general public as a result of unrestrained economic activities' (Kapp [1950] [1963] 1977: 95). Due to the co-existence of the private and public sector social costs are harmful effects of private and public economic decision-making (Kapp [1965a] 1983: 10). Kapp argued that 'the decline of […] salmon fisheries […] is another example of substantial social losses [i.e. social costs]' (Kapp [1950] [1963] 1977: 140).

'The consequences will be not only a rapid and cumulative exhaustion but an irreversible process which may have far reaching adverse effects for the prosperity of entire industries and communities' (Kapp [1950] [1963] 1977: 93). One of the adverse effects, for example, is that alternatives of economic activities open to a social group are eliminated. Enforced specialization in economic development and arrested growth are serious consequences and constitute substantial social losses. 'Thus communities may be left stranded and ghost towns may take the place of formerly striving settlements' (Kapp [1950] [1963] 1977: 93). And even where restoration is technically feasible, salmon depletion can be economically irreversible owing to its prohibitively high costs (Kapp [1950] [1963] 1977: 94). This process of social costs is tipped off by resource depletion and cumulatively leads to societal crisis and economic stagnation. This is precisely what Myrdal's CCC analysis described as a vicious circle or 'social waste,' leading to growing regional economic inequalities and poverty[89] (Myrdal 1957: ch. 3).

However, salmon depletion has led to a relatively new 'social cost-phenomenon,' i.e. aquacultures and farmed salmon. When Kapp described disruptive farming practices, he could just as easily have meant farmed salmon:

> these operations may have harmful effects which often fail to be considered by those interested in increasing [...] [the yield of salmon]. Indeed, if carried out on a large scale and without protective measures in response to a rapidly growing demand for [...] [salmon], the process of bringing [...] [farmed salmon] into use may endanger the very prosperity which it seeks to promote. (Kapp [1950] [1963] 1977: 94)

The artificial abundance of salmon stocks produced by means of salmon farming emerges as a result of unnatural depletion of wild salmon so that both become cumulative causes of significant social costs that are ultimately born by society at large, third parties and future generations. The salmon analysis supports Kapp's tenet that competitive conditions fail to guarantee that the harvest of salmon will not be intensified beyond a safe minimum rate. They also lead to more devastating practices aimed at making up for declining returns:

> Not even [...] lower returns resulting from excessive production will necessarily lead to a curtailment of output. Quite the contrary, lower yields may actually prove an incentive to greater efforts [...], inducing them [fishing industry] to make up for their declining return by still greater output. (Kapp [1950] [1963] 1977: 111)

The price system as such can be considered incapable of rationally defining an ideal output position regarding renewable resources, and has a devastating tendency to accelerate the rate of use of resources. In fact, reliance on the price system may lead to maximizing future costs and minimizing future benefits (Kapp [1950] [1963] 1977: 113).

Evidence of the problematic relationship between the 'free' price system and the degradation of renewable resources that enter the process essentially as free gifts of nature has been found by Marx long ago, in particular with regard to price fluctuations: 'the whole spirit [...] toward the immediate gain of money contradicts agriculture [and fisheries], which has to minister to the entire range of permanent necessities of life required by a network of human generations' (Karl Marx, *Capital*, Vol. III; Kapp [1950] [1963] 1977: 101). Likewise, Veblen recognized that the 'American plan or policy is a settled practice of converting all public wealth to private gain on a plan of legalized seizure' (Veblen, Absentee Ownership; Kapp [1950] [1963] 1977: 139). 'Business enterprise has run through that range of natural resources, the fur-bearing animals [and salmon], with exemplary thoroughness and expedition and has left the place of it bare. It is a [...] concluded chapter of American business enterprise' (ibid.: 137).

In the tradition of Veblen's *Theory of Business Enterprise* (1904), Kapp's institutional analysis identifies the situation of the modern (food) corporation as the main underlying cause of social costs. That is the application of modern technology under the guidance of pecuniary drives that are firmly entrenched in the system of business enterprise, coupled with a lack of effective public controls to safeguard ecological and social balance. According to this perspective, social costs are neither accidental, nor minor side-effects that can be fixed by ad hoc measures. Instead, they are systemic effects of the competitive system caused by a situation of pecuniary exigencies. The latter result from the capitalization of productive equipment and putative future earnings as collateral for monetary debt contracts (capitalization is based on an accounting system in terms of exchange value). The growth-logic of the interest rate requirement of debt contracts means that the corporation needs to generate a permanent and increasing flow of financial returns and is thus forced to increase its earning capacity. This requires a minimization of idleness in the expensive production process operating with extremely productive modern technology on a large scale (economies of scale) (Kapp, unpublished). In this perspective the corporation's drive for increasing pecuniary returns is institutionalized in the competitive system via a self-reinforcing causation of large-scale modern technological and monetary debt relations.

Applied to biotic resources, this growth rationale causes depletion because the sustainable harvest rate is relatively stable. Georgescu-Roegen's production theory explains why renewable biotic 'funds' exhibit a specific service rate that does not grow exponentially

(Georgescu-Roegen 1971). The pressure of the time value of money in property-based market regimes encourages depleting renewable resources that grow at a rate below the market interest rate (Steppacher forthcoming; Swaney 2006: 116). Salmon farming may be seen as an attempt to encourage biotic resources to conform to these technological and pecuniary exigencies, making fishing results predictable at a growing flow rate. This can, however, only work to the advantage of the individual firm when it is legal to ignore negative ecological effects and to legally shift these costs to society at large. The costs of depleting natural salmon, pollution and ecological degradation are unpaid for by the business enterprise, i.e. they are socialized. The now cheaply available farmed salmon further contributes to the creation of irrationally high consumer demand for salmon via sales promotion. In fact, this kind of ecologically harmful consumption may be considered the result of technological and pecuniary exigencies of the corporation. The latter is forced to find ever new outlets for its enormous productive capacity as well as new sources of pecuniary profits (Kapp [1950] [1963] 1977; Steppacher forthcoming). Kapp's social costs theory points out that shifting costs to society where no charges for waste and depletion of food webs are levied is often a precondition for maintaining the earning capacity of the business enterprise. In such a system, pecuniary profits are made via wasteful production and the promotion of wasteful consumption, while society's capacity to provide for its social reproduction and that of future Veblen, who defined waste not by means of a moral standard but as those practices that 'do not serve human life or well-being on the whole' (Kapp [1950] [1963] 1977; Veblen [1899] 1917: 97). In this case profits and waste are not a contradiction but, in fact, condition one another.

13.5 CCC's 'real term' method and its implications for the theory of social costs

Kapp's findings lead him to develop a theory of social costs that stresses 'the cumulative character and complexity of the causal sequence which gives rise to environmental disruption and social costs' (Kapp 1970a: 837) and 'the delicate system of interrelationships' (Kapp [1950] [1963] 1977: 94). His theory can in this sense be coined a CCC theory or complexity theory of social costs that is able to deal with less tangible yet important effects and interrelationships (Özveren 2007: 203-4). Kapp emphasizes that social costs cannot be considered as minor side-effects in relatively isolated locations, but have to be seen as all-pervasive effects. He even formulates a historical hypothesis: 'as the economy becomes more complex, non-market interdependencies are likely to assume greater significance. For this reason social costs are bound to become increasingly important' (Kapp [1965a] 1983: 5).

Kapp's theory of social costs implies a holistic view of the quality of life (i.e. of the whole situation of private and social costs and benefits), and the dependence of societal reproduction on states of socio-ecological balance. It may also be called 'substantive' in the sense that it aims at revealing negative effects on society's reproductive capacity and on the satisfaction of fundamental human needs in real terms (Berger 2008b). This is in the tradition of Myrdal's CCC-based insight that only a real term analysis as opposed to a monetary analysis can capture social costs and the condition of the whole situation (Myrdal 1957). Any deficiencies in this regard are a substantive indicator of social costs in real terms. Kapp's and Myrdal's argument for a substantive accounting of social costs is in the broad tradition of classical and institutional economics and their approach to surplus and distribution (Kapp, unpublished).

Kapp's rejection of utilitarian and formal solutions to social costs (i.e. his critique of the Pigouvian and Coasian frameworks) is partly the consequence of the complex CCC perspective. The CCC perspective gives rise to a specific conceptualization of the problem of social costs that is much broader and follows the subject matter more closely and stays closer to the real facts. 'An element of inescapable indeterminacy may remain either due to the lack of homogeneity of the facts or of people's valuations or due to a lack of knowledge about causal interrelationships' (Kapp [1972] 1977: 309). Kapp pointed out why, in particular, circular cumulative causation in the ecological system and fundamental uncertainty render formal approaches inappropriate.

Pollution and the disruption of the environment are the results of a complex interaction which have their own specific regularities. Moreover, pollutants from different sources act upon one another and what counts are not only the effects of particular effluents and toxic materials but the total toxological situation. [...] Those who have studied these complex relationships know that environmental disruption can easily become cumulative with pervasive and disproportionate effects per unit of additional pollutants. (Kapp [1972] 1977: 314-15)

Under such conditions the price system cannot identify a viable output position because complexity and uncertainty make it largely impossible for 'the individual to ascertain the full range of short and long run benefits of environmental improvements, or for that matter, of the full impact of environmental disruption upon his health and well-being' (Kapp [1972] 1977: 314). On the other hand, leaving out less tangible social costs because they cannot be priced would make economics an incomplete, i.e. an irrational system of thought. Referring to Myrdal, Kapp reminded us 'that statistical convenience and measurement must *not* be permitted to set limits to concept formations and thus to exclude relevant elements [...] to define the concept more precisely than is justified is logically faulty' (Kapp [1972] 1977: 309-10).

Kapp rejected the application of the monetary calculus that is based on the utilitarian principle (i.e. the willingness to pay or accept compensation), and assigns monetary exchange values to ecological effects. This method is, according to Kapp, as arbitrary as the distributional inequality which it expresses because the 'willingness to pay' depends on the 'ability to pay' and has nothing to do with the objective and real exigencies of states of socio-ecological balance.

> The use of the willingness to pay as criterion of quantifying and evaluating the quality of the environment has the insidious effect of reinterpreting original human needs and [socio-ecological] requirements into a desire for money and of evaluating the relative importance of such needs in terms of criteria which reflect the existing inequalities and distortions in the price, wage and income structure. (Kapp [1972] 1977: 313)

Kapp endeavored to show that monetary criteria, such as the willingness to pay, are not appropriate because they do not evaluate the characteristics which define the quality of the environment and its potentially negative impact on human health, human well-being, and human survival (Kapp [1972] 1977: 316).

Neither Coase nor Pigou aim to guarantee the fulfillment of the requirements of socio-ecological balance or the satisfaction of basic human needs but prescribe a fixed behavioral rule that is assumed to solve the problem. Their solutions are predetermined by their formal apparatus and apply only ex-post. This 'catching-up' with the effects ex-post can be too late if damaging effects are irreversible, and can be too little as their closed system methodology prevent them from taking into account the whole range and full extent of repercussions:

> making the content and extent of the control of environmental quality dependent upon individual willingness to pay could at best lead to piece-meal measures and an ineffective formal sub-optimization if it does not become the pretext for endless delays or a policy of doing too little too late. (Kapp [1972] 1977: 315)

13.6 From increasing pecuniary returns to sustainable socio-economic and ecological returns: the quest for new forms of democratic governance

Social costs raise questions regarding the Kaldorian current of CC theory: how far is the promotion of increasing pecuniary returns sustainable and at what point does the system actually exhibit greater total costs than total benefits (total including the sum of social and private)? In other words, where are the limits of increasing pecuniary returns? Interestingly, Kaldor's theory of increasing returns notes that 'agriculture (and mining) [and fisheries] produces both direct and indirect inputs for industry – basic materials and food. If agriculture is subject to the Law of Diminishing Returns, agricultural output may be constrained by land and the available technology' (Kaldor 1974 [1978]: 206). However, Kaldor also stated ambiguously that 'total output can never be confined by resources' (Kaldor 1972 [1978]: 194) while 'a maximum rate of growth […] must be on account of the scarcity of natural resources, and the impossibility of substituting capital goods for natural resources at more than a certain speed' (Kaldor 1972 [1978]: 195). Based on his distinction between manufacturing industry (increasing returns) and agriculture (diminishing returns), Kaldor elaborates the consequences for development, competition, price formation, and trade (Kaldor 1978: xxii–xxiii). Yet, unlike Kapp, he does not analyze the social costs that result from a manufacturing system that attempts to generate increasing pecuniary returns by harvesting funds of renewable resources at a rate that is faster than their rate of reproduction. In addition, the fundamental difference between manufacturing and agriculture as well as the limits this imposes for economic growth were elaborated more accurately by Georgescu-Roegen (Georgescu-Roegen 1965 [1976], 1970). Thus, CC theories of increasing returns need to be embedded in a wider ecological and institutional perspective in the tradition of Kapp and Georgescu-Roegen.

As a solution to the problem of social costs, Kapp proposes safe minimum rates for the utilization of resources and maximum tolerance levels for pollution. He considers the latter to be social minima because they help avert the severe social consequences of resource depletion and pollution, such as arrested economic development and structural depression of entire regions.[90] The social minimum standard serves as a bench-mark for policy makers to evaluate private practices and public policies. It also serves to monitor the effects of different institutional and technological set-ups (Kapp [1950] [1963] 1977: 114). Kapp proposes the adoption of more selective practices of resource use that are in harmony with the life and growth cycle of salmon fisheries:

> A wide variety of measures are available ranging from educational persuasion, closed seasons for [...] [fishing], specific interdictions, the subsidization of substitutes in plentiful supply, taxation, price control, rationing and outright prohibitions placed on the use of certain materials for low priority uses [i.e., luxury]. (Kapp [1950] [1963] 1977: 154)

The determination of social minima and the means to achieve them takes place in democratic political processes with the help of the sciences and economics. Kapp describes this as a process of democratic political economics (Berger and Forstater 2007; Berger 2008a) which contributes important political elements to EE (Özveren 2007: 190). Political economics also addresses the problems and exigencies that power asymmetries and vested interests inherent in the economic system pose for this democratic process (see Kapp's application on François Perroux' theory of the 'domination effect' (Perroux 1950); Kapp 1968).

13.6.1 Prospects for an institutional-political EE approach to fisheries

While many ecological economists consider Kapp an exceptional economist whose very early emphasis on basic uncertainty and interdependencies of social and environmental systems is foundational to EE, the relatively weak influence of this branch of institutional economics (Røpke 2005: 278-9) has led to an integration based mainly on the neoclassical branch of new institutional economics. CCC's contribution and potential regarding the importance of 'interdependence' in relation to environmental problems seems to be largely overlooked (see e.g. Paavola and Adger 2005: 354-7). Despite the fact that institutional economics in the US has not had an unproblematic relationship with EE (Swaney 1985: 854; Swaney 2006: 113, 122 n. 12)[91] both are increasingly being integrated (Barnes 2006). In Europe, on the other hand, institutional economics in the tradition of Kapp and Georgescu-Roegen synthesized ecological political economy in the tradition of Marx and Georgescu-Roegen (Guha and Martinez-Alier 1997, Steppacher forthcoming). In fact, Kapp had identified the common concerns of Marx and Veblen about ecological degradation early on. In particular, parts of Volume III of Marx's *Capital*, which deal with soil degradation, share similarities with Georgescu-Roegen's work on viable agriculture (Kapp [1950] [1963] 1977: 101; Foster 2000; Georgescu-

Roegen 1965). Several European contributions also adopt Karl Polanyi's concepts of 'embeddedness,' 'fictitious commodities,' and 'substantive economics' as a basis for integrating institutional economics and EE (Barthelemy and Nieddu 2007; Adaman *et al.* 2003). Similarities between Polanyi's and Kapp's concepts exist (Swaney and Evers 1989; Berger 2008b) and are considered to have potential for a further integration of institutional economics and EE (Özveren 2007: 191).

Looking at how EE explores sustainable institutional arrangements for resource utilization shows the close links to Kapp's work. EE applies economic policy analysis to empirically elaborate institutional settings that work to conserve the resources (Ostrom 2006: 760). EE evaluates institutional performance according to multiple criteria including efficiency, sustainability, and equity. According to Dietz *et al.*, economic efficiency focuses on the total relationship of individual and social benefits versus individual and social costs, and does not presuppose exact quantitative measurement (Dietz *et al.* 2002: 25). The focus on social costs and social minima is considered to be a result of the complexity perspective (Stern *et al.* 2002: 463). In all of this, the goal of sustainability and livelihood in general prevails over individual economic profit making (Tietenberg 2002: 199-200; Plummer and Armitage 2007: 69).

Nevertheless, the question remains how to scientifically elaborate social minima in complex systems under conditions of fundamental uncertainty. The scientific determination of social minima is complex because much information is needed that often relies on experience, knowledge, and participation of the users themselves. This process works best when all participants take an interest in an integrated approach towards resource preservation that considers interspecies relationships and ecological balance. In general, research into complex systems finds that different problem contexts require different caps (social minima) and that intense use should be followed by an early shift away from the resource at signs of trouble, allowing the resource to recover (Rose 2002: 241). With varying ecological conditions there is also no single institutional blueprint and the idea that there is only one best solution is a great obstacle against creativity when the development of regimes is at stake. 'This is the case for those saying that private ownership and market allocation is always the best solution, as it is for those believing that the state can allocate all goods or that more community is the solution to any problem' (Vatn 2005: 417-18). Consequently, EE proposes a diversity of methods to achieve collaborative environmental management.

13.6.2 Free market environmentalism and EE's critique

Contrary to EE, free market environmentalism (FME) which is a branch of neo-classical environmental economics proposes one single 'cure-all' approach, i.e. individual tradable quota regimes (ITQs). ITQs are individual property rights and are supposed to lead to sustainable practices due to the self-interested actions of the owners. The argument is that 'Command and Control' regimes run by the state are 'economically inefficient.' The main focus of FME is – as is not surprising – directed towards increasing the pecuniary profitability of the resources. FME proponents display almost no concern for the actual compatibility of this regime with the specificities of the resources and ecological balance. Its beneficial character is simply taken for granted or assumed: perhaps as an example of ecological 'invisible hands.' From the CCC perspective, the main problem of ITQs is that they tend to neglect a long-run focus and complexity. Simple individual tradable property rights that can manage complex resources efficiently are hard to design because externalities are interlinked, so that complex institutional settings are needed for complex resources and complex user communities (Stern *et al.* 2002: 463). Overall, FME seems to ignore the implications of CCC. However, even FME presumes a total allowable catch, i.e. the safe ceiling that can be harvested (cf. also Adaman *et al.* 2003: 363; Swaney 2006: 119). Existing ITQ regimes set total caps based, e.g. on historic practices and negotiations (Rose 2002: 236, 241). Unfortunately, FME proponents, such as Leal, do not explain how the total allowable catch is determined and do not address the apparent theoretical inconsistency (Leal 2005: 6). Social minima constitute a break with the market mechanism because they are social and community rights, and the government is more involved than in rights for commodities and individual property rights. The political process has to determine a schedule that specifies ceilings for each year going forward, and decides how they are allocated/distributed, also considering the possibility of technological controls to observe the ceiling (Swaney 2006: 118, 120).

13.6.3 From 'command and control' to 'community-based management' regimes

A case study from Alaska which hosts one of the few remaining sources of wild Pacific salmon is an example of a 'command and control' regime. Alaska's salmon resources as a whole are still relatively fecund. In the past 25 years Alaskan wild salmon harvests have remained high, and have even enjoyed a slight increase. This maintained productivity may be attributed to Alaska's tight regulation of its 26 fisheries, using a 'limited entry' program,

> which was established in the 1970s to limit growth in the number of people fishing in the salmon industry. [...] In each fishery, fishermen may use only the type of gear specified by the permit. There are also numerous other restrictions on boats and gear. For example, in Alaska's Bristol Bay drift gillnet fishery boats may not exceed 32 feet in length and gillnets may not exceed 150 fathoms (900 feet) in length. Individuals may hold more than one salmon permit, but they may participate in only one salmon fishery per season. A boat may only be used in one salmon fishery per season. (Knapp *et al.* 2007: vi)

The future of Alaska's salmon fishery is however still subject to uncertainties, because like all other fisheries, sustained yield is not a reliable indicator of a sustainable fishery and, in fact, most fishery collapses exhibit high or moderate production until their crash rather than a slow decline (Mullon *et al.* 2005: 111).

Despite its fundamental uncertainty problem, the dominant approach to fisheries management today is still this kind of 'command and control' regime that tries to maintain the competitive system by, for example, determining shortened harvest seasons and caps on total allowable catch. However, even if the state succeeds in enforcing a sustainable limit of total catch, experience shows that maintaining competitive conditions in a common pool resource can be uneconomical and irrational. The reason is that without further technological-institutional support, such a system leads to a rush for fish where each fisherman tries to maximize his catch, and a need to invest in the latest technology that leads to heavily overcapitalized fleets. This means an extreme duplication of material and a wasteful excess capacity so that the whole industry is operating at greater costs than benefits. In addition, the whole annual amount of total allowable catch is brought ashore in just a few days, and the race-like process leads to the waste of a high percentage of the caught fish.

In several instances this dilemma triggered the formation of cooperatives in fishing communities to reduce overexploitation and duplication. Paradoxically, the competition of cheap farmed salmon has also supported this trend towards sharing profits and efforts in co- ops to become more cost-efficient (Leal 2005: ch. 1; Wilen 2005: 50, 54-5). As a result of anti-trust law and opposition to supply curtailment, however, some governments impede self-organization to the detriment of ecologically beneficial arrangements (Adler 2005: 153). Anti-trust law is a legal institution that is used to prevent the creation of ecologically important associations. Ecology is not valued in the deliberation process (Adler 2005: 165). In places where anti-trust law is effective, co-ops have been allowed to prosper only where the state had already enacted strict catch limits that limited quantity regardless of the co-ops (Adler 2005: 162).

Limiting the spread of co-ops in these places is unfortunate from a normative EE standpoint since more complex forms of co-management between the government and co-ops, and community-based management regimes (CBMR) often reflect an attempt to save the ecosystem (Rose 2002: 250-1; Yandle 2005: 216-17). Another advantage of CBMR is that they successfully solve the problem of 'command and control' regimes that caused the fishermen to only keep large fish and waste by-catch, ignoring important interspecies relations. 'Co-management is a continuous problem-solving process, rather than a fixed state, involving extensive deliberation, negotiation and joint learning in problem-solving networks' (Plummer and Armitage 2007: 70). These are similar to traditional systems because they allow for resource-related variations and have turned resource conservation into an adaptive system (Rose 2002: 244), as, for instance, in New Zealand where the total allowable catch is defined in terms of percentage of resource (Rose 2002: 242) based on experience from historical practices and interactions with the resource base. Where CBMR has been enacted the role of the state has been to help facilitate solutions, such as limiting entry or fostering producer agreements (Townsend 2005:142-5).

13.7 Conclusion

This chapter underlines the renewed relevance of Kapp's and Myrdal's CCC by identifying common characteristics between CCC and the pre-analytical vision of EE in the area of fisheries. This propels the necessary integration of socio-economic and ecological knowledge based on a world view of real interrelations as well as an awareness of cumulative causation that can jeopardize societal reproduction and the satisfaction of fundamental human needs (Kapp 1961). It also shows that CC theories of increasing returns must be embedded into the substantive CCC approach to elucidate whether or not the wealth-diminishing effects of social costs are so large that they actually offset gains in pecuniary increasing returns. In addition, Kapp's CCC-based analysis of salmon depletion and remedies for social costs are broadly compatible with EE. Therefore, the chapter supports an integrated ecological-institutional approach and at the same time advocates a greater role for the political economy of Kapp and Myrdal concerned with democracy and economic power.

References

Adaman, F., Devine, P. and Ozkaynak, B. (2003) 'Reinstituting the Economic Process: (Re)embedding the Economy in Society and Nature,' *International Review of Sociology*, 13, 2: 357-72.

Adler, J. H. (2005) 'Antitrust Barriers to Cooperative Fishery Management,' in D. R. Leal (ed.) *Evolving Property Rights in Marine Fisheries*, Oxford: Rowman & Littlefield Publishers.

Barnes, W. (2006) 'Ecological and Institutional Economics: Building on Common Ground,' paper presented at the Annual Meeting of the Association for Institutional Thought, Phoenix, April.

Barthelemy, D. and Nieddu, M. (2007) 'Non-trade Concerns in Agriculture and Environmental Economics: How J. R. Commons and Karl Polanyi can help us,' paper presented at the Annual Meeting of the Association for Evolutionary Economics, Chicago, January.

Berger, S. (2008a) 'K. William Kapp's Theory of Social Costs and Environmental Policy: Towards Political Ecological Economics,' *Ecological Economics*, 67: 244-52.
(2008b) 'Karl Polanyi's and K. William Kapp's Substantive Economics: Important Insights from the Polanyi–Kapp Correspondence,' *Review of Social Economy*, 66, 3: 381-96.

Berger, S. and Elsner, W. (2007) 'European Contributions to Evolutionary Institutional Economics: The Cases of Cumulative Circular Causation (CCC) and Open System Approach (OSA) – Some Methodological and Policy Implications,' *Journal of Economic Issues*, 41, 2: 529-37.

Berger, S. and Forstater, M. (2007) 'Towards Political Institutionalist Economics. Kapp's Social Costs, Lowe's Instrumental Analysis, and the European Institutionalist Approach to Environmental Policy,' *Journal of Economic Issues*, 41, 2: 539-46.

Clay, J. (2004) *World Agriculture and the Environment: A Commodity by Commodity Guide to Impacts and Practices*, Washington, DC: Island Press.

Daughton, C. G. and Ternes, T. A. (1999) 'Pharmaceuticals and Personal Care Products in the Environment: Agents of Subtle Change?' *Environmental Health Perspectives*, 107, 6: 907-38.

De Groot, S. J. (2002) 'A Review of the Past and Present Status of Anadromous Fish Species in the Netherlands: Is Restocking the Rhine Feasible?,' *Hydrobiologia*, 478: 205-18.

Dietz, T., Dolsak, N., Ostrom, E. and Stern, P. C. (2002) 'The Drama of the Commons,' in E. Ostrom, T. Dietz, N. Dolsak, P. C. Stern, S. Storich and E. U. Weber (eds) *The Drama of the Commons*, Washington, DC: National Academy Press.

Foran, J. A., Carpenter, D. O., Hamilton, M. C., Knuth, B. A. and Schwager, S. J. (2005) 'Risk-based Consumption Advice for Farmed Atlantic and Wild Pacific Salmon Contaminated with Dioxins and Dioxin-like Compounds,' *Environmental Health Perspectives*, 113, 5: 552-6.

Foster, J. B. (2000) *Marx's Ecology: Materialism and Nature*, New York: Monthly

Review Press.

Galtung, J. (1975) 'Development From Above and the Blue Revolution: The Indo-Norwegian Project in Kerala,' in *International Peace Research Institute*, Oslo: PRIO Publication No. 2-12.

Georgescu-Roegen, N. [1965] (1976) 'Process in Farming vs. Process in Manufacturing: A Problem of Balanced Development,' in *Energy and Economic Myths – Institutional and Analytical Economic Essays*, New York: Pergamon.

— (1970) 'The Economics of Production,' *American Economic Review*, 60, 2: 1-9.

— (1971) *The Entropy Law and The Economic Process*, Cambridge, MA: Harvard University Press.

Guha, R. and Martinez-Alier, J. (1997) *Varieties of Environmentalism: Essays North and South*, London: Earthscan Publications.

Helfield, J. M. and Naiman, R. J. (2001) 'Effects of Salmon-derived Nitrogen on Riparian Forest Growth and Implications for Stream Productivity,' *Ecology*, 82, 9: 2403-9.

Hildebrand, G. V., Farley, S. D., Schwartz, C. C. and Robbins, C. T. (2004) 'Importance of Salmon to Wildlife: Implications for Integrated Management,' *Ursus*, 15, 1: 1-9.

Kaldor, N. [1972] (1978) 'The Irrelevance of Equilibrium Economics', in N. Kaldor (ed.) *Further Essays in Economic Theory*, New York: Holmes & Meier Publishers.

— (1978) 'Introduction,' in N. Kaldor (ed.) *Further Essays on Economic Theory*, New York: Holmes & Meier Publishers.

— [1974] (1978) 'What is Wrong with Economic Theory,' in N. Kaldor (ed.) *Further Essays on Economic Theory*, New York: Holmes & Meier Publishers.

Kapp, K. W. (1950) *The Social Costs of Private Enterprise*, Cambridge, MA: Harvard University Press.

— (1961) *Toward a Science of Man in Society – A Positive Approach to the Integration of Social Knowledge*, The Hague: Martinus Nijhoff.

— [1965a] (1983) 'Social Costs in Economic Development,' in J. Ullman (ed.) *Social Costs, Economic Development and Environmental Disruption*, Lanham, MD: University Press of America.

— (1965b) 'Social Economics and Social Welfare Minima,' in T. K. N. Unnithan et al. (eds) *Towards a Sociology of Culture in India, Essays in Honor of Dr. D. P. Mukerji*, New Delhi: Prentice Hall of India.

— (1968) 'In Defense of Institutional Economics,' *Swedish Journal of Economics*, LXX, l: 1-18.

— (1970a) 'Environmental Disruption and Social Costs: A Challenge to Economics,' *Kyklos*, 23, 4: 833-48.

— [1970b] (1983) 'Environmental Disruption: General Issues and Methodological Problems,' in J. Ullman (ed.) *Social Costs, Economic Development and Environmental Disruption*, Lanham, MD: University Press of America.

— (1972) 'Social Costs, Neo-classical Economics, Environmental Planning: A Reply,' *Social Science Information*, 11, 1: 17-28; reprinted in *The Social Costs of*

Business Enterprise (1977), Nottingham: Spokesman.

[1973] (1974) 'Environmental Indicators as Indicators of Social Use Value,' in K.W. Kapp (ed.) *Environmental Policies and Development Planning in Contemporary China and Other Essays*, Paris/The Hague: Mouton.

(1976) 'The Open-system Character of the Economy and its Implications,' in K. Dopfer (ed.) *Economics in the Future*, London: Macmillan.

(1950; 2nd edn 1963; 3rd edn 1977) *The Social Costs of Business Enterprise*, Nottingham: Spokesman University Paperback.

Unpublished manuscript. *The Foundations of Institutional Economics*, Kapp Archive, Basel (CH).

Knapp, G., Roheim, C. and Anderson, J. (2007) *The Great Salmon Run: Competition between Wild and Farmed Salmon*, Washington, DC: TRAFFIC North America, World Wildlife Fund. Online. Available at: (accessed January 2007).

Kocik, J. F. and Sheehan, T. F. (2006) 'Atlantic Salmon,' *Status of Fishery Resources off the Northeastern US*. NOAA Publication. Online. Available at: (accessed January 2007).

Leal, D. R. (2005) 'Fencing the Fishery: A Primer on Rights-based Fishing,' in D. R. Leal (ed.) *Evolving Property Rights in Marine Fisheries*, Oxford: Rowman & Littlefield Publishers.

McGinnity, P., Prodöhl, P., Ferguson, A., Hynes, R., Maoiléidigh, N. O., Baker, N., Cotter, D., O'Hea, B., Cooke, D., Rogan, G., Taggart, J. and Cross, T. (2003) 'Fitness Reduction and Potential Extinction of Wild Populations of Atlantic Salmon, Salmo salar, as a Result of Interactions with Escaped Farm Salmon,' *Proceedings: Biological Sciences*, 270, 1532: 2443-50.

Mercer, D. (2006) 'Human Destruction of the Marine Commons: The Case of Fisheries Collapse in the North Atlantic,' *GeoDate*, 19, 4: 5-7.

Mullon, C., Fréon, P. and Cury, P. (2005) 'The Dynamics of Collapse in World Fisheries,' *Fish and Fisheries*, 6, 2: 111-20.

Myers, R. A. and Worm, B. (2003) 'Rapid Worldwide Depletion of Predatory Fish Communities,' *Nature*, 423: 280-3.

Myrdal, G. (1957) *Economic Theory and Under-developed Regions*, London: Gerald Duckworth.

(1976) 'The Meaning and Validity of Institutional Economics,' in K. Dopfer (ed.) *Economics in the Future*, London: Macmillan.

(1978) 'Institutional Economics,' *Journal of Economic Issues*, 12, 4: 771-83.

Naylor, R. L., Goldburg, R. J., Mooney, H., Beveridge, M., Clay, J., Folke, C., Kautsky, N., Lubchenco, J., Primavera, J. and Williams, M. (1998) 'Nature's Subsidies to Shrimp and Salmon Farming,' *Science Magazine*, 282, 5390: 883-4.

O'Hara, P. A. (2007) 'Principles of Institutional-evolutionary Political Economy – Converging Themes from the Schools of Heterodoxy,' *Journal of Economic Issues*, 41, 1: 1-42.

Ostrom, E. (2005) *Understanding Institutional Diversity,* Princeton, NJ, and Oxford: Princeton University Press.

(2006) 'Bookreview – Institutions and the Environment, by Arild Vatn,' *Land Economics,* 82, 2: 316-19.

Özveren, E. (2007) 'Where Disciplinary Boundaries Blur: The Environmental Dimension of Institutional Economics,' in S. Ioannides and K. Nielsen (eds) *Economics and the Social Sciences: Boundaries, Interaction and Integration,* Cheltenham, and Northampton, MA: Edward Elgar.

Paavola, J. and Adger, W. N. (2005) 'Institutional Ecological Economics,' *Journal of Ecological Issues,* 53: 353-68.

Patnaik, U. (1979) 'Neo-populism and Marxism: The Chayanovian View of the Agrarian Question and Its Fundamental Fallacy,' *The Journal of Peasant Studies,* 6, 4: 375-420.

Perroux, F. (1950) 'The Domination Effect and Modern Economic Theory,' *Social Research,* 17: 188-206.

Plummer, R. and Armitage, D. (2007) 'A Resilience-based Framework for Evaluating Adaptive Co-management: Linking Ecology, Economics and Society in a Complex World,' *Ecological Economics,* 61: 62-74.

Røpke, I. (2005) 'Trends in the Development of Ecological Economics from the Late 1980s to the Early 2000s,' *Ecological Economics,* 55: 262-90.

Rose, C. M. (2002) 'Common Property, Regulatory Property and Environmental Protection: Comparing Community-based Management to Tradable Environmental Allowances,' in E. Ostrom, T. Dietz, N. Dolsak, P. C. Stern, S. Stonich and E. U. Weber (eds) *The Drama of the Commons,* Washington, DC: National Academy Press.

Saunders, R., Hachey, M. A. and Fay, C. W. (2006) 'Maine's Diadromous Fish Community: Past, Present, and Implications for Atlantic Salmon Recovery,' *Fisheries,* 31, 11.

Steppacher, R. (forthcoming) 'Property, Mineral Resources and Sustainable Development,' in O. Steiger (ed.) *Property Rights, Creditor's Money and the Foundation of the Economy,* Marburg: Metropolis.

Stern, P. C., Dietz, T., Dolsak, N., Ostrom, E. and Stonich, S. (2002) 'Knowledge and Questions after 15 years of Research,' in E. Ostrom, T. Dietz, N. Dolsak, P. C. Stern, S. Stonich and E. U. Weber (eds) *The Drama of the Commons,* Washington, DC: National Academy Press.

Swaney, J. A. (1985) 'Economics, Ecology, and Entropy,' *Journal of Economic Issues,* 19, 4: 853-65.

(2006) 'Policy for Social Costs: Kapp vs. Neo-classical Economics,' in W. Elsner, P. Frigato and P. Ramazzotti (eds) *Social Costs and Public Action in Modern Capitalism – Essays Inspired by Karl William Kapp's Theory of Social Costs,* London and New York: Routledge.

Swaney, J. A. and Evers, M. A. (1989) 'The Social Cost Concepts of K. William Kapp and Karl Polanyi,' *Journal of Economic Issues,* 23, 1: 7-33.

Taylor, B. (1999) 'Salmon and Steelhead Runs and Related Events of the Clackamas River Basin – A Historical Perspective,' Portland General Electric Company. Online. Available at: www.portlandgeneral.com/community_and_

env/hydropower_and_fish/clackamas/history/clackamas_river_history_full.pdf (accessed December 2008).

Tietenberg, T. (2002) 'The Tradable Permits Approach to Protecting the Commons: What Have We Learned?,' in E. Ostrom, T. Dietz, N. Dolsak, P. C. Stern, S. Stonich and E. U. Weber (eds) *The Drama of the Commons,* Washington, DC: National Academy Press.

Townsend, R. E. (2005) 'Producer Organizations and Agreements in Fisheries: Integrating Regulation and Cosean Bargaining,' in D. R. Leal (ed.) *Evolving Property Rights in Marine Fisheries,* Oxford: Rowman & Littlefield Publishers.

Vatn, A. (2005) *Institutions and the Environment,* Cheltenham: Edward Elgar.

Veblen, T. B. [1899] (1917) *The Theory of the Leisure Class – An Economic Study of Institutions,* New York: Macmillan.

— (1904) *The Theory of Business Enterprise,* New York: Charles Scribner's Sons.

Wilen, J. E. (2005) 'Property Rights and the Texture of Rents in Fisheries,' in D. R. Leal (ed.) *Evolving Property Rights in Marine Fisheries,* Oxford: Rowman & Littlefield Publishers.

Willson, M. F. and Halupka, K. C. (1995) 'Anadromous Fish as Keystone Species in Vertebrate Communities,' *Conservation Biology,* 9, 3: 489-97.

Wilson, J. (2002) 'Scientific Uncertainty, Complex Systems, and the Design of Commonpool Institutions,' in E. Ostrom, T. Dietz, N. Dolsak, P. C. Stern, S. Stonich and E. U. Weber (eds) *The Drama of the Commons,* Washington, DC: National Academy Press.

Worm, B., Barbier, E. B., Beaumont, N., Duffy, J. E., Folke, C., Halpern, B. S., Jackson, J. B. C., Lotze, H. K., Micheli, F., Palumbi, S. R., Sala, E., Selkoe, K. A., Stachowicz, J. J. and Watson, R. (2006) 'Impacts of Biodiversity Loss on Ocean Ecosystem Services,' *Science,* 314, 3: 787-90.

Yandle, T. (2005) 'Developing a Co-management Approach in New Zealand Fisheries,' in D. R. Leal (ed.) *Evolving Property Rights in Marine Fisheries,* Oxford: Rowman & Littlefield Publishers.

Notes

1. The author adopts Mirowski's definition of neoliberalism as a political movement that promotes a set of tenets surrounding the idea of the market as superior information processor. (Mirowski and Plehwe 2015).
2. Kapp's secondary school teacher, the notable German novelist and poet Ernst Wiechert, writes in his post–World War II autobiography that Kapp played a leading role in the school's socialist youth organization.
3. Research in the Kapp Archive has shown no evidence that Kapp accepted the invitation. The present author's inquiries with the institute on this matter have not been answered.
4. See also Marc Tool's and Wilfred Beckerman's special recognition of Kapp as augur of the environmental crisis (Berger 2012).
5. For a brief comparison between Kapp's economics and the early land ethic of Aldo Leopold, see Swaney 2006. See also Goodwin 2008 for a more detailed account of Leopold's early ecological economics, which exhibit striking similarities to Kapp's approach.
6. For Kapp's substantive economics, see Berger 2008.
7. Kapp's social minima approach can also be viewed as a science-based social-democratic alternative to Hayek's nondisgressionary rules argument (Burczak 2011).
8. For the social epistemology adopted here, see Mirowski and Nik-Khah 2008 and Mirowski 2013.
9. The first time the manuscript is referred to in the literature is in a dissertation reconstructing Kapp's economics: R. Heidenreich, *Economics and Institutions – a reconstruction of K. W. Kapp's social economics* (Ökonomie und Institutionen – Eine Rekonstruktion des wirtschafts- und sozialwissenschaftlichen Werks von K.W. Kapp), Frankfurt am Main 1994.
10. S. Berger, *European Institutionalism – The Significance of Open System Approach and Circular Cumulative Causation for Evolutionary Institutional Economics with special consideration of the works of Nicholas Georgescu-Roegen, K. William Kapp, Adolph Lowe, Gunnar Myrdal, and Karl Polanyi* (Europäischer Institutionalismus – Die Kernkonzepte Open System Approach und Circular Cumulative Causation und ihr Beitrag zur modernen evolutorischen institutionellen Ökonomie. Unter besonderer Berücksichtigung der Beiträge von Nicholas Georgescu-Roegen, K. William Kapp, Adolph Lowe, Gunnar Myrdal, and Karl Polanyi), Frankfurt am Main: Peter Lang Verlag, 2007; R. Rorty, 'The Historiography of Philosophy: Four Genres,' in R. Rorty et al. (eds) *Philosophy in History – Essays on the Historiography of Philosophy*, Cambridge 1984.
11. G. Hodgson, *The Evolution of Institutional Economics – Agency, Structure and Darwinism in American Institutionalism*, London 2004; M. Rutherford, 'Institutional Economics: The Term And Its Meanings,' in W. Samuels and J. Biddle (eds) *Research in the History of Economic Thought and Methodology – A Research Annual*, Amsterdam 2004; B. Chavance, *Institutional Economics*, Routledge 2009.

12. W. Elsner, Pietro Frigato and Paolo Ramazzotti (eds) *Social Costs Today – Institutional Economics and Contemporary Crisis*, Routledge (forthcoming). Elsner, Wolfram et al. (eds), *Social Costs and Public Action in Modern Capitalism – Essays inspired by Karl William Kapp's theory of social costs*, Routledge 2006.
13. K. W. Kapp, *Hindu Culture, Economic Development and Economic Planning in India – A Collection of Essays*, Asia Publishing House, Bombay et al 1963.
14. This was just before his second visit to India as a Fulbright Professor to the University of Rajasthan, Jaipur in 1961/62. His first research visit as a Fulbright Research Professor had been to the Gokhale Institute of Politics and Economics in Poona in 1957/58.
15. For an analysis of the cooperation between the two economists, see S. Berger, 'Karl Polanyi's and K. William Kapp's Substantive Economics: Important Insights from the Polanyi-Kapp Correspondence,' *Review of Social Economy* 66, 2008, pp. 381-396.
16. Kapp to Polanyi on November 4, 1960.
17. This was probably presented to Brooklyn College in the early 1960s and was found in the Karl Polanyi Archive with Polanyi's handwritten remarks (see appendix).
18. K. W. Kapp, *History of Economic Thought – A Book of Readings*. New York: Barnes & Noble, 1963, p.381.
19. Letter to John Gambs, February 23, 1965.
20. The organization was eventually named Association for Evolutionary Economics (AFEE).
21. Weber's concept occupies a central place in Kapp's intellectual project since the early 1960s. See his article 'Social Costs and Social Benefits – A Contribution to Normative Economics,' in E. v. Beckerath and H. Giersch (eds) *Probleme der normativen Ökonomik und der wirtschaftspolitischen Beratung*, Verein für Sozialpolitik Berlin: Duncker & Humblot, 1963
22. See also S. Berger, 'K. William Kapp's Theory of Social Costs and Environmental Policy: Towards Political Ecological Economics,' *Ecological Economics* 67, 2008, pp. 244-252.
23. January 19, 1963.
24. S. Berger, *Foundations of Non-Equilibrium Economics – The Principle of Circular and Cumulative Causation*, Routledge, 2009.
25. Further evidence for this importance is the incorporation of the CCC section of Myrdal's *Rich Lands and Poor* in the 'Social Economics' section of Kapp's *History of Economic Thought*. Unfortunately, Kapp did not complete the planned chapter on CCC for his book manuscript, so the editors decided to add an abridged version of his last published work on CCC to the appendix.
26. K. W. Kapp, 'Friedrich List's Contribution to the Theory of Economic Development,' in *Hindu Culture, Economic Development and Economic Planning in India – A Collection of Essays*, Asia Publishing House, Bombay et al. 1963.
27. Dec. 5, 1966
28. The argument for minimum adequate living conditions is linked to Kapp's

proposal for a science of man in society based on a bio-cultural concept of man (Kapp 1961) and his plea for a humanization of economics (Kapp 1967).
29 Interestingly Myrdal accepted AFEE's Veblen-Commons award in 1976, delivering a speech that refers to Kapp's concept of the open system character of the economy while bypassing Veblen and Commons.
30 February 1, 1968.
31. Biological metaphors and the accentuation of 'evolution' have played a problematic role, inviting several misinterpretations, the introduction of hidden biases, and the alienation of more progressive economists. Eventually, the *Association for Institutional Thought* was formed in the US. Also, the formation of the *Union of Radical Political Economy* can be seen as a failure to form a broader organization of those concerned with progressive institutional change. See also A. G. Gruchy, 'Institutional Economics: Its Development and Prospects,' in R. Steppacher, B. Zogg-Walz, H. Hatzfeldt (eds) *Economics in Institutional Perspective – Memorial Essays in Honor of K. William Kapp*, Lexington (MA) 1977. Today, the European *Association for Evolutionary and Political Economy* (EAEPE) also attracts economists with a variety of 'evolutionary' approaches, including conservative and neoliberal ones.
32 S. L. McDonald, E. Zimmermann, 'The Dynamics of Resourceship,' in: R. J. Phillips (ed), *The Texas Institutionalists*, JAI Press 1995.
33. March 8, 1968.
34. May 8, 1968.
35. Kapp to Jacoby on June 3, 1968.
36. Kapp to Myrdal on July, 19 1968.
37. Kapp to Junker on February 16, 1968.
38. January 9, 1969.
39. January 21, 1969.
40. June 16, 1969.
41 December 19, 1969.
42 July 29, 1970.
43. This important chapter was missing from the manuscript. The editors decided to add Kapp's last article on social costs, as well as his work on substantive rationality, within the appendix.
44. August 14, 1970.
45. Letter to Myrdal August 14, 1970.
46. Kapp spent a research semester at the École des Hautes Études en Sciences Sociales in Paris in 1972/73.
47 Personal correspondence with Ken Coates (President of the Bertrand Russel Peace Foundation). Kapp's essay was recently republished in the hundredth number of the foundation's 'Spokesman' ('Democracy – Growing or Dying') as one of the most influential papers in the publication's history.
48. July 29, 1975.
49. P. Mirowski and D. Plehwe, *The Road From Mont-Pelerin: The Making of the Neoliberal Thought Collective*, Harvard University Press 2009. EAEPE's 2009

Kapp-Prize winning paper points out how effectively G. Stigler pursued his neoliberal political-economic agenda as a pillar of the Chicago School: E. Nik-Khah, 'Getting Hooked on Drugs The Chicago School, the Pharmaceutical Project, and the Construction of Medical Neoliberalism,' Conference Paper, EAEPE, 2009. Another example is how the discourse on environmental disruption and social costs was taken over by the neoliberals; see S. Berger, 'The Discourse on Social Costs: The Kapp Theorem vs. Neoliberalism,' in W. Elsner, P. Frigato and P. Ramazzotti (eds) *Social Costs Today – Institutional Economics and Contemporary Crisis*, Routledge (forthcoming).

50. See Kapp's interpretation of Karl Polanyi's 'double movement' as a social protective movement: 'The political history of the last 150 years can be interpreted as a revolt of large masses of people (including small businesses) against social costs.' K. W. Kapp, *Social Costs of Business Enterprise*, Asia Publishing House, 1963, p. 15
51. K.W. Kapp, 'Economic Development, National Planning and Public Administration,' in *Hindu Culture, Economic Development and Economic Planning in India – A Collection of Essays*, Asia Publishing House, Bombay et al. [1960] 1963; G. Myrdal, *Asian Drama – An Inquiry into the Poverty of Nations*, New York: Pantheon Books, 1968; S. Berger, 'Myrdal's Institutional Theory of the State: From Welfare to Predation – and Back?,' *Journal of Economic Issues*, Vol. 43, 2009.
52. Quote by K. William Kapp in an interview with 'The Economist' in 1967.
53. Neoliberalism is defined here as the set of principles of a political movement (Mirowski 2009; 2013)
54. For the influence of Polanyi on Kapp see Berger 2008. It remains an open question why Kapp does not cite or reference Polanyi's work in his dissertation.
55. This chapter is an interview conducted in 1962 most likely as part of a survey on the Japanese economy by the magazine 'The Economist.' It shows how Kapp perceived the genealogy of his SC/SB project.
56. Bellagio conferences included Hayek's renowned analogy symposium in 1966 (Caldwell 2004, p. 308) and Machlup's Bellagio group for world monetary reform between 1964-1977 (Connell 2012).
57. '*Wirtschaftlichkeit vom Standpunkt der Gesellschaft*'.
58. Kapp builds on Menger's enlarged and revised second edition of *Principles of Economics*, published posthumously by his son.
59. Kapp had emigrated with his wife, Lore, to the United States in 1937, where he was initially affiliated with Columbia University, the workplace of John M. Clark.
60. Kapp also referred to Marx's way of viewing capitalism: 'No matter how economical capitalist production may be in other respects, it is utterly prodigal to human life. [...] Capitalism loses on one side for society what it gains on another for the individual capitalist' (Marx, *Capital III*, 1909: 104, in Kapp 1970: 844).

61. Dieter Plehwe has identified Beckerman as part of the neoliberal thought collective; personal conversation 2010.
62. For an elaboration of Kapp's institutional argument against the return of liberalism and the reaction of leading neoliberal economists, refer to Berger (2012).
63. It is noteworthy that the financial support for institutional economists waned since the 1950s, with the Ford Foundation being the last to quit funding institutional research by the early 1960s (Rutherford 2011). Myrdal's and Kapp's project to start an international association of institutional economists was denied funding by the Swedish Research Council in 1968 (for details concerning Kapp's intellectual project, see Berger and Steppacher 2011). This may be seen as a consequence of changes in the way economic science was funded with several foundations increasingly supporting neoliberal ideas, for example, the Volcker Fund and the Walgreen Foundation (Mirowski and Plehwe 2009; Nik-Khah 2011).
64. See also Swaney and Evers (1989), who have located this important concept at the core of the institutional theory of social costs.
65. Clark's 'Accelerator Principle' is based on the idea of self-reinforcing causation (vicious circle) or circular and cumulative causation, which is one of the key concepts of non-equilibrium economics (Berger 2009).
66. This issue was at the heart of the European socialist accounting debate in the 1920s (Kapp 1936).
67. The Kapp-Clark correspondence – retrieved from the Kapp Archive – contains five letters. Two letters deal with Kapp's article on consumer theory, 'Rational Human Conduct' (1943), and three letters concern Kapp's book manuscript 'Social Costs of Private Enterprise' (1950). The present analysis only refers to the latter set of letters.
68. The section on social returns was never published. In this, Kapp provides an institutional version of Paul Samuelson's neoclassical 'public goods' argument (Samuelson 1954).
69. Leading authors using the institutional argument on social costs in the tradition of Kapp work are Swaney and Evers (1989), Swaney (2006), Sherman et al. (2007), Foster (2000, 2010), and Martinez-Alier (2002).
70. For a similar thesis, see Swaney and Evers (1989) and Franzini (2006).
71. Today Kapp's approach resembles in important ways Amartya Sen's 'capabilities approach' and Max Neef's human needs matrix.
72. Recent archival research has elevated the role played by Stigler as a key protagonist of the Chicago School with a coherent agenda in the areas of law and economics, and science and technology (Nik-Khah 2011), contributing to the demise of the institutional argument on social costs.
73. The Kapp-Polanyi correspondence remained unknown to the Polanyi Archive until 2006 and has not yet been fully published, although parts have been published in Heidenreich (1994). This paper works with yet unpublished material found in the Kapp Archive.

74. A good discussion in the English Language of Kapp's German dissertation can be found in Cangiani 2006.
75. Among them was Adolph Lowe whose work on political economics Kapp sees to be in line with his attempt to reconstruct a modern political economy. See: Berger and Forstater (2007). Kapp also became close friends with Pollock, exchanging letters on Lowe's political economics amongst other issues (Kapp-Pollock Correspondence, Kapp Archive). In addition, Kapp cites the work of members of the Frankfurt School, such as Adorno, Fromm, Habermas and Horkheimer throughout his work.
76. Especially Veblen's Theory of Business Enterprise (1904) made for Kapp's specific institutionalist approach to the problem of social costs. In the introduction of the revised and enlarged 1963 edition of The Social Costs of Business Enterprise Kapp explains that the change of the title is in reference to Veblen.
77. Kapp's close friends called him Ted.
78. Menger uses the German word 'unmittelbar,' which directly translates into 'immediate.'
79. Translation by the author in collaboration with Judith Ryan (German Department, Harvard University)
80. According to a letter written by K. William Kapp to Ernst Wiechert on March 31, 1948, Lore Kapp presented her essay under the title, 'The German Poet Ernst Wiechert,' at the meeting of a club that is not specified. Kapp quotes the president of the club as having commented: 'We all feel humble in the presence of such a great man' (Kapp's 1948, from a letter)
81. For the various meanings and applications of this concept see Berger (2009).
82. The emphasis CCC places on interrelatedness is closely related to conceptual developments in the social sciences (e.g., systems theory, system dynamics, cybernetics, complexity theory): Myrdal and Kapp considered the economic system to be an open system in reciprocal interaction with the surrounding systems (Myrdal 1976, 215; Kapp 1976a) implying the possibility of disruptive effects that are potentially threatening to human survival (Kapp 1975a; Berger and Elsner 2007).
83. Kapp also used the concept of 'social reproduction' developed by the Physiocrats and later adopted by Marx and Engels, which he considered a tool for the elaboration of useful hypotheses regarding defects and inefficiencies of a social system (Kapp [1973b] 1974, 132, 134-5).
84. The CCC exhibits similarities to the development theories of F. Perroux ('domination effect') and J. Galtung ('center-periphery'). The CCC, according to Kapp, however, seems to be more generally applicable.
85. Being the economist of the Social Research Institute at Columbia and a member of the Frankfurt School, Pollock was a close friend of Lowe and Kapp. Lowe was the 'liason officer' who mediated the contacts between the New School for Social Research and the Social Research Institute (Krohn 1996, 144), and the latter was affiliated with the Social Research Institute and taught at Columbia.

86. In this context it is interesting that the importance of K. Polanyi's 'substantive' meaning of 'economic' has been emphasized more recently because of its usefulness for the integration of modern heterodox economics, such as neo-marxist and neo-institutionalist approaches (O'Hara 2000:128-134).
87. This is analogous to Polanyi's concept of 'commodity fiction' (Polanyi 1947).
88. This transfer of fish protein away from protein-poor countries to already protein-rich countries for purposes of farming is described in Kapp (1976).
89. Galtung focuses on the exploitation of the periphery by the center to explain the depletion of fisheries and the ensuing regional poverty (Galtung 1975).
90. The consequences of resource depletion for social reproduction and unequal development are addressed by holistic economists, taking a socio-economic and ecological view of the development process (Galtung 1975), or focus on distribution conflicts (Guha and Martinez-Alier 1997).
91. Two important controversies center around Georgescu-Roegen's application of the entropy law to economics and his views on agrarian economics. The latter controversy is rooted in the conflict between Narodniki and Marxists (Guha and Martinez-Alier 1997: 25; Patnaik 1979).